THE NEW ENGLISH TABLE

200 Recipes from the Queen of Thrifty, Inventive Cooking

Rose Prince

PHOTOGRAPHS BY LAURA HYND

FOURTH ESTATE • *London*

First published in Great Britain in 2008 by
Fourth Estate
An imprint of HarperCollins*Publishers*
77–85 Fulham Palace Road
London W6 8JB
www.4thestate.co.uk

This edition first published in 2010 by Fourth Estate

1

A catalogue record for this book is available
from the British Library

ISBN 978 0 00 725094 3

Text designed by Terence Caven

Printed and bound in Hong Kong by
Printing Express Ltd.

In memory of
Mary Goloubeff Kapnist and her white farmhouse

A man dies and is buried, and all his words and actions are forgotten, but the food he has eaten lives after him in the sound or rotten bones of his children.

George Orwell, *The Road to Wigan Pier* (1937)

Contents

Acknowledgements

The guidance of Louise Haines, my editor at Fourth Estate, has been extraordinarily valuable. Once again I am so grateful for her patience and enthusiasm. Designer Julian Humphries' unique and special talent has, I believe, produced a book that is beautifully different, and Laura Hynd's photography has stand-alone quality – I am so proud to be working on her first book. In spite of the long time span of this project, it has been fun, as always, to work with a delightful and thoughtful team that includes Jane Middleton, Silvia Crompton, Terence Caven, Robin Harvie and the many others at Fourth Estate who keep you cheerful and encouraged throughout.

At home, there would be no inspiration without Dominic and my two children, Jack and Lara. The help of Maria Taylor, Hayley Hedges and Amy Higgs has also been invaluable, especially during photography sessions.

Thanks, too, for the patience and advice of Carolyn Hart, Michele Lavery, Kathryn Holliday and Summer Nocon of the *Telegraph Magazine*, and also to Casilda Grigg and Jon Stock, my editors on the *Telegraph* Weekend section. The work I do for them, and also for Veronica Wadley on the *Evening Standard* and Catherine Pepinster on the *Tablet*, doubles as precious research for this book. Without their backing I would be a much less travelled, less knowledgeable food writer. Joyce Prince was a mine of good-quality information, her help with historical fact was vital, and Bec Huxtep did a great job digging up the bad and good news on foods.

I am so grateful, also, for help and cheer from the following: Andrew Ashenden, Carole Bamford, Sophia and Tim Beddow, Marlene and Rodney Belbin, Joanna Blythman, Rosie Boycott, Phil Britten, Bill Brogan and St John's College, Cambridge, James and Rose Campbell, Sam and Sam Clark, Sarah Clarke, Alex and Katie Clarke, Caroline Cranbrook, Andre Dang,

Alan Dangour, Meredith Etherington Smith, John Franklin, Rex Goldsmith, David Hammerson, Chris and Ali Hirst, Vivienne Jawett, Laura Jeffreys and especially Tom Jeffreys for his beaming smiles, Jeremy Lee, Tania Littlehales, Jason Lowe, Jack O'Shea, David Mellor's shop, Retrouvius, Nigel Slater, Rachel Simhon, William Sitwell, Olly Smith, Matthew Stevens, Andrew Whitley, and Andrew and Sybille Wilkinson.

Lastly, a salute to the Chelsea Physic Garden. Many quiet afternoons spent there, sitting reading among the thousands of nourishing and life-saving species, sparked an idea.

RP

Acknowledgements xii

Introduction

My one table is two tables. Mostly it is an everyday table, a busy junction where plates arrive and leave, sometimes in a hurry, sometimes late. But they leave empty, I hope. Food for every day might be an economical bean and herb soup; juicy threads of braised ham hock beside a pile of buttery potato, or something good rehashed from something left over. But every now and then we sit at the 'other' table, for a weekend lunch or dinner, supper with others or a seasonal feast. Then we eat dishes cooked with ingredients that are more luxurious and precious: a whole baked Cornish fish, or roast game birds; a dish of new-season asparagus and pea shoots; a creamy pudding piled with summer berries and decorated with flowers.

It is a rhythm of eating that I enjoy. I have been good, so I can be bad; some meals are tempered, so others can be rich. It rejuvenates the old concept of 'fast and feast' and has become quite natural. But oscillating between those dishes of leftovers, cheap cuts and humble raw materials on the one hand and richer meals based on more valuable ingredients on the other is not just a feel-good diet; it forms part of a solution to a wider predicament.

There is a strong bond between good human health and the health of the environment. What you choose to eat has both an intrinsic and an ecological impact. If, in place of eating fillets of chicken, you decide to cook a whole chicken, eat the meat, then make an ambrosial broth from the bones to use in a creamy soup scented with tarragon, you can afford to buy a traditionally reared bird that has been fed on natural forage. Feeding chickens grass rather than cereals not only saves considerable quantities of fossil fuel (used in fertiliser and processing) but also benefits you: grass-fed livestock have a higher proportion of essential fatty acids in their meat, which are good for heart health and help guard against becoming overweight. There is also the diversity factor in this equation. As well as reducing uneconomic waste, recycling food left over from other meals encourages the use of many more appetising ingredients, such as herbs, salad vegetables and pulses. Growing a greater variety of crops and so eating a more diverse diet is again a plus for both people and planet. The meals on our table form part of a cycle that can, collectively, make a positive difference.

Currently, the main challenges and threats we face are food related. 'Peak oil' – the point after which demand for fossil fuels outstrips supply – has pushed food prices up, and inflation on some foods is now as high as 20 per cent. Rising levels of obesity are costing the National Health Service an estimated £1 billion per year; in children the obesity epidemic is especially tragic and poignant. But in our own warm kitchens, we can go some way to addressing issues that the authorities seem uninspired, or politically afraid, to deal with.

The problem of methane-emitting food waste and higher prices can be tackled by turning, say, some surplus cooked beef into a rich braise, enlivened with puréed tomatoes, red wine, garlic and thin shreds of wild fungi, to eat with buttered pasta ribbons.

One answer to the peak oil question lies in an earthily delicious dish of home-grown purple sprouting broccoli and tender green lentils, both of which are crops with a low environmental impact.

Given the known benefits of eating a more diverse menu than red meat, white bread and King Edwards potatoes, poor diet can be addressed by exploring a wider variety of foods, trying new types of grain, sprouted seeds and leafy green vegetables. We can do good by choosing from battalions of pretty squashes, rare potato and apple breeds, less familiar seafood and game birds – even edible flowers. If any of the above were medicine, it would taste of honey and lemon.

But what to put on the table… what is English, or British? A peculiar aspect of our progress over centuries, during which artists have created works of genius and scientists have developed life-saving cures, is that the English larder has become culturally primitive. Once we were imaginative and knowledgeable about the art of food, and more democratic in the share of it. Now, the majority paint by numbers in crude colours.

So this is a book of ingredients: how and when to buy them, all the many things that can be made with them and, in many cases, how to use up what is left. There is an economic divide between the foods listed. Some are obvious candidates for an occasional feast, others plainly everyday items.

Some fall between the two – they can be cheaper to buy in a glut moment, or depending on where you live. Many are recognisably home grown – beef, Cheddar, wheat and watercress, for example. Some are produced here but are underexploited – sardines, sweetbreads, barley and rabbit. Others could be grown here commercially but are not – buckwheat, lentils, quince and chestnuts. Others cannot be produced here but are non-controversial imports embedded in our history – olive oil, tea, lemons and rice. All these foods belong here, or were English once. Have confidence. There's no need always to look to the Mediterranean for something good.

With your new knowledge and ideas, choose when is right to eat what. Try new things. Add herbs, leaves, flowers and spices to the kaleidoscope and suddenly the English table has food on its plates that is interesting, pretty, honest and so good to eat. Choosing to cook and not waste a diverse range of foods, in a rhythm that is economical and healthy in every sense, will become the essence of a New English Table.

APPLES

Apple Soup
Apple, Red Cabbage and Watercress Salad
Hot Apple Juice
Russet Jelly Ice

An apple is often the earliest of our food memories. From the moment an infant takes its first carefully sieved apple purée, to the apple in the lunchbox or the one pinched from a tree in next door's garden, apples are always close by. For busy students and workers, they are a constant – reliable pocket fodder or desktop picnic regular. Apple turnovers and doughnuts are just another, naughtier, form of the fruit. Then young families make their first apple crumble, and over time come apple snow, pies, tarts and charlottes. Non-pudding eaters never tire of apples with cheese. Then after this lifetime with a fruit that is a symbol of the heart, some of us will face the end with the occasional bowl of apple purée again. I hope I do, teeth or no teeth.

Apples are an emblem of what is wrong and what is right about our food supply. There are thousands of varieties but only a handful of them are grown commercially – a monoculture that squanders custom and harms the environment. But this dent in diversity is now – slowly – reversing, with apple farmers bringing traditional varieties to city markets and even supermarkets putting a few unfamiliar apples on their shelves. There has been a revival of apple customs, community orchards and 'Apple Days', when children can taste some odd things made with apples and adults get squiffy on farmhouse cider. Yet Britain grows a shamefully small crop. It was once enormous, but the creation of a free market with other European countries in the 1970s saw British farmers chop down every tree, grub them up and plant a more valuable crop. Did they know at the time that to destroy an orchard is to terminate the survival of a menagerie of wildlife, including the vital wild bee population? They do now, and so does Defra (the Department of Food and Rural Affairs), which is offering incentives to farmers planting orchards. So there's hope – a long way still to go, but I feel optimistic.

Sold in every greengrocer's, every paper shop, everywhere, apples have become an everyday thing to take for granted – eating one is like brushing your teeth or taking a bus. Like it or not. I like it when the home crop is in season and varieties jig in and out of the autumn and winter months, but *not* when the stickers on the fruit show that it has travelled long haul even though our own are in season. I'd rather feel the rough skin of a Russet on my lip and taste its firm, mellow flesh than have my face sprayed with the acidic juice of an import that has been bred for looks but not taste. I am happy not to eat peaches in late summer, preferring to wait for those anonymous native apples that drop off local trees, whose red skin stains their white insides pink. That's what I call exotic.

But why are English apples just that bit better? Here is a fruit that, unlike tomatoes, *likes* its adopted country. The chemistry between the apple tree, our climate and our soil yields a fruit that has intricate melodies of taste and texture. Commercially grown French apples have tarty PVC skin and astringent flesh; our ordinary Cox's, on the other hand, are dressed for the weather, with sturdy, windcheater hides holding in their mellow juices.

Perhaps we should rethink when to eat apples. For almost ten months of the year, from late July to early May, there is the home-grown supply: the Pippins, Pearmains, Russets and other esoteric types. There are even free apples if you can get at some windfalls. You don't have to own a tree, but good contacts help. My mother-in-law brings us hers when she visits us in town. Fallen apples are not always the best to eat in the hand, having been bashed about a bit, but they cook well.

Buying apples

For the interesting ones, visit your local farmers' market and buy lots. Store them in the dark, where they will keep well, then it won't be the end of the world if the weekly market trip cannot be made. To find a farmers' market, look at your local council website or at www.farmersmarkets.net (for a nationwide list). London markets can be located at www.lfm.org.uk. There are other independently run produce markets, such as Borough Market in southeast London, and you will sometimes find locally grown apples in ordinary street markets across the country. Look out also for country markets, run by the WI – your nearest can be located on www.country-markets.co.uk.

A novel way to buy apples is by post. Try Broomfields Apples (www.broomfieldsfarmshop.co.uk; tel: 01905 620233). For information about starting or locating community orchards, or learning about apple varieties and customs, contact the Dorset-based organisation, Common Ground (www.commonground.org.uk).

Which apple to use

The season for British apples runs from July to May. Early varieties ripen on the tree and do not store well, then the later ones start to come in. Some of these can be eaten immediately, but others need time in storage for the sugars to develop. Sometimes this can take months, hence the long apple season. Cox's, for example, are picked in late September but are not ripe until late October. Modern storage facilities have also lengthened the season. There are a few varieties that are specifically for cooking (like the Bramley) but the truth is that you can cook with any eating apple. It is best, though, to cook them when they are still a little unripe, so the flavour will be stronger.

Good apples tend to be very good on the inside but a little knobbly in looks. They may have rough bumps, come in odd shapes or have some pest damage but, providing the flesh is not bruised or discoloured and the juice is sweet, this will not affect the way they cook.

Familiar native apples

Bramley The prototypical cooking apple, tart and firm, but not the one with the most interesting taste. Bramleys have a thick skin, normally pared away for cooking, and a flesh that cooks to a pale and puffy soft purée. They always need sweetening and are traditionally used in pies and crumbles. I prefer to bake smaller dessert apples, but a baked Bramley with its foaming hot flesh is something of a classic.

Cox's Orange Pippin An eating apple (that can also be cooked) with a mellow, yellow-tinted flesh and a slightly rough, red- and green-tinted skin. British commercial growers like to grow Cox's because they last until March in storage. They are a good apple, sweet enough to cook without sugar yet they work well with savoury things, too (see Bacon and Apples on page 19). When shopping, look out for their Pippin relatives for new aromas, colours and flavours.

Egremont Russet Their smallness makes these eating apples irritating to prepare for cooking but, used slightly underripe, they have a beautiful sharpness and can hold their shape. I put them in tarts, and make an ice with a jelly prepared from whole Russets (see page 10). They are ideal for the soup recipe on page 7. They ripen in late October and there is a good supply until December.

Discovery My favourite apple to eat raw. The pink from the skin tints the flesh and they have a knockout scent. Use in salads with toasted pumpkin seeds and fruity cheeses like Cheddar, or cook them with blackberries. They ripen on the tree in July/August and must be eaten quickly.

Worcester Pearmain This is the classic bright-red striped English eating apple, available in winter (but rarely after Christmas). The juice is sharp and fragrant. The colour fades when cooked, so Worcesters are better eaten raw. Use them in salads, with walnuts and blue cheese.

Unfamiliar native apples

Blenheim Orange These eating apples are often mentioned in old cookery books as excellent cooking apples, too. They cook down to a drier, more textured purée than regular cooking apples and are thought to be ideal for charlottes (a fruit pudding baked in a straight-sided dish lined with buttered bread, then turned out to serve).

Newton Wonder A sweet cooking apple that ripens in late December and is available through January. Remove the core, stuff the cavity with dried figs and treacle, then bake in a low oven and eat with good vanilla ice cream.

Laxton's Fortune An early eating apple with Pippin ancestors, this ripens in September and should be eaten quickly, raw.

Tydeman's Late Orange A dry-skinned Russet with plenty of aromatic juice, this eating apple ripens in January. Core it, stuff the cavity with raisins, wrap in shortcrust pastry, then brush with egg and bake. Eat with custard or sweetened cream cheese.

Scarlet Pimpernel An adorable small, fragrant apple that ripens in August. Fry them in a pan, sprinkle with brown sugar and serve with barbecued pork chops. Or eat raw, with cobnuts (see page 134).

Ashmead's Kernel An eating apple that doubles as a cider apple, with yellow, firm-textured flesh that keeps well. Good for making Apple Soup (see page 7), or peel, core and braise with duck and haricot beans for a sweet, winter dish.

Crab apple The parent species of every apple, crab apples are always sour, very fragrant and have a nice habit of turning rusty pink when cooked. The best possible use for them is to make a syrup or jelly. Put the quartered apples in a pan with some water and simmer until soft. Suspend a muslin jelly bag over a chair, place a bowl beneath and tip the cooked apples into the bag. Do not force it; let the juice drip through naturally. Measure the juice, add 500g/1lb 2oz granulated sugar for every 600ml/1 pint liquid, boil for about 15 minutes then put into jars. It will set into a delicate pink jelly.

Breakfast apple There isn't any such species but I use this as a catch-all word for apples I cannot identify. I peel and core them (using a clever machine available from www.decuisine.co.uk; tel: 0870 850 5395) and then cook them to a soft purée. This is my regular breakfast, which I eat with honey, yoghurt and linseed.

Apple Soup

This is a buttery, sweet and sour soup that makes an ideal everyday lunch reheated from the fridge. It can be made with any apple but it is better if they are slightly unripe or sour. Its flavour will change depending on the apple variety, and it is a good way to use up those wrinkly apples that have been sitting in the fruit bowl for too long. I recommend using a food processor to chop the fruit and vegetables. You don't have to use homemade chicken stock – water or even apple juice is fine. If you use water, you will probably need to add more salt.

For a bigger meal, put this soup on the table with bread and cheese, or ham or potted meat (see page 325) with toast.

Serves 4

85g/3oz unsalted butter, plus extra to serve
1 large or 2 small white onions, roughly chopped
2 garlic cloves, chopped
12 apples, peeled, cored and chopped small
2 celery sticks with their leaves, chopped

leaves from 2 sprigs of thyme
5 allspice seeds, ground in a mortar and pestle (or ½ teaspoon ready-ground allspice)
1.2 litres/2 pints chicken stock (see page 116), pressed apple juice or water
sea salt and freshly ground black pepper

Melt the butter in a large pan and add the onion, garlic, apples, celery, thyme leaves and allspice. Cook over a low heat until the onion and apples soften. Add the stock, bring to the boil and cook until the apples are quite tender. This should take about 15 minutes – don't overcook it or the fresh flavours will be lost. Add black pepper, then taste and add salt if necessary. Serve with a knob of creamy unsalted butter melting in each bowlful.

Kitchen note
To make the soup richer still, stir in a splash of apple brandy or strong cider and put a spoonful of double cream into each bowlful when serving. For a different kind of soup, fry small pieces of smoked bacon or black pudding and add to each bowl. Adding a teaspoonful of toasted medium oatmeal will give this soup more muscle still.

Apple, Red Cabbage and Watercress Salad

I want to eat smaller, mayonnaise-bound salads instead of large bowls of rocket and mizuna dressed with olive oil and smothered in cheese. I like those spiky salad leaves but, after 10 years of enthusiasm, it is nice to turn instead to neat forkfuls of vegetables, herbs, nuts, fruits, perhaps cured meat or leftover chicken, clinging together with the help of an oil–egg emulsion like mayonnaise. Even a small amount fills and fuels you through an afternoon. These salads keep for 2 or 3 days in the fridge, so are a useful everyday graze. Leaves need not be left out. In the following recipe, they are part of the dressing.

This apple-based salad is lovely eaten alone but good, too, with hot boiled gammon, cold ham or cured sausage.

Serves 4

6 apples (the red skins of Worcesters are effective with the cabbage)
a squeeze of lemon juice
¼ red cabbage
2 tablespoons walnut halves
a little oil
sea salt and freshly ground black pepper

For the dressing:
2 egg yolks
1 heaped teaspoon Dijon mustard
2 bunches of watercress, chopped
300ml/½ pint light olive oil, sunflower oil or groundnut oil
1–2 tablespoons white wine vinegar, to taste
1 tablespoon cornichons (baby gherkins), drained and finely chopped

First make the dressing: put the egg yolks and mustard into a bowl and mix well with a small whisk. Add the chopped watercress, then beat in the oil, a few drops at a time to begin with, then adding it a little faster once a third of it has been incorporated. If you add the oil too quickly it may curdle. Mix in the vinegar with the cornichons and set to one side.

Quarter the apples, remove the cores and slice them thinly, leaving the skins on. Dress with a little lemon juice to stop discoloration. Shred the cabbage as finely as possible, keeping the crunchy stalk. Put both the apple and cabbage into a bowl, then pour over enough of the dressing to give a good covering (set the rest aside; it will store well in a jar in the fridge).

Mix the salad gently so the apple slices do not break. Taste a little and add salt if necessary. Season with black pepper.

Toast the walnut halves in a pan with a little oil over a medium heat, then grind them in a pestle and mortar or chop them to a rough consistency. Scatter the nuts over the plates of salad as you serve it, spooning the salad on to the plates in appetisingly high mounds.

Hot Apple Juice

I am no fan of flasks filled with old tea for car journeys, but it is good to stop and sip something hot that was not bought at gross prices from service stations. This is a family invention to solve the problem. Pressed apple juice, with a little spice and light muscovado sugar, lasts all day as long as there is a decent Thermos to store it in. Try to use the best pressed apple juice, not one made from concentrate – juice made from concentrate can taste metallic. I sometimes buy direct from farmers' markets in the city, although you can buy pressed apple juice in supermarkets, too.

Heat 1 litre/1¾ pints apple juice to boiling point and add ½ teaspoon ground cinnamon and a tiny pinch of ground cloves. Sweeten with light muscovado sugar to taste. If you are putting the juice into a flask, remember to wash it out first with boiling water.

 Kitchen note
Hot cider is the adult alternative for non-drivers, and can be made using the same spices and sugar to sweeten, as above.

Russet Jelly Ice

I like this ice when it has a slightly bruised, windfall scent, like the musty inside of an apple store. The base is a jelly, extracted from whole apples or leftover apple peelings. Fresh apple is grated into the jelly before freezing but not before allowing it to brown a little – for that orchard-floor taste.

This is not a quick recipe but it is a very worthwhile one, especially if you use up windfalls. Try it with various apple varieties, including crab apple – you should see some interesting fluctuations in taste. Using slightly unripe apples will heighten the flavour.

Serves 6–8

10 Russet apples, plus 6 more to grate in at the end

golden granulated sugar
2 egg whites

Chop the 10 apples into quarters, leaving the cores, stalks and skin on, and put them into a big, heavy-bottomed pan. Cover (only just) with water, bring to the boil and cook very slowly – it should murmur and bubble rather than simmer fast. This ensures the apples do not change flavour, and they will turn a pretty, rusty-pink colour. When you have a thick, sloppy purée, line a colander with muslin and set it over a bowl (or use a jelly bag, if you have one). Spoon the purée into the muslin. Do not push the purée or stir it; just let the juice drip naturally into the bowl through the cloth. Make sure the cloth is high above the bowl so it will not touch the juice in the bowl as it fills. This can take at least a couple of hours or overnight – you need to extract every last bit of juice.

Measure the volume of juice and add 450g/1lb granulated sugar for every 600ml/1 pint. Put it into a saucepan and bring to the boil. Simmer for about 10 minutes – the liquid will clarify as it boils and become syrupy. Allow to cool down to about 40°C/104°F (hotter than bathwater). Meanwhile, grate the flesh and skin of the 6 remaining apples – leave to brown a little, then add to the syrup. Whisk the egg whites until stiff and fold them into the apple mixture. Pour into a container and place in the freezer. After an hour or so, stir to loosen the ice, then freeze again (or use an ice-cream maker if you have one). Serve with Pistachio Biscuits (see page 311) – made with another nut (walnut, for example), if you prefer.

ASPARAGUS

Asparagus with Pea Shoots and Mint
Boiled or Steamed Asparagus

Being one of those slow-growing vegetables with a short (eight-week) glut, British asparagus comes at a price too high for it to be anything but a treat. Having said that, I would be happy to live off bread and lentils at that time if I could eat asparagus by the kilo. Its arrival in the shops is a happy moment, an affirmation of spring. When the supply begins to dwindle and the spears begin to look a little hairy and overblown, it's like the end of a birthday.

British asparagus should be all over the place in season, which, depending on the weather, runs from late April to the third week of June. Look for it in greengrocer's shops and supermarkets; the boxes are usually heavily emblazoned with Union Jacks. Buying asparagus locally not only supports farmers in the region where you live, it also makes sense in terms of freshness. Competing with it will be the Spanish. I have to say I am not unhappy about using Spanish asparagus *before* the British season begins because it can be very good. Air-freighted baby Peruvian and Thai asparagus is tasteless and pointless.

Buying asparagus

To find your nearest asparagus grower, see www.british-asparagus.co.uk (tel: 01507 602427). To find a farmers' market, check your local council website or www.farmersmarkets.net – or www.lfm.org.uk for London markets.

For mail-order asparagus, contact Sandy Patullo, who grows exceptional asparagus and sea kale (another delicious edible stalk) in Scotland: Eassie Farm, By Glamis, Angus DD8 1SG; tel: 01307 840303.

All the major supermarkets sell British asparagus in season.

Asparagus with Pea Shoots and Mint

Pea shoots are an established vegetable now. They have been stocked by Sainsbury for the past three years and I often see them in markets. They are increasingly available in good food shops, too, and you can get them via mail order from Goodness Direct (www.goodnessdirect.co.uk; tel: 0871 871 6611).

When they are cooked – lightly fried in a little oil or butter, or even steamed for a minute – they have all the taste of a good, sweet garden pea, or indeed a frozen pea, but with the added bonus of being lively plants. They appear around the same time as English asparagus and, while I am always happy to eat asparagus plain, the combination of the sweetness in the pea shoots and the unique grassy flavour of the asparagus is joyfully vernal.

Serves 4–6

1kg/2¼lb new-season asparagus
2 tablespoons extra virgin olive oil
4 punnets of pea shoots
a few small mint leaves
finely grated zest of ½ lemon
sea salt and freshly ground white
  pepper

For the sauce:
1 shallot, chopped
a grating or two of nutmeg
2 wineglasses of white wine
1 teaspoon white wine vinegar
225g/8oz unsalted butter,
  softened

Pare away the outer skin of each spear, taking off about 6cm/2½ inches from the base of the stem. Bring a large, shallow pan of water to the boil. Before cooking the asparagus, however, make the sauce. Put the shallot, nutmeg, white wine and white wine vinegar in a small saucepan and bring to the boil. Cook until the liquid has reduced to about 3 tablespoons, then strain it through a sieve and return it to the pan, discarding the shallot. Add the butter, about a teaspoon at a time, whisking it into the liquor over a low heat. When all the butter has been used, the sauce should be thick and creamy.

Add the asparagus to the pan of boiling water; it will need about 5 minutes' simmering to become just tender. Meanwhile, put the oil in a small frying pan and fry the pea shoots in it until they collapse slightly.

Using tongs, lift the asparagus out of the water and drain on a cloth (I find asparagus breaks up if you tip it into a colander, and that it needs the cloth to get rid of excess water, which can make it soggy). Divide the asparagus between 4–6 warm serving plates and heap the pea shoots over the tips. Give the sauce one final whisk over the heat to amalgamate it (it will split a little if left, but it will 'come back'), then pour it generously over the asparagus. Season with a little salt and pepper and scatter the mint leaves and lemon zest over the top. Eat immediately and, if you are in festive mode, serve as a starter before Fried Megrim Sole (on page 260) or the lamb with spring vegetables on page 235.

Boiled or Steamed Asparagus

I cook asparagus loose, either in boiling salted water in a shallow pan or in a steamer. Today's varieties seem to take only about 5 minutes for a thick stem. If you have time, pare away the outer skin of the spears up to about 6cm/2½ inches from the base before cooking. This enables you to eat the whole spear, and allows the butter to sink in. Melt about 30g/1oz butter per person, pour it over the cooked asparagus and serve with loose sea salt.

BACON

Unhappiness reigns if there is no bacon in the house. It is my mainstay meat, the inexpensive strip of flesh that is the difference between having nothing to cook with and the ability to produce a meal quickly for everyone. It glamorises and adds body, not least its great and addictive flavour, to things such as lettuce and spring greens, and it keeps for weeks.

But be fussy about the bacon you buy. The food industry's record in the cheap pig meat business is abysmal on both welfare and quality grounds. Pigs reared intensively in Holland and Denmark, major providers of budget pork products to the UK, suffer some unacceptable conditions. Two-thirds of sows (mothers) are tethered and confined in stalls with hard, slatted floors for all their lives. The idea is to make pig rearing super efficient and tidy, to the miserable detriment of the pigs themselves. They are no more than breeding machines, expected to shoot out three litters a year until their bodies pack up. Stalls and tethers are not permitted in indoor pig farms in the UK but sows are kept in farrowing crates during birth and for four weeks after, before being transferred back to a pen – a system that is not ideal but is less cruel. Feed for pigs in both systems is high protein, often heavy in soya (these omnivores consume little flesh), which grows the animal to its bacon weight in swift time so that it will become a highly profitable pig. Processing this meat into bacon, and maximising profit, means injections of brine and phosphates; liquid that you will see seeping from the rasher as it cooks. A big, heavy pack of Danish bacon, the supposed great budget buy, will become shrunken watery slivers in the pan. It is hard to see what is economical about that for the consumer but we assume the industry that produced it is laughing all the way to the till. There is better value in a pack of best smoked streaky from a pig that has been kindly and naturally reared; best of all, if the streaky is cured on the butcher's premises. Ask for it to be sliced very thinly, so that all the rind is edible and the bacon cooks to a crisp stained-glass window in just a few minutes. Back rashers have their place, too, and it is good to have both cuts at the ready. Smoked bacon tends to be less salty, as it goes through two curing processes, and its flavour pervades other ingredients in recipes in a non-aggressive way. But these flavour comments are personal. Like tea, everyone likes bacon in a different way.

Buying bacon

Buy dry-cured bacon made as near as possible to your home. Ask butchers where they source either the bacon they sell or the pork they make their own from. If you cannot buy anything local, one of the best bacons via mail order is made by Peter Gott, at Sillfield Farm near Kendal in Cumbria (www.sillfield.co.uk; tel: 015395 67609). The flavour of his dry-cured bacon and 'pancetta' is beautifully balanced, and is made with pork from free-range rare-breed pigs and wild boar. Furness Fish, Poultry and Game Supplies deal with the mail order: www.morecambebayshrimps.com; tel: 015395 59544.

Bacon and Shellfish

Bacon can switch from being stock food to something exceptional when it is put in the pan with one of its most natural partners. Spend a happy hour piling through a bowl of shell-on North Atlantic prawns that have been added, at the last minute, with 2 tablespoons of butter to a frying pan of bacon. Throw over a handful of chopped dill as you serve. Big king scallops, griddled on a hot plate, can be put on the same plate as streaky bacon 'sugar canes': rashers of very thin bacon that are twisted before being roasted in the oven or cooked in a pan over a medium heat for 10 minutes. Serve the scallops and bacon with small beet leaves or baby chard. Tabasco on the table – as it often seems to be.

Bacon and Potatoes

A rasher of bacon, wrapped around a lump of butter or cream cheese with chopped parsley and placed inside a part-baked potato, will, once returned to the oven wrapped in foil for a further 20 minutes' cooking, make a supper eons more exciting than a wrinkled brown pebble with a sad lozenge of butter sliding around on the top.

Bacon Gravy for Sausages

I use bacon to make instant onion gravy for bangers and mash when I have no stock. Put a chopped rasher into the pan with a chopped onion, add a little butter or oil and cook over a low heat until the onion turns golden. Add a teaspoon of flour, stir well over the heat until it browns a little, then slowly add about 150ml/¼ pint water, stirring all the time. The result is a pale, buff-coloured sauce, not gravy brown, but it tastes fine.

Light Bacon Stew

Smoked pork belly can be cut into chunks, browned in a pan with garlic, onion and celery, then simmered in stock until tender. Serve with boiled potatoes and plenty of parsley. If you have any joints of poultry or fresh rabbit, add and simmer with the bacon.

Bacon and Apples

An easy small lunch dish that can be woven into a plate of cooked yellow lentils and a slice of Appleby Cheshire cheese. Nearly perfect. It will be no good, though, made with any one of that terrible trinity of juice bombs – Gala, Braeburn or Granny Smith – and, sad to say, Bramleys will fall to bits. Cox's Orange Pippins are best, or another apple with a good, fibrous texture and matt skin (see page 3).

I prefer to use thinly cut smoked streaky bacon for this, but if you like a thick cut, or prefer to use back or middle rather than streaky, that's fine, too.

Serves 2

a large knob of butter
4 rashers of smoked streaky bacon,
    cut into 2cm/¾ inch strips (remove
    the rind first if they are cut thick)
2 eating apples, cored and cut into
    segments
light brown muscovado sugar
freshly ground black pepper

Melt the butter in a frying pan, add the bacon and cook until it loses its transparency and becomes crisp. Add the apples and fry both for 4–5 minutes until the apples are tender, gently turning them occasionally but not too often or they will break up. Sprinkle a pinch of muscovado sugar over the apples, then twist over some black pepper. With the bacon, salt is not needed.

Serve with yellow-brown Umbrian lentils – cooked as for green lentils on page 252 but substituting real ale, more stock or water for the wine.

Bacon and Potato Salad with Green Celery Leaf and Cider Vinegar

Be sure to chop the celery leaves finely for this warm salad so there is all the flavour and no fibrous texture. This is a perfectly good and economical dish to eat alone – the bacon means you need no other protein, but you could follow it with some cheese and buttered oatcakes.

Serves 4

20 new potatoes
6 rashers of smoked streaky bacon, cut very thin, or the rind cut off
1 teaspoon sugar
1 tablespoon Dijon mustard
175ml/6fl oz light olive oil or sunflower oil

1 tablespoon cider vinegar or apple vinegar
2 tablespoons water
a handful of celery leaves, finely chopped
2 shallots, chopped
sea salt and freshly ground black pepper

Cook the potatoes in boiling water until just tender but not too soft. Drain, cut each one in half and set aside. Meanwhile, cut the rashers in half and put them in a frying pan (with no fat). Place over a medium heat and cook for about 10 minutes, turning once or twice, until crisp as a cracker.

Put the sugar, mustard, oil, vinegar and water in a bowl and mix until well emulsified. Stir in the celery leaves and shallots. Taste and add salt if necessary, then season with black pepper.

Put the potatoes in a big bowl, throw the crisp rashers over the top and pour over the dressing. Mix well. It doesn't matter if the rashers break up – that way it just tastes better.

BARLEY

Barley Cooked as for Risotto

Pot Barley and Lamb Broth

Pearl Barley with Turmeric, Lemon and Black Cardamom

Barley Water (the Queen's Recipe)

Spiced Barley with Leeks, Root Vegetables, Oregano,
Nutmeg, Allspice and Butter

Barley in Breadcrumbs

Superseded by wheat in almost all recipes, and now mainly used in brewing, barley is an ideal grain to rediscover from the annals of lost food plants and bring back into use in modest, everyday recipes. Now is a good time to think about eating grains other than the obvious ones, and to enjoy as many food plants as possible.

Before getting on to the science bit, I have to start by saying that since using new grains in my kitchen, life has got a lot more interesting. After years of pasta, risotto and pilav, suddenly I am tasting something with a totally new feel, scent and taste. I am yet to get some of these new grains past my children, who are happier to fork up basmati and penne. But my mother, who tried to feed us the then unfashionable Puy lentils in the 1970s, provoked a memory that must have steered me towards them when they properly arrived on the scene nearly 20 years later. So now when I put the new grains on the table and hear the inevitable refusal from the children, I know that *they hear* adults praise the dish, and I hope their curiosity will one day provoke them to have a try. I am sure they will do it when I am not looking, but I have learned that there is no point in making a child eat something when they are not ready.

Discovering, cooking and eating new grains matters. According to scientists at Biodiversity International, the organisation campaigning to preserve the gene bank of 'lost' foods, we depend on wheat, rice and maize for 50 per cent of our diet – a fact that challenges human health and opens to question our ability to deal with the effects of climate change. They say that people who eat more diverse diets are less prone to killer diseases, such as cardiovascular illness, cancer and diabetes. They also claim that avoiding the bank of over 7,000 edible plants means we miss out on essential nutrients.

It's a bit of a tall order to expect anyone to keep 7,000 foods in their larder, but the basic message is that the balance of our diet has been lost. Daily bread should not always be wheat but occasionally another grain or, better still, a combination of several. In terms of the environment, demand for a diverse diet encourages more innovation in agriculture. The monoculture dominated by wheat, rice and maize is vulnerable to disease and pests but widening the range of crops 'confuses' these threats – one crop's enemy is not that of another. A pest that destroys a certain breed may not touch others. Hence less need to treat with pesticides, a longer season (given that different strains of species ripen at intervals) and so more food. There is also evidence that cultivating a greater number of grains, vegetables and fruits can benefit the wealth of farming communities in developing countries. It's obvious, though, isn't it? With just three main grain plants dominating the food chain, and every country fighting to make money from farming and be a part of the global marketplace, there are going to be those at a natural disadvantage – namely those farmers who do not receive subsidies and nations who pay levies on exports.

In the UK, the range of grains we can include in our own diet includes rye, oats, spelt and the various strains among these species. Likewise we could expand our repertoire on the vegetable and fruit front, too (see Apples, page 1). Barley is a good starting point. It is the oldest cultivated grain in not only Europe and the Middle East but also possibly the world. Some historians believe that it may have been grown in China before rice. Looking at my store of pearl and pot barley, I wondered about this. Pearl barley, like white rice, has had all the bran milled away, leaving a mild-flavoured grain; pot barley still retains some bran, whose oils turn up the flavour volume. Barley has lower protein levels than wheat, hence its gradual decline – it was thought the poor could never be fed on such a grain – but it is sad to miss out on its delicate nature. Why not use it in a recipe and divert attention away from rice for a change?

Buying barley

Pearl barley is available in every supermarket but you may have to go to a wholefood store for pot barley – the one with the bran. The Infinity Foods brand of organic pot barley is widely available (www.infinityfoods.co.uk; tel: 01273 424060).

Barley Cooked as for Risotto

White pearl barley can be treated in exactly the same way as Arborio rice to make an Italian-style risotto. For 2 people, melt a tablespoon of butter in a heavy-bottomed pan, then add 1 finely chopped shallot. Cook for a minute, then add 150g/5½oz pearl barley. Cook for another 30 seconds, then pour in a wineglass of white wine and bring to the boil. Begin to add either chicken, vegetable or veal stock a ladleful at a time, allowing the barley to absorb the stock before adding more. When the barley is tender, beat in another tablespoon of butter. Season with salt and pepper and serve with grated cheese. For an indigenous dish, use a British hard, aged ewe's milk cheese, such as Lord of the Hundreds or Somerset Rambler, or a cow's milk cheese such as Twineham Grange (a Parmesan taste-alike made in the southeast). Add a vegetable, if you wish – the green kernels of broad beans, or Cos lettuce. The barley would also be good with shellfish, omitting the cheese: add North Atlantic prawns at the second butter stage, first using their shells to make the stock that 'feeds' the barley.

Pot Barley and Lamb Broth

More soup to eat regularly, leaving a store of it in the fridge and returning to it until it is finished. This time a broth, heartened with lamb or mutton. You don't want a soup that is too thick and grainy here but a clear, brown broth, with just enough pearl barley to make it a lunch. The sauce will brighten it, dragging a winter dish into spring. If you use mutton instead of lamb, be aware that there is often a lot of fat on it. If you make the broth the day before you eat, skim off the hardened fat but leave a little – it is not only very good for you but carries a robust, muttony taste.

Serves 4

1 teaspoon dripping
1kg/2¼lb shank of lamb, or mutton
   (neck, shank), including the bone
1 large carrot, roughly chopped
1 onion, roughly chopped
1 celery stick, roughly chopped
1 bay leaf
1 sprig of thyme

6 tablespoons pearl barley
sea salt

To serve:
1 garlic clove, peeled and cut in half
4 sprigs of flat-leaf parsley, very finely
   chopped
3 tablespoons olive oil
freshly ground black pepper

Heat the dripping in a large casserole, add the meat and brown on all sides. Add the vegetables and herbs, then pour in enough water to cover and bring to the boil. Skim away any foam that rises to the surface. Simmer for about 1½ hours, until the stock has taken on the flavour of the lamb – taste it – and the meat is falling from the bone. Strain the contents of the pan through a large sieve or colander, retaining the broth. Put the broth back into the pan. Discard the vegetables and herbs and pick the meat off the bone. Add the meat back to the pan with the barley. Bring to the boil again and simmer gently for 25 minutes, until the barley is cooked. It should be slightly chewy in the centre. Taste the broth and add salt if necessary. Skim off any surplus fat.

Rub the garlic clove around the inside of a small bowl to release its juice but no flesh. Add the parsley, oil and black pepper and stir. Add a teaspoon to each bowl of hot broth as it is served.

Pearl Barley with Turmeric, Lemon and Black Cardamom

We eat this as an alternative 'lemon rice' with curries and dals, or with grilled meat and fish. It is quite possible to adapt this recipe to other grains, such as basmati rice, oat groats, spelt grains or quinoa, if you wish. I like the feel of barley in the mouth – little springy cushions of grain that easily absorb the flavours of whatever they are cooked with.

Serves 4

2 tablespoons sunflower oil
1 white onion, finely chopped or grated
1 teaspoon black mustard seeds

1 black cardamom pod
2 level teaspoons ground turmeric
200g/7oz pearl barley
juice of ½ lemon
sea salt

Heat the oil in a pan, add the onion and mustard seeds and cook over a medium heat until the onion begins to take on some colour – the mustard seeds will make a popping sound. Add the other spices, stir and add the barley. Stir the barley to coat it with the oil and spice mixture, then pour in enough water to come just over 1cm/½ inch above the surface of the barley. Bring to the boil, cover the pan, then turn the heat right down and cook for 25 minutes. Have a peep from time to time – you may need to add a little more water if it is becoming too dry.

When the barley is just tender, add the lemon juice, then taste and add salt if necessary. Try to avoid eating the black cardamom – while it smells heavenly, it is a nasty thing to chew.

Kitchen note
Eat with the curries on pages 122, 124, 161, 349, Spiced John Dory (see page 223) or Skewered Spiced Mutton (see page 231).

Barley Water (the Queen's Recipe)

Jeremy Lee is a chef who likes to be called a cook. He grew up with good food in his mother's kitchen and is now dedicated to making it for others. Since meeting him and eating at his restaurant, the Blueprint Café in London, I have been awed by his knowledge, and love his simple approach to good ingredients. He is one of those chefs who resist the temptation to add another ingredient to a dish, and he makes a mustardy salad dressing that will activate your tear ducts at 20 paces. The table and cooking of his mother, Eileen Lee, must have rubbed off; you will always find bottled fruit and pickles lined up on shelves in his restaurant and they are not there for décor. Eileen died suddenly in 2006 but, during a conversation that strayed inexplicably to barley (my, how you'd enjoy my company), Jeremy told me about the barley water she would make for her 'little clucks', keeping it in a glass jug in the fridge. 'The recipe, which was called the Queen's barley water, was pulled from a newspaper,' he wrote when he sent me the recipe. 'It was so refreshing, nourishing and also very good for your skin.' Making it yields a nice little by-catch – a dish of barley to dress with olive oil, shallots and herbs.

> 225g/8oz approx. pearl barley
> 2.5 litres/4 pints water
> 6 oranges
> 2 lemons
> Demerara sugar to taste

Wash the barley well. Tip it into a pot and cover with the water, then bring to the boil. Lower the heat to a gentle simmer and cook gently for up to an hour, until the barley is tender. Strain the barley (reserve it for another dish) and leave the liquid to cool. Stir in the grated zest of 3 oranges and 1 lemon, then the juice of all the fruits. Add sugar to taste; it should not be too sweet. Pour into a jug and keep in the fridge, drinking within a day or two.

Kitchen note
Add the cooked barley, which will be quite soft, to a broth with vegetables, or dress it with olive oil, finely sliced shallot, plenty of chopped parsley (as much as it will take before becoming more parsley than barley) and lemon juice. Serve with Flatbreads (see page 232) or grilled or barbecued fish or meat.

Spiced Barley with Leeks, Root Vegetables, Oregano, Nutmeg, Allspice and Butter

Another useful way to eat barley. For 2 people, sweat (gently fry) 1 thinly sliced young leek in butter until soft, then add 150g/5½oz pot barley with a large pinch each of dried oregano, ground nutmeg and ground allspice. Cook for a minute, then add dried root vegetables such as Jerusalem artichokes, beetroot, turnips or squash. Cover with water and simmer for 20 minutes, until the barley is tender. Eat with roast meats – poultry, game birds and lamb – or try with a little fresh soft goat's cheese, briskly mixed with the barley just as you sit down to eat. A little leafy salad beside...

Barley in Breadcrumbs

Leftovers of the above barley recipe and the recipe on page 24 can be rolled into small balls, dipped in seasoned flour, then beaten egg, followed by breadcrumbs, then fried and eaten as a little appetiser.

BEANS

Rifling through the bags of beans in the kitchen drawer, it's easy to imagine how a geologist feels about his collection of favourite pebbles. Beans make funky percussion noises as they fall around in the bags, a hollow sound reminding us that here is a dry store, a useful source of food. And they are so pretty. Spotty like bird's eggs, black, purple, white, red and green – it's a glamorous palette for a humble, economic food. But what a food. My week never passes without a foray into the drawer for one type or another and, depending on whether I use dried beans or canned cooked ones, a pan will soon be simmering with something good under the lid. White beans, garlic and tomatoes are a classic combination; meaty-flavoured brown beans taste good with a hint of sweet-sourness and the richness of added pork; Mexican black beans are a favourite, because they are not too floury; green flageolet beans with shallots and butter is a dish I will keep going back to all my life. More recently, I have discovered that mung bean sprouts are lovely in herby soups.

However, with names like flageolet, haricot and cannellini, we are not talking of one British pulse. All beans sold dried or cooked and canned are imported. But they belong in our kitchens on various counts. One is that we do not grow them – we could, and should, develop some varieties, however – and the other is that we, the British, not famous for eating any beans other than Heinz, would discover that they make a valuable addition to our diet. Beans, along with lentils, grains and peas, need to become a central quotidian food. This is why:

Buying into beans is a humanitarian deed. They are the ultimate low-impact food, being as good for the places where they grow as they are for human nourishment. Their virtues are remarkable: they need little water compared to other food crops, tending to grow well in dry climates (major producers are Africa, India, Pakistan, Turkey and the Middle East); there are hundreds of varieties, so they are a diverse, anti-monoculture food crop whose cultivation benefits soil fertility and increases protection against disease and pests; bean plants also fix nitrogen in the soil, and so are intrinsic to traditional crop rotation as a 'green manure' – they also grow well without chemicals in an organic system and tend to be grown with the assistance of pesticides only when the farmer can afford it. A pulse grown in a developing country is usually free of spray. When last tested by the UK's pesticides residue committee, only 11 out of 81 samples tested positive for residues. These results are quite favourable for the consumer, but it is easy to buy pulses from an organically certified source.

On the downside, beans are still largely a commodity crop and there are very few fairly traded beans on the British market, although Suma, an organic supplier, sells fairly traded aduki and black beans.

On a more selfish note, we should eat more beans because they are so good for us. They are a low-cost way of eating a high-protein food containing plenty of healthy complex carbohydrates. They are packed with vitamins, iron and calcium. It is important to note, however, that while fresh beans are very high in vitamin C, dried beans contain virtually none. The good news is that canned beans, which tend to be cooked using fresh pulses, retain about 50 per cent of their vitamin C. I was delighted to discover this, as I have always felt guilty about buying canned beans, believing I should virtuously go through the whole cooking process. The truth is I rarely have the time, although it must be said that there is a much wider range of dried beans available, including some rare ones like appaloosa beans from America and black turtle beans from China.

Buying beans

I buy from Infinity Foods, a workers' co-operative in Brighton that sells a vast range of high-quality pulses. (See www.infinityfoods.co.uk; tel: 01273 424060). Monika Linton imports great beans for her London-based business, Brindisa, both dried and bottled, rather than canned (www.brindisa.com; tel: 020 8772 1600).

Basics when preparing dried beans

Unlike lentils, beans need to be soaked before cooking or they will split. If you soak them in cold water for several hours or overnight, then boil them for the correct amount of time, they should stay intact and slip lightly around the pan, mixing well with the other ingredients. It would be good to have a chart of cooking times for beans but no such thing can exist. The cooking time depends on size and type and also, more crucially, on how recently the beans were picked and dried – the older a bean is, the longer it takes to cook. It must be said that most beans sold in the UK are fairly aged, so expect to leave them for a good 1½–2 hour simmer. Test after about 50 minutes, though, just in case they are done. Overdone beans are floury and disgusting.

Bean Sprout and Herb Soup

A light soup, finished with a herb sauce. With a supply of fresh chicken stock, brewed from the bones after the roast (see page 116), this broth can be made in about 5 minutes. I have used mung bean sprouts, which are popular in Southeast Asian cooking. It is easy to buy fresh ones, but I have a three-tier clear plastic seed 'sprouter', known to the family as the 'farm', in which the beans grow to a useable sprout within a week or so. Mung beans have very little flavour when raw but take on a delicate, fresh, beany taste as soon as they land in the pan.

Serves 2

2 tablespoons extra virgin olive oil
2 spring onions, chopped
1 garlic clove, chopped
2 handfuls of mung bean sprouts and seed sprouts (any kind)
225g/8oz canned or cooked lentils (see page 252), drained of any liquid
600ml/1 pint chicken stock (see page 116)
sea salt

For the sauce:
leaves from 3 sprigs of parsley, finely chopped
1 teaspoon chopped chives
4 basil leaves, torn
2 tablespoons freshly grated Parmesan cheese (or other mature cheese, such as Twineham Grange or pecorino)
1 tablespoon pine nuts, toasted in a dry frying pan until golden
3 tablespoons extra virgin olive oil

Heat the oil in a pan, add the spring onions and garlic and cook for about 2 minutes, until soft and translucent but not browned. Add the sprouts, lentils and stock and bring to the boil. Simmer for 1 minute and then remove from the heat. Taste and add salt if necessary.

Mix the sauce ingredients together, breaking up the pine nuts as much as possible with the back of a wooden spoon. Spoon the sauce over the soup once it is ladled into bowls.

Baked Beans with Bacon, Molasses and Tomato

The nation's favourite canned meal was once a pottage, which was exported to the Americas by early settlers and became Boston baked beans – a dish of salt pork and haricot beans sweetened with molasses (but not tomatoes, which I have added here to keep up with modern tradition). An earthenware pot or cast-iron casserole with a well-fitting lid prevents the beans and sauce drying out during cooking. Try to find good bacon – dry-cured from naturally reared pork will let a gentle meaty flavour seep into the beans.

Serves 4

175g/6oz white haricot or navy beans
4 tablespoons cold-pressed
   sunflower oil (or extra virgin
   olive oil)
2 thick slices of green (unsmoked)
   back bacon
1 onion, finely chopped or grated
1 garlic clove, finely chopped
200ml/7fl oz passata (puréed
   tomatoes)
1 dessertspoon molasses
1 tablespoon English mustard
1 tablespoon Worcestershire sauce
sea salt

Soak the beans in plenty of water overnight or for 24 hours, then drain.

Preheat the oven to 150°C/300°F/Gas Mark 2. Heat the oil in a casserole and add the bacon, onion and garlic. Cook over a medium heat until soft. Add the beans, then the passata, plus enough water to cover the beans by 3cm/1¼ inches. Add the molasses and bring up to a simmer. Cover, place in the oven and bake for about 3 hours, until the beans are tender. You may need to add more water to prevent them drying out. About half an hour before you eat, add the mustard and Worcestershire sauce. Finally, add a little salt to bring out the flavour of the beans. Eat with fried eggs or any type of hot sausage, including black pudding.

Pinto Beans and Venison

The suet in this dish is optional but it does give it an amazing flavour. This is a good braise to eat with polenta or wild rice. Alternatively, serve with boiled long grain rice, or sourdough bread that has been brushed with oil and toasted.

Serves 6

225g/8oz pinto or Mexican black beans
1 tablespoon beef dripping or extra virgin olive oil
1kg/2¼lb venison, cut into 1cm/½ inch cubes
2 heaped tablespoons grated beef suet (optional)
2 onions, finely chopped
4 garlic cloves, chopped

4 chipotle chillies, soaked in hot water for 30 minutes, then deseeded and chopped
2 teaspoons ground cumin
½–1 teaspoon cayenne pepper (to taste)
½ teaspoon ground cloves
600ml/1 pint beef stock – plus more to make it soupy, if necessary (see page 64)
sea salt and freshly ground black pepper

Soak the beans in plenty of water overnight or for 24 hours. The next day, drain the beans and put them in a pan. Cover with fresh water, bring to the boil and simmer for 1–1½ hours, until tender. Drain and set aside.

Heat the dripping or oil in a large casserole (preferably cast iron) and brown the meat well over a reasonably high heat. Lower the heat, then add the suet, if using, plus the onions, garlic, chillies and spices and cook for 2–3 minutes. Cover with the stock and simmer with the lid partly on for approximately 1 hour, until the meat is tender. Add the beans and cook over a very low heat for 15 minutes. Skim off any fat that floats on the surface. Taste for seasoning and serve.

White Bean Broth with Buttered Tomato and Lettuce

White beans make textured soups that keep their elegance. They are the favourite bean of Italian cooks for this purpose. They have a mild, slightly floury taste and texture that absorbs the flavours of other ingredients.

Use cannellini beans or white haricots for this soup. Haricots are usually only available dried; they are a round bean, staying firm and smooth even after a long simmer in the pan. Cannellini are kidney shaped and can become quite soft. They are the better choice for busy cooks, since canned ones are easily available. The best lettuce to use is Cos, sometimes called Romano, or the heart of any other large-leaf lettuce.

Serves 4

4 tablespoons extra virgin olive oil
2 garlic cloves, chopped
1 white or red onion, finely chopped
1 celery stick and leaves, chopped
1 small fennel bulb and leaves, chopped
1–2 pinches of dried oregano
2 cans (about 470g drained weight) of white cannellini beans, drained – or use 200g/7oz dried haricot beans, soaked in cold water overnight, then simmered in fresh water for 1–1½ hours, until tender
1.2 litres/2 pints vegetable or meat stock (see pages 64, 116 and 238)
sea salt

To serve:
55g/2oz butter
1 garlic clove, chopped
4 small Cos hearts, cut into quarters, or the hearts of 2 larger lettuces, roughly chopped (use the outer leaves for salad)
4 plum tomatoes, skinned and diced
4 tablespoons grated Twineham Grange cheese (English Parmesan), or a hard ewe's milk cheese such as Lord of the Hundreds or Somerset Rambler – or real Italian Parmesan
a small handful of basil leaves
a little extra virgin olive oil

Heat the oil in a large pan and add the garlic, onion, celery, fennel and oregano. Cook over a low heat for about 2 minutes until their edges begin to soften. Add the beans and stock and bring to the boil. Cook for about 5 minutes, then taste for salt.

Melt the butter in a separate pan, add the garlic and lettuce hearts and cook gently until soft; add the tomatoes and stir once. Divide the soup between 4 serving bowls and spoon the lettuce-tomato mixture on top. Scatter the grated cheese over the top with the basil. Shaking over a few drops of extra virgin olive oil will turn up the flavour.

 Kitchen note
Omit the tomatoes and use lovage for this recipe if you grow it. Lovage has a floral celery scent and is a rare treat.

Bean and Herb Salads

Plain cooked beans, either drained straight from the can or from a store you have prepared yourself, can be mixed with herbs, olive oil and lemon juice then seasoned to make a salad that can be eaten with almost anything. I tend to choose either white haricot beans or cannellini beans for this job because they have the tenderest skins. You can make an exotic and piquant version, however, with black Mexican beans (unavailable canned but will cook in about an hour), chopped grilled peppers, garlic, red chilli and coriander. It is very important not to overcook the beans. Their skins should remain intact and the 'kernels' inside must not be floury but should have a little bite to them.

Quick Braised Butterbeans

I can buy tins of butterbeans from the late-night grocer's across the road. Drained, then flung into a pan with a couple of tablespoons of olive oil, a chopped garlic clove and spring onion, a teaspoon of organic Marigold stock powder and a little water, they make a bean stew in no time. I throw over a chopped hot red chilli, shake on some extra virgin olive oil, then eat them from a bowl.

BEEF

The cheap cuts

Grilled Goose Skirt with Salad Leaves and
   Berkswell Cheese

Top of the Rump with Lemon and Parsley Butter

Flank with Tarragon Butter Sauce

Braised Shin of Beef with Ale

Cold Salt Beef and Green Sauce

The valuable cuts

Roast Rare Aged Beef Sirloin with a Mustard and
   Watercress Sauce

Raw Beef with Horseradish, Sorrel and Rye Bread

Leftovers

Beef with Horseradish Sauce on Crisp Bread

Beef with Pumpkin Seeds and Carrot

Sauce for Pasta

Braised Beef and Fungi

Beef Stock

Dripping

My attitude to beef has recently moved into a new phase. It is easy to pinpoint when my original decision to eat less but better beef was made, because it was at the same time that I had the urge to write about food. My first piece 15 years ago was about a butcher. At the time I was motivated by the plight of the closing high-street butcher's shops. They were – on the whole – the best place to source delicious beef, but they were closing down due to the arrival of the larger 'superstores'. I was equally motivated by the matter of welfare: free-ranging animals, travelling only a short distance to the slaughterhouse, produce beef with a low PH and so more tenderness. When livestock are stressed, the acidity in their muscles is raised, affecting the finished result when cooked. But then, a year later, the BSE scandal exploded, when the link was made between the cattle disease bovine spongiform encephalitis and the human form, vCJD, and the whole subject of beef once more needed some examination. Two significant events had come to light. The first was that, revoltingly, beef animals had been fed the remains of their own species. This had been done purely in the name of profit – give an animal high-protein feed and it will grow at an alarming rate, becoming ready for slaughter, with lots of meat on its bones, nice and quick. The full, disgraceful disclosure of the participation of the livestock feed industry and the attitude of the Ministry of Agriculture (now Defra) and many (but not all) farmers was mind-blowing. The second significant event was the remedy introduced by the authorities to wipe out the disease in the British herd.

Meat changed by a scandal

The remedy dreamt up by the Ministry and its scientific advisers became known as the Over-Thirty-Month Scheme (OTMS), and simply meant that no cow – dairy or beef – was allowed to live longer than 30 months, because scientists said that the disease only developed in animals over this age. This had the peculiar effect of shortening the time farmers had to fatten up their beef steers, putting them under pressure in a way that has damaged the quality of beef and the national herd itself. Every farmer had to comply with it, including the substantial number who had never fed their beef animals meat and bone meal. It is not known whether the OTMS was actually responsible for reducing the number of cases; it was rumoured to be the idea of the supermarket chains, which wanted a clear-cut strategy that would boost consumer confidence.

It is nearly impossible for farmers to get their beef animals up to a saleable weight in just two and a half years. So what can they do? They can't feed meat and bone meal protein, because that is now banned – so in comes the cereal diet: soya, maize and other grains that are high in proteins and speed up growth. They then cross breeds with large, fast-growing Continental-type cattle and take the animals off that windy hill where they burn up far too many calories, instead making sure they spend more time in the shelter of a barn, getting pig-fat. Out of this the consumer gets flavourless, loose-grained meat, unsuitable for British butchers' cuts (the only exception is when butchers take the trouble to hang the meat on the bone for as long as possible). Consumers are further compromised because such beef, even though cross bred with non-native cattle, is still called by its British breed name – Aberdeen Angus, for example.

This news has altered my view of beef again. I now choose beef guided by three principles:

* Pure native breed
* Naturally slow grown
* Grass fed

Slow grown means that, where possible, I buy 'aged' beef that is over 30 months old – the OTMS was lifted in November 2005. The farmers who rear such beef must jump through hoops to do this: completing extra paperwork, moving livestock in separate transportation from others, and using abattoirs specially dedicated to the slaughter of older animals. Farmers who produce 'aged' beef complain that it is hard to profit from the extra effort, but the resulting meat is well worth it in terms of flavour. What really matters now, however, is the third principle: grass fed. Feeding beef animals grass ticks all the boxes in terms of healthy environment and healthy consumers.

Grass-fed beef is good food. The fat that is marbled through it contains higher levels of essential omega-3 fatty acids, including the nutritionally important EPA and DHA. Beef animals fattened on a high-protein (from grain such as soya and maize), high-energy diet, rather than on grass, will have a low ratio of omega-3 in their fat compared to other fats. To be healthy, humans need to eat fats in the correct proportion or the risk of disease, specifically heart disease, is increased. It is now thought that it is not so much burger culture that made one in four Americans fat and unhealthy but the way in which beef steers were reared. Eating meat containing the right balance of the right fats raises dietary levels of conjugated lineolic acid (CLA), protecting against cancer and – essentially – discouraging weight

gain because our bodies know exactly how to process such fat: burning it and not storing it as body fat.

US beef farmers are great proponents of maize feed, and 'park' their cattle in 'feedlots' – sheds or grassless fields where they are literally stuffed with maize. If you have been fed beef with yellow fat, you will recognise this beef. In the UK there is often that depressing sensation as you drive through the countryside that the crops growing in fields are mostly there to feed animals and not you. Even the wheat in the field could be for the feed bin rather than the bread bin. Compare the amount of pasture you see to the quantity of grain crops. We also import great quantities of cereal across the Atlantic to feed livestock, especially soya – much of it GM – which is high in protein and used to fatten beef animals before slaughter.

Feeding cattle grass slows down their growth. If it were the only feed available, there would be fewer beef animals on the market. We would be healthier, and so would the economy, unburdened by the cost of an obesity epidemic. However, the price of all beef would rise steeply towards the price now paid for organic and grass-fed beef. This is unavoidable, but using beef differently in the kitchen will help offset the cost. Learn to identify which are the cheap cuts to enjoy regularly and which are special. Pay more but make better use of the beef you buy. Use up leftovers, learn ways with cold beef, make stock and cook with the dripping (see page 64).

Buying beef

For beef to cook well, it must be hung properly. Hanging beef on the bone in temperatures just above 2°C breaks down the tough fibres – the meat is slowly decomposing. Beef should be hung for at least three weeks but I have bought joints from sides that have hung for up to five weeks. This beef will be visibly darkened by oxidisation on the outside but don't be put off – it will taste delicious. Always ask if the beef has been actually hung and not matured in plastic bags stacked in a freezer. This method never has the same effect but meat is increasingly matured this way, partly due to new regulations that insist that the cuts destined to be beef mince should not be hung for as long as the roasting joints. This means the sides have to be cut up and jointed early, and cannot physically hang.

It is impossible to choose good beef by inspection alone, but joints of native beef tend to be small and the grain finer. The colour of beef flesh varies and does not always relate to a long period hanging on the bone. This is why it is better to buy beef and other meat from a place where you can ask questions about feed, breed and welfare. Ideally, you want to hear that the animal, a native breed, was slowly reared on grass or forage, at a local farm.

Buying beef from local farms reduces carbon emissions, shortens journeys, reducing stress to the animals, and supports the local economy. To find locally reared beef, speak first to your nearest high-street butcher or visit a local farmers' market. If no joy, look at www.bigbarn.co.uk, put in your postcode and check their area maps, which highlight local producers – but ask specific questions about feed and breed before buying from any of their suppliers.

In London I buy beef from the butcher Jack O'Shea, at 11 Montpelier Street, London SW7 1EX (www.jackosheas.com; tel: 020 7581 7771). He hangs it for weeks and knows everything about cutting in both the Continental and the British way. He is an expert on cheap cuts that can be put on the grill, worth a visit for this alone (see recipes below).

Buying beef via home delivery is another option. Below are producers that I have used regularly:

* Pipers Farm in the West Country rears handsome Devon Ruby cattle, then hangs and butchers them expertly: www.pipersfarm.co.uk; tel: 01392 881380.

* Donald Russell is another great butcher whose beef is carefully matured and cut: www.donaldrussell.com; tel: 01467 629666.

* Blackface.co.uk in Dumfries and Galloway rears Galloway beef on the hill for up to four years, well beyond the OTM limit: www.blackface.co.uk; tel: 01387 730326.

* Edwards of Conwy sells Welsh beef, including cuts from native Welsh Black cattle: www.edwardsofconwy.co.uk; tel: 01492 592443.

* Andrew and Sybille Wilkinson at Gilchester Organics rear cattle on their organic pasture in Northumberland: www.gilchesters.com; tel: 01661 886119.

Beef – the cheap cuts

With beef I need to solve a problem. It is not a meat I eat often because, much as I love it braised for hours until tender, the truth is that I cannot always plan ahead. The kind of beef that it is best to buy, the slow-reared native breeds fed on grass, is pricy stuff. The sirloin, forerib, rib eyes and rump steaks are the easiest meals to make but come at an extraordinary cost. So, to find pieces of the best beef that are affordable for routine meals yet quick to cook, what is needed is an exceptional butcher. Most butchers insist that all cheap cuts must be minced or cut into cubes and slow cooked, but butchers who understand Continental cutting know differently. If the side of beef has been well hung – and this is almost the single most important element in successful beef cookery – it is quite easy to fast cook some of the more extreme cuts.

Cheap cuts on the grill

The following is a new series of recipes, the basic ideas borrowed from European butchery and cooking but adapted to British ingredients. They rely on your willingness to eat the meat medium rare or rare. All are cooked as whole pieces of meat and then sliced. If they are brown all the way through – 'well done', as the oxymoron goes in this context – the effect is ruined.

Grilled Goose Skirt with Salad Leaves and Berkswell Cheese

Goose skirt is a dark meat with a wide grain (it is a different cut from the plain flank or skirt in the recipe on page 51). It is essential that the beef has been well hung. If seared quickly, it will be very tender. Serving it with leaves and a hard, mature ewe's milk cheese is a good antidote to the richness of gravies and butter sauces. You could substitute Lord of the Hundreds, Somerset Rambler or Italian pecorino for the Berkswell.

Serves 4

750g/1lb 10oz goose skirt steak, left in
  whole pieces
4 large handfuls of young salad
  leaves

4 tablespoons extra virgin olive oil
115g/4oz mature Berkswell cheese,
  pared into thin slices
sea salt and freshly ground black
  pepper

Have ready 4 warm (but not hot) plates. Season the beef with salt and pepper. Heat a ridged grill pan until smoking, then sear the beef for about 2 minutes per side. Ideally, it should be eaten very rare in this dish. Transfer to a wooden board, leave to rest for a minute and then slice thinly. Lay the slices on the warm plates, scatter the leaves on top and shake over the olive oil. Put the pared cheese over the top and eat immediately.

Top of the Rump with Lemon and Parsley Butter

This is a tender muscle, taken from the cheaper end of the rump, with a strip of fat attached. In Portugal and Brazil it is known as the *picanha*, and thought far superior to a rib-eye or fillet steak. Unlike the skirt and flank in the previous and following recipes, it is grilled in individual helpings. If you like a peppery taste, add a tablespoon of crushed pink or green peppercorns to the butter.

Serves 4

4 top rump steaks

For the lemon and parsley butter:
140g/5oz unsalted butter, softened
juice and grated zest of ½ lemon
a large handful of very finely
    chopped parsley
freshly ground black pepper

First prepare the butter, putting all the ingredients in a bowl and stirring carefully until well mixed. Place the mixture between 2 sheets of greaseproof paper (or 2 butter papers). Roll it to about 1cm/½ inch thick and put it in the fridge to harden. When hard, remove from the fridge and use a small, round biscuit cutter to cut out discs (or other shapes). Leave the discs in the fridge.

Grill or fry the steaks, seasoning them with a little black pepper first. Ideally they should be served rare (see guide on page 52). Leave to rest in a warm place for about 10–15 minutes. Warm 4 plates. Serve the steaks with a disc of the lemon and parsley butter melted on top. Have some English and Dijon mustard ready on the table.

Flank with Tarragon Butter Sauce

Sometimes called skirt or *bavette*, flank is a cut taken from the diaphragm muscle of the beef animal. Here it is grilled whole, then sliced and served with a buttery sauce sharpened with shallots and vinegar. It must be cooked so it is rare in the centre or it will be dry. If you like steaks well done, I am afraid you will have to use conventional rump or sirloin.

Making the sauce requires a certain amount of patience, and a small, heavy-bottomed pan to prevent overcooking. It can be made in a food processor, however, if the butter is melted first and trickled in warm. Serve with green vegetables – the courgette salad on page 149 is good, fried potatoes even nicer ...

Serves 4–6

2 whole pieces of flank
a little olive oil
freshly ground black pepper

For the tarragon butter sauce:
4 tablespoons tarragon vinegar
4 tablespoons dry white wine

2 shallots, finely chopped
3 egg yolks
175g/6oz unsalted butter, at room
    temperature
a small handful of French tarragon
    leaves, chopped
sea salt and freshly ground black
    pepper

Season the beef with pepper, then rub it with a little olive oil. Set to one side (leaving it at room temperature).

Put the vinegar, white wine and shallots into a small, heavy-bottomed pan and heat to boiling point. Simmer until the liquid has reduced to 1 tablespoon, then remove from the heat and add 2 tablespoons of cold water. Leave to cool, then mix in the egg yolks.

Return the pan to a very low heat and whisk in the butter, one hazelnut-sized piece at a time, until the sauce is thick and glossy. Add the tarragon, then taste and season with salt and pepper. If it becomes grainy or begins to 'split', add a dessertspoon of iced water and whisk hard. Once made, the sauce will remain stable for half an hour or so if kept in a warm place; just whisk again before serving.

To grill the meat, set a ridged grill pan over a high heat. When it begins to smoke, lay the meat on the pan and cook for 2–3 minutes on each side, turning down the heat a little if it becomes too smoky. The meat will be rare in the centre. Remove from the heat and leave to rest in a warm place for 10 minutes. It should not be so warm that the beef continues to cook. Meanwhile, warm some dinner plates.

To serve, slice the beef across the grain and place a few slices on each plate, with a dollop of sauce beside it.

How to grill or fry meat

Very rare Sear the steak on both sides; a finger pressed on the surface will leave an indentation.

Rare Sear one side, then continue to cook until droplets of blood are visible on the surface. Turn the meat and cook the other side for an equal time. Some resistance should be felt when pressing a finger on to the surface.

Medium Sear one side, wait until juices (not blood) begin to emerge on the meat surface, then turn and cook the other side.

Other cheap cuts

The *onglet* is a muscle that connects the last rib to the kidney. It is brownish in colour and there is a faint delicious flavour of kidney. It is not generally used as a grilling steak in the UK, but if you visit a Continental butcher they will know it immediately – if not as *onglet* (the French name), then perhaps as *lombatello* (Italian), or *solomillo de pulmón* (Spanish). In America it is known as the hanging steak. A keen British butcher, with experience in cutting the Continental way, may be able to prepare it for you. Have a discussion when he hasn't got an enormous queue.

The *onglet* weighs about 500g/1lb 2oz and, when trimmed of gristle, it can be grilled or roasted whole (but left rare in the centre), then sliced and served with any of the sauces in the previous two recipes.

In Cork City in Ireland, butchers cut a muscle from the shoulder called the Jewish fillet. It is removed whole and totally trimmed of any connecting tissue or gristle, then – as with the other cuts – grilled whole and sliced. It can be served with the lemon and parsley butter on page 50, or with the tarragon butter sauce on page 51.

Other butchers elsewhere will have different names for the cuts in the recipes above. I once saw an Italian butcher cut the shoulder muscle as above, but my Italian was too appalling to ask about the name for it. Some butchers call *onglet* thin steak, others call it feather steak, because it is a V shape with grains leading from a central join. Disagreement over the terms leads only to a healthy debate between butcher and customer – I advise getting stuck in.

Cheap cuts in the pot

Almost any forequarter beef or shin meat is suitable for a slow braise. This is easy territory for butchers, who have loads to spare and are longing to get rid of it. If you can make time, encourage the butcher to give you some of the bones, to roast and then simmer with water the day before the braise so you have a ready supply of stock. Preparing stock takes just minutes – then all you have to do is wait until the pot has done its work.

Braised Shin of Beef with Ale

A slow simmer of beef is the best winter food. Supplemented with mash and piles of roasted root vegetables, a little goes a long way towards feeding a big table of people. Bread brushed with dripping or olive oil and rubbed with garlic, then baked until crisp, can be put in baskets on the table. Make sure you have handfuls of parsley to scatter over the top. If you want to be more adventurous still, grate a little orange zest into the parsley. In February use the zest of blood orange, which is somehow just right with red meat.

Serves 6–8

5–6 tablespoons olive oil or
   dripping
2 garlic cloves, chopped
2 onions, finely chopped
2 celery sticks, finely chopped
2kg/4 1/2lb braising beef, cut into
   4cm/1 1/2 inch chunks

1 bay leaf
a pinch of dried thyme
2 parings of orange peel
600ml/1 pint real ale
2 tablespoons plain flour
beef or other meat stock, to cover
   (see page 64)
sea salt and freshly ground black
   pepper

Heat about a third of the fat in a large, deep pan and gently cook the garlic, onions and celery in it until soft. Remove the vegetables with a slotted spoon and set aside. Add more of the fat to the pan, turn up the heat and brown the beef on all sides, cooking it in batches and setting it aside as soon as it is done. Add more fat as necessary. Add the herbs, orange peel and ale to the pan and bring to the boil, scraping away at the base of the pan with a wooden spoon to deglaze it. Return the meat and vegetables to the pan, sprinkle with the flour and stir well. Add enough stock to cover, then stir and bring to the boil, skimming off any foam that rises to the top. Turn down the heat to a slow bubble and cook, covered, for 1½–2 hours, until the meat is tender. Skim off any fat. Season with salt and pepper to taste.

Cold Salt Beef and Green Sauce

If you are lucky enough to know a butcher who puts brisket and silverside in a brine cure, it is an easy and quite economical dish to cook for one meal. Hopefully, there will be leftovers for following days, to eat in sandwiches with mustard or as a salad with a herb sauce.

Serves 6–8

1.5–2kg/3¼–4½lb piece of boned, rolled salt-cured silverside or brisket
1 clove
1 star anise
1 bay leaf

For the green sauce:
5 sprigs of parsley, chopped (or chervil, if you can find it)
3 sprigs of tarragon, chopped
4 sprigs of basil, chopped
about 2 tablespoons chopped chives
1 tablespoon chopped cornichons (baby gherkins)
1 heaped teaspoon capers, rinsed and chopped
1 teaspoon Dijon mustard
6 tablespoons olive oil
sea salt and freshly ground black pepper

Soak the beef in cold water for a few hours or overnight, changing the water once or twice. Drain the beef and put it in a large pan with enough water to cover. Add the clove, star anise and bay leaf, bring to the boil, then turn the heat down so the water is barely boiling – 'murmuring' is a good description. Simmer for 2–3 hours, until the meat is tender when pierced with a knife. Lift out, wrap in foil and leave to rest for a good hour.

To make the sauce, mix all the ingredients together, seasoning with salt and pepper to taste.

Serve slices of the lukewarm beef with the sauce and a potato salad. You could make the bacon and potato salad on page 20, omitting the bacon.

Beef – the valuable cuts

Now and again I turn to the special parts of beef for food to feast on – the sirloins, fillets, rump steaks and forerib. All can be cooked quickly, can be eaten rare and never toughen. Eating a grilled steak is an easy task – sometimes too easy with fillet steak, which can be tender to the point of dullness and lacks the flavour of a good rump steak.

These cuts form a small percentage of the meat on a beef animal, and have prices that match their economy of scale. Economic to buy they are not. It is not unusual to see well-trimmed fillet sold at over £35 per kilo. That's more than £8 per helping, so it is a meal that I will not serve for supper any old day.

What matters is to recognise that these are not cuts that should be eaten every day, even if your means make them affordable. A farmer goes to immense trouble over the years to rear a steer to perfection, yet there is only enough fillet to feed about 20 people from it. A butcher must trim off a good proportion of the fillet once it has been extracted from the carcass, because it is unsaleable with the untidiness of stray pieces of beef and some membrane. This meat is chucked into the mince and sold for pence, not pounds. For every fillet in a beef side there's an awful lot of much less valuable meat that is a hard job for the butcher to sell. It's not really acceptable for someone who says they love beef to eat only the fillet or sirloin. Demand for fillet is a demand for a whole animal to be reared and slaughtered and there is – bossy as it sounds – a collective responsibility to find uses for the other cuts. I am not suggesting buying the whole cow, but you can buy beef boxes from some butchers and mail-order services. You can also ask for bones. They are free, and a source of good stock, marrow or even canine happiness. Butchers and meat producers pay to have bones and waste material removed and disposed of.

So, if I haven't made you feel too guilty...

Roast Rare Aged Beef Sirloin with a Mustard and Watercress Sauce

Now that the Over-Thirty-Month rule has been lifted, it is possible once again to buy beef from steers that have reached their full maturity. So we now have four-year-old beef and it is unbelievably good, both to cook and in its vintage flavour. I buy four-year-old well-hung Galloway beef from Ben Weatherall, of Blackface (see Buying beef on page 46). Its texture and the way it cooks so beautifully, barely losing an ounce as it roasts, is confirmation that growing an animal slowly is the best approach to rearing beef.

When you buy your sirloin, ask the butcher for the 'cradle' of detached ribs for it to sit in as it roasts; they can be used to make stock for other dishes.

Serves 6

1.25kg/2¾lb whole piece of rolled sirloin
fennel seeds
6 small sprigs of thyme
sea salt and freshly ground black pepper

For the mustard and watercress sauce:
leaves from 2 bunches of watercress
1 tablespoon English mustard powder
2 tablespoons white wine vinegar
4 tablespoons chicken stock (see page 116)
1 shallot, roughly chopped
1 garlic clove, roughly chopped
200ml/7fl oz olive oil
lemon juice

Allow the beef to come to room temperature before you begin roasting. Preheat the oven to 240°C/475°F/Gas Mark 9.

Season the beef all over and put it in a roasting tin. Scatter the fennel seeds and thyme on top. Put in the oven and roast for 10 minutes, then turn the heat down to 175°C/350°F/Gas Mark 4 and continue roasting for about 30 minutes. Remove from the oven and test for doneness. To do this, insert a skewer into the thickest part of the meat, leave it there for 1 minute, then take it out and test the temperature of the skewer by touching it with your finger where it would have been in contact with the centre of the sirloin.

For rare beef, it should be above blood temperature (about 50°C/125°F if you use a meat thermometer) – this is not a dish to eat well done. If the meat is cooked, remove from the oven and leave for a good 20 minutes to rest. If not, return it to the oven for 10 minutes and then test again.

Meanwhile put the watercress, mustard, vinegar, stock, shallot, garlic and oil in a liquidiser and blend until smooth. Taste and add salt if necessary. Finish with a squeeze of lemon juice and stir well.

Carve the beef in thick slices and serve with the sauce in a bowl on the table so everyone can help themselves. Serve mustard, too – and have a big leafy salad afterwards.

 Kitchen note
The same sauce can be eaten with roast whole fillet or a rolled forerib roast.

Raw Beef with Horseradish, Sorrel and Rye Bread

Two years ago I travelled to Copenhagen on an assignment. The story was a young chef whose restaurant, Noma, was attracting much attention. Rene Redzepi has since won awards for his curious cooking, which uses only Nordic raw materials on a strictly seasonal basis. He made a 'tartare' similar to this one, and advised that we should eat it with our fingers. I recommend it (if occasion allows); somehow the absence of a cold fork is just right. It is a nice primitive way to eat a dish that feels northern European down to its boots, yet would not be out of place in Venice.

Redzepi made this with the fillet of a Musk Ox, a native Greenland breed. With none to hand, seek out any of the pure native British breeds: Angus, Hereford, Red Poll, Galloway, Devon, Highland, Welsh Black, White Park, Dexter and so on. Use only beef that has been hung for a minimum of three weeks, preferably four.

Serves 4

450g/1lb prime fillet beef
4 small pinches of sea salt
4 thin slices of rye bread, each slice
    trimmed of the crust and cut into
    4 squares (pumpernickel is the
    closest alternative to Danish rye
    bread)
4 tablespoons olive oil
2 tablespoons grated fresh
    horseradish
a handful of sorrel leaves – or sorrel
    sprouts (see Kitchen Note below)
2 shallots, very thinly sliced

1 tablespoon juniper berries
1 teaspoon coriander seeds
1 teaspoon caraway seeds

For the tarragon sauce:
6 sprigs of tarragon
1 tablespoon white wine vinegar
1 tablespoon chicken stock (see
        page 116) or water
½ shallot
½ garlic clove
150ml/¼ pint olive oil
lemon juice
sea salt

Begin with the tarragon sauce. Put the tarragon, vinegar, stock or water, shallot, garlic and oil in a liquidiser and blend to a smooth cream. Season to taste with salt and a few drops of lemon juice, then refrigerate.

Using a very sharp knife, 'scrape' the meat into fine strips along the grain, parting the grain. Divide it between 4 serving plates. Sprinkle each portion with a small pinch of salt. Fry the rye bread lightly in the oil, then scatter it randomly over the beef, followed by the horseradish. Finish off with the sorrel and sliced shallots.

Heat the spices in a deep frying pan until they begin to brown, then grind to a fine powder using a mortar and pestle or a redundant coffee bean grinder. Put a large pinch of the spice mixture on the side of each plate. Serve with little bowls of the sauce to one side of each plate, eating the tartare with your fingers by taking a pinch of the raw meat and dipping it first in the sauce, then in the spice.

Kitchen note
Sorrel takes just 2 or 3 weeks to grow in a bed or pot but is sometimes available from specialist greengrocers. Alternatively, try a peppery leaf such as rocket or even cress, instead of the lemon-flavoured sorrel.

Beef leftovers

In 2006 a stunning statistic revealed that the average person throws over £400 worth of food away each year, and I'll bet a proportion of that will be leftover meat, carcass bones and fat. If, after reading the introduction to the beef section, you are convinced that spending more on naturally reared beef is essential, then absorb the extra spend by making use of the leftovers. This food is a bonus, and a strong point in favour of the argument that good eating is more a question of knowing what to do with food than one related to money.

Cold meat

Beef with Horseradish Sauce on Crisp Bread

Making sandwiches with cold beef seems dull when you could brush a piece of bread on both sides with olive oil, then toast it in a pan, turning once. Meanwhile, make a sauce for 2 people by mixing together 2 teaspoons of mustard (English, French, whichever is your favourite), 1 tablespoon of grated horseradish or a teaspoon of 'Gentleman's Relish', a chopped shallot, about 3 tablespoons of double cream or crème frâiche, ½ teaspoon of cider vinegar and some salt. Place a slice of cold roast beef rolled up with 1 tablespoon of the sauce on the crisp bread, and throw over some chopped herbs or cress – or other salad leaves.

Beef with Pumpkin Seeds and Carrot

I have become as fond of green pumpkin seeds as pine nuts, and have a weakness for the sweet sourness of grated carrot, mixed with lemon and oil, then seasoned with salt. For 2 people, put 2 tablespoons of olive oil in a pan and toast 2 tablespoons of pumpkin seeds in it until they are tinged with gold. The oil will turn a beautiful green. Grate 2 carrots, dress them with about 3 tablespoons of olive oil and the juice of ½ lemon, then add a pinch of salt. Stir well. Divide between 2 dishes. Place slices of beef on top, then spoon over the seeds, with their lovely oil. Black pepper is essential.

Minced cold meat

Sauce for Pasta

Mince the cold beef using an old-fashioned mincer (available in hardware shops) or chop it into small pieces. For 4 people, fry approximately 450g/1lb mince with 1 finely chopped onion, 2 chopped garlic cloves and 2 chopped chicken livers. Add 2 pinches of dried thyme, a wineglass of white wine and a tin of tomatoes and cover with beef stock (see page 64). Simmer for about 1 hour, then taste and add salt. Serve with spaghetti, noodles or penne – and have a bowl of grated Parmesan cheese ready.

Braised Beef and Fungi

Make as for the sauce above, but omit the chicken livers and tomatoes, adding a handful of dried porcini that have been steeped in a mug of boiling-hot water until soft (add the soaking water, too). Simmer for an hour and serve with rice, or the cooked barley on page 24, or the farro on page 445. Use fresh mushrooms instead of dried, if you wish, and add a mugful of stock.

Beef Stock

To make beef stock, put the bones left over from a roast into a deep saucepan with a carrot, an onion, a celery stick and a bay leaf. Cover with water and bring to the boil. Simmer for about 1½ hours. Skim off surplus fat. Don't be put off by the time this takes; once everything is in the pan and simmering, the stock makes itself and you have a bountiful supply to use in other recipes. I like to call stock a half-made meal.

Dripping

Once the beef has been roasted, pour off the dripping (fat) through a sieve into a little bowl and store in the fridge. Use it to fry or roast potatoes. Spread the jelly that sets underneath the fat on to hot toast and throw over some sprouting seeds – broccoli seeds are perfect for this. You can buy them from Goodness Direct (www.goodnessdirect.co.uk; tel: 0871 871 6611).

Blackcurrants

Blackcurrant Tarts

Venison Marinated in Blackcurrants

Redcurrant Cake

I went on a radio programme once to discuss 'blackcurrants as a superfood' with a representative of the Blackcurrant Foundation. Asked by Jenni Murray, of BBC Radio 4's Woman's Hour, where the fruit originated, the expert said France. Well, it seemed rather rude to embarrass this blackcurrant expert in front of millions of people so I buttoned my lip. But it is not true. Blackcurrants, like white and redcurrants, are very northern – and originally grew wild all over Europe and Northern Asia, including Nordic countries. They love our climate, and grow well in Scotland. It is nice, for once, to look at a fruit and not think of it as better grown in France or Italy, like peaches, apricots and grapes. Blackcurrants are high in vitamin C, and the subject of many glowing tabloid health claims, since they have a high level of antioxidants (nutrients that help protect against cancer). The only problem with these claims is that currants of all colours usually taste even nicer with rather a lot of refined white sugar, which negates the goodness somewhat. But as a treat, puddings made with blackcurrants are among my favourites: their midnight inkiness, the rich and delicate flavour of the juice, the heaven that is blackcurrant jam, and the way you can use the leaves to add more blackcurrant flavour. And don't forget white and red currants – the latter make an extraordinary cake.

Buying blackcurrants

I see a lot of blackcurrants during the season, in vegetable markets and farm shops, and they are an excellent buy at pick-your-own farms. Double check the label – it is better, and always cheaper, to buy British.

Blackcurrant Tarts

Sweet, intensely flavoured little tarts. Serve them warm after baking and spoon some vanilla ice cream on top. Alternatively, if the season for blackcurrants lingers on into that for cobnuts, try them with Cobnut Ice (see page 138). If you don't feel like making pastry, a West Country producer will come to your rescue. Dorset Pastry is made with proper butter and all natural ingredients. Its sweet shortcrust pastry is impressive – available from Waitrose, or contact Dorset Pastry for other stockists: www.dorsetpastry.com; tel: 01305 854860. It is also available via mail order from Cornucopia Foods (www.cornucopiafoods.co.uk; tel: 08450 633699).

Makes 24

For the jam:
1kg/2¼lb blackcurrants, plus
    6 blackcurrant leaves
1kg/2¼lb granulated sugar

For the sweet pastry:
55g/2oz icing sugar
250g/9oz plain flour, plus extra for
    dusting
a pinch of salt
125g/4½oz softened unsalted butter,
    plus extra for greasing
1 large egg yolk
1–1½ tablespoons double cream

Make the jam the day before. Pull the blackcurrants off the stalk using a fork, then put them in a ceramic or stainless steel bowl. Cover with the sugar, give them a stir and leave for an hour or so to soften. Then put them in a pan, bring to the boil slowly and boil for 15 minutes. You don't need to boil it to a traditional jam setting point – sloppy jam is much better. Leave it to cool and set overnight.

To make the tarts, you will need 2 bun trays, greased lightly with butter (if you don't have any bun trays, it is possible to make one large tart in a 20cm/8 inch tart tin). For the pastry, put the icing sugar, flour and salt into a food processor and whiz for a few seconds. Add the butter and egg yolk, plus enough double cream to form a paste when the mixture is whizzed briefly. Do not overwork it. Remove from the food processor, place on a well-floured board and lightly work into a ball. Wrap in cling film and leave to rest in the fridge for about 1 hour.

Roll out the pastry on a well-floured surface, dusting the rolling pin frequently with flour, until it is about 3mm/⅛ inch thick. Work lightly and quickly – this is a rich pastry that can become greasy and difficult to handle. Using a glass or a pastry cutter that is about 2cm/¾ inch wider than the circumference of the bun moulds, cut out 24 circles of pastry. Press them into the bun trays, then refrigerate for about half an hour, until cold and solid.

Preheat the oven to 200°C/400°F/Gas Mark 6. Remove the pastry cases from the fridge and fill each one three-quarters full with jam. Bake for about 20 minutes, until the pastry is crisp. Remove them from the oven, leave for a minute or two, then lift the tarts out on to a cooling rack. Serve warm.

Venison Marinated in Blackcurrants

There is something very right about eating deer accompanied by berries. Deer can be a pest, roaming the countryside on an endless raid. They nibble the young shoots of brambles, preventing them cropping, and given half a chance will do the same with cultivated fruit in gardens. There is only one way to combat deer break-ins, and that is to feast on the intruders themselves. Revenge is a dish served hot.

Serves 4–6

1.25kg/2¾lb well-hung venison
   saddle, boned and rolled
450g/1lb fresh blackcurrants
2 tablespoons extra virgin olive oil
2 garlic cloves, chopped
1 small onion, chopped
85g/3oz butter, at room temperature

sea salt and freshly ground black
   pepper

For the vegetables:
55g/2oz butter
2 shallots, finely chopped
200g/7oz pot barley
450g/1lb curly kale, shredded into
   fine strips

Put the venison in a ceramic dish and cover with the blackcurrants. Leave to marinate in the fridge for several hours, turning occasionally.

Preheat the oven to 240°C/475°F/Gas Mark 9. Lift the venison out of the marinade and put it in a roasting tin. Season with black pepper, place in the oven and roast for about 10 minutes, then turn the heat down to 175°C/350°F/Gas Mark 4 and roast for another 20 minutes. Test with a skewer (see the roast beef recipe on page 57) or a meat thermometer. Rare venison should give a reading of about 50°C/125°F in the centre. Leave the meat to rest for 20 minutes, covered with foil in a warm place.

While the venison is roasting, prepare the vegetables: melt half the butter in a pan, add the shallots and cook until soft. Add the barley, stir-fry for a minute or two, then cover with water. Bring to the boil, turn down to a simmer and cook for about 15 minutes. Add the kale and cook for another 10 minutes, until both barley and kale are tender. Beat in the remaining butter and season with salt and pepper. To make the sauce, put the oil in a pan, add the garlic and onion and cook gently until tender. Add the blackcurrants from the marinade and cook until they are soft. Beat in the butter and season with salt and pepper to taste.

Have ready some warm plates before you carve the venison, as it cools very quickly. Serve a few slices to each person, with a little sauce and the barley and kale beside.

Redcurrant Cake

Due to their extraordinarily high nutrient content, more blackcurrants are grown in Britain than their relatives, red or white currants. Both have a more subtle, elegant flavour – especially redcurrants, which are delicious used in fools, ice cream and also in this pudding, which I like to call a biscuit that becomes a cake after it has sat for a while. It is quite easy to make, needing patience more than anything, but the end result will look like the work of a master pâtissier. Eat it with clotted cream or thin, creamy vanilla custard.

Serves 8

225g/8oz softened unsalted butter
70g/2¹/₂oz light brown muscovado
 sugar
175g/6oz ground almonds
225g/8oz superfine plain flour or
 Italian '00' flour, plus extra for
 dusting

a few drops of vanilla extract, or the
 seeds scraped out from ¹/₂ vanilla
 pod
approximately 450g/1lb redcurrants,
 pulled off the stalks with a fork (you
 can use previously frozen fruit)
caster sugar

Cream the butter and sugar in a mixer or using an electric beater until light
and fluffy. Fold in the ground almonds, followed by the flour and vanilla,
and mix to form a dough. Wrap the dough in a plastic bag and put in the
fridge to rest for about 1 hour.

Preheat the oven to 150°C/300°F/Gas Mark 2. Divide the dough into
quarters. Roll out each on a piece of baking parchment dusted with a
small scattering of flour. Use a 23cm/9 inch plate as a template and cut
around it, discarding the pastry trimmings to leave a neat round. Transfer
each sheet of pastry to a baking sheet and bake for 12–15 minutes, until
golden. The colour of the biscuit is important; it should be reasonably 'high
baked' – so a good golden colour without being burnt. Leave to cool on the
baking sheets.

To build the cake, transfer the least perfect biscuit round to a flat plate.
Scatter a third of the redcurrants over the whole surface in an even layer.
Sprinkle just a little caster sugar over them before lowering the second
biscuit on top. Repeat with the remaining layers, using all the redcurrants
so the top of the cake is biscuit, not fruit. It really does not matter if layer
1, 2 or 3 breaks (the biscuit is necessarily fragile) but try to keep number
4 intact for looks purposes.

Leave the cake to sit for at least 2 hours – the juice from the redcurrants
will seep into the biscuit and the whole thing should amalgamate nicely
into a crumbly cake you can cut (using a very sharp knife) into slices and
serve with cream or custard.

BROCCOLI

Purple Sprouting Broccoli with Little Brown Lentils
Creamed Broccoli Soup
Romanesco Salad

I could write poetry to welcome purple sprouting broccoli, when the fresh new season's spears hit the shops. It is just at that moment when potatoes are getting big and carrots enormous; the frosts are killing the softer vegetables and no other way can be found to eat squash. I have written before how purple sprouting, at its best, jostles for position with asparagus as a favourite seasonal pleasure – it wins because it is cheaper.

Buying broccoli

Farmers' markets are the best source of the freshest broccoli, both purple sprouting and the boring kind. Supermarkets sell plenty, but the delay as the broccoli travels from farm to depot for cleaning, trimming and packing is reflected in its slight toughness and reduced sweetness. To find a farmers' market nationally, see www.farmersmarkets.net or, for a London farmers' market, see www.lfm.org.uk.

Purple Sprouting Broccoli with Little Brown Lentils

When you want vegetables to sit patiently and ready on the table while you get on with other things, this is the way to do it. When I made this originally, I liked it a lot, but when I ate the leftovers as I did the washing up I liked it ten times more – so make in advance and leave it. Do not refrigerate; if it is served chilled, the flavour is lost. For a warm dish, reheat any leftovers the next day, when the broccoli will darken and the whole thing amalgamate. Eat with red chilli and lumps of fresh acidic cheese.

Choose broccoli that feels tender right down to the tip of the stem and whose flowers are still closed. The leaves should not be enormous, but young enough for the flower heads to be visible.

Serves 4

200g/7oz small brown lentils
2 garlic cloves, peeled and pressed
    with the flat side of a knife to crack
    them a little
2 wineglasses of red wine

water or chicken stock (see page 116)
2 sprigs of thyme
450g/1lb purple sprouting broccoli
6 tablespoons extra virgin olive oil
2 tablespoons red wine vinegar
sea salt and freshly ground black
    pepper

Put the lentils in a pan with the garlic and wine, then cover with enough water or stock to come about 1–2cm/½–¾ inch above the pulses. Add the thyme, bring to the boil and simmer for about 25–35 minutes. Test – the lentils should be soft in the centre but the skins should not be falling off.

Strip any big tough leaves from the broccoli, and peel away any tough skin on the stalk using a potato peeler. Bring 4cm/1½ inches of salted water to the boil in a large pan and add the broccoli. Cook until just tender, then lift out with a slotted spoon and leave to drain on a dry cloth.

Put the broccoli in a bowl. Stir the oil and vinegar into the lentils, then season with salt and black pepper if necessary. Tip this mixture over the broccoli and leave the whole dish to perform its alchemy.

Creamed Broccoli Soup

When very lightly cooked until it is just tender and still grass green, then blitzed with stock and finished with a lemon-scented cream, broccoli soup is a heavenly way to eat what can be a tedious vegetable. The key to giving this soup a light, fresh spring vegetable flavour is in timing the cooking perfectly, and gentle reheating.

Serves 4–6

2 tablespoons olive oil
1 white onion, chopped
1 garlic clove, sliced
1 litre/1¾ pints chicken or vegetable
  stock (see page 116)
2–3 whole broccoli heads, weighing
  approximately 700g/1lb 9oz,
  separated into spears

4 tablespoons double cream
sea salt and freshly ground black
  pepper

To serve:
4–6 tablespoons double cream
  withgrated zest of ½ lemon or
  Greek-style yoghurt

Heat the oil in a large saucepan, add the onion and garlic and cook over a medium heat for a few minutes, until soft and translucent but not browned. Add the stock and bring to the boil. Simmer for a minute, then add the broccoli. Simmer until the stalks are just tender when pierced with a knife – they should still have some 'bite'. Remove from the heat immediately and transfer to a bowl so the soup cools a little faster. Liquidise the soup with the cream until smooth. Taste and add salt and pepper if necessary.

To serve, mix the cream with the lemon zest. Just before you eat, reheat the soup gently, then serve straight away with a spoonful of the lemon cream, or yoghurt, in every bowl.

Romanesco Salad

I sometimes see this pointy, pale-green vegetable in local greengrocer's shops and farmers' markets. Although it is a relative of the cauliflower, it is known as Romanesco broccoli, and has a delicate flavour somewhere between cauliflower and broccoli. It is delicious served raw, for dipping into sauces, and when cooked it needs very little treatment at all except a drizzle of olive oil and lemon juice and parings of a hard cow's or ewe's milk cheese. Cut into quarters, then steam it for about 8 minutes. Test the stalk with the point of a knife – you do not want it too soft or the flower head will turn to mush. Much better that there is a firm stalk. Slice into big chunks, then serve in bowls with the oil, lemon, salt and cheese.

BUCKWHEAT

Kasha Salad

Buckwheat Pancakes

Herrings in Buckwheat Groats

My first encounter with buckwheat came in the form of a plate of blini, the Russian pancakes eaten with caviar or smoked fish. My step-grandfather was a Russian émigré, who adored them but liked them thick and heavy. My mother then found an authentic recipe in the Time-Life Russian cookbook – it was a revelation. Light, airy yeast pancakes with a taste of wholesome grain. Spoonfuls of melted butter, smoked fish and dollops of soured cream went on top; this was richness and earthiness combined. So you see, I am a fan of this brown flour with its dark flecks, but then recently I found kasha, the whole grains of buckwheat. They are shaped like a spearhead and are pale green. They need a short boil, then a wash to remove the starch. Added to salads or eaten hot with a dressing of oil, butter and fresh dill, they are exciting and totally different.

Buckwheat is not a wheat at all, but the grains from a flowering plant dating back thousands of years. It can, though, be used to make bread (with other flours) and noodles, notably soba noodles.

Buying buckwheat

Wholefood stores usually stock buckwheat flour, and often the groats as well. Organic buckwheat is available from Infinity Foods of Brighton. For stockists, contact them on www.infinityfoods.co.uk; tel: 01273 424060.

Kasha Salad

Kasha is whole buckwheat grains, sometimes sold as buckwheat groats. It has a green tinge and a fresh vegetable flavour, and cooks conveniently in a very short time. This simple salad has a gentle, grassy flavour. It is lovely with cold chicken, smoked fish or soft-boiled peeled eggs (bring eggs and cold water to the boil and cook for 4 minutes, cool in cold water, then peel).

Serves 4

2 garlic cloves, peeled
a pinch of dried thyme
200g/7oz buckwheat groats
1 ripe avocado

juice of 1 lemon
6 tablespoons extra virgin olive oil
a small bunch of dill, roughly chopped
sea salt and freshly ground black pepper

Put the garlic cloves, thyme and buckwheat in a saucepan and cover with water. Bring to the boil, turn down to a simmer and cook for about 15–20 minutes, until the buckwheat is tender but not a mush. Drain and rinse quickly in cold water to remove any foamy starch. Leave to drain for a few minutes; it should not be wet.

Peel, stone and dice the avocado. Put it in a salad bowl and dress with the lemon juice, then add the olive oil, buckwheat, dill and seasoning and toss quickly. Do not make this salad too far in advance or the avocado will discolour.

Buckwheat Pancakes

These are my English blini, adapted from the Russian recipe of my childhood made in an English kitchen. Earthy but light, thanks to the use of both whipped egg whites and yeast, they should be drizzled with melted butter and eaten with smoked fish (see the Cured Mackerel on page 257), chopped dill and soured cream. Freshly ground black pepper is a must. They could also be eaten with Bacon and Apples (see page 19) or perhaps a little thin slice of dry-cured beef, in which case serve with chopped spring onions and a little melted butter.

Serves 4–6

125g/4½oz brown buckwheat flour
250g/9oz fine white flour (if you want
    gluten-free pancakes, you could
    use rice flour)
½ teaspoon fine sea salt
30g/1oz fresh yeast
1 teaspoon caster sugar
450ml/¾ pint lukewarm milk
3 eggs, separated

2½ tablespoons soured cream
2½ tablespoons melted butter, plus
    extra for brushing

To serve:
smoked fish of any sort
fried mushrooms
chopped dill
300ml/½ pint soured cream
175g/6oz butter, melted

Put the flours in a bowl with the salt and leave in a warm place. Mix the yeast with the sugar until it breaks down to a paste, then add the milk. Leave for about half an hour, until the yeast is activated and a foam forms on the top. Make a well in the centre of the flours and pour in the yeast mixture, beating as you go. When you have a smooth batter, leave the mixture to rise for about 1½ hours, covered with a tea towel, until doubled in size.

Beat in the egg yolks and fold in the soured cream and melted butter. Leave in a warm place for 20 minutes. Whisk the egg whites until they form stiff peaks, then very carefully fold them into the bubbly pancake mixture. You do not want to break down the bubbles made by the yeast.

Heat a flat griddle or pancake pan and brush with a little melted butter; it should be hot but not smoking. Drop a tablespoonful of the mixture on to the pan and cook until bubbles rise to the surface and pop. Flip the pancake over and cook until puffed. Do not allow the pancake to burn – keep the heat steady. You should be able to cook 3 pancakes at a time in an average-sized pan. Keep the pancakes warm in a bowl lined with a tea towel, or eat them as you go, with any of the accompaniments listed above, finishing with chopped dill, a dollop of soured cream and a little melted butter drizzled on top.

Herrings in Buckwheat Groats

Herring fillets rolled in eggs and buckwheat, then shallow-fried and eaten with a good, piquant sauce. It is essential to buy very fresh herring. Herring roes are also good prepared like this.

Serves 4

200g/7oz buckwheat groats
4 large or 8 small herring fillets
1–2 eggs, lightly beaten
sunflower oil
sea salt and freshly ground black
   pepper

For the sauce:
2 egg yolks
2 teaspoons Dijon mustard
300ml/½ pint light olive or sunflower
   oil
lemon juice, to taste

3 hardboiled egg whites, chopped
   (see Kitchen Note below)
1 tablespoon capers, rinsed,
   squeezed and chopped
5 cornichons (baby gherkins),
   chopped
1 shallot, finely chopped
leaves from 1 sprig of parsley,
   chopped
leaves from 2 sprigs of tarragon,
   chopped
leaves from 2 sprigs of chervil,
   chopped (if available)

First make the sauce. Put the egg yolks in a bowl with the mustard, then gradually whisk in the oil bit by bit until you have a thick emulsion. Add the remaining sauce ingredients, taste and add a pinch of fine sea salt if necessary. Set to one side.

Season the groats with salt and pepper. Dip the herring fillets in the beaten egg, then roll them in the buckwheat groats. Pour enough oil into a heavy-bottomed frying pan to cover the base well. Heat the oil and fry the herrings over a medium to high heat for about 2 minutes on each side, until the groats are golden and the fish is firm. Eat hot, with the sauce.

 Kitchen note
Grate the hardboiled egg yolks over the braised chicory on page 132, to make a richer dish.

BUFFALO MILK

Buffalo Milk Yoghurt with Lavender Honey and Pear Salad

There has been an invasion, a friendly one, that has won the hearts and minds of food lovers everywhere. Buffalo roam the English fields – but not the entire countryside, thank goodness. They like to wallow to cool their muscles and, while it is a cute sight to see their ears and nostrils poking above the water in rivers and shallow ponds, it is a terrible job for the herdsmen to winch them out of their happy, wet haven and milk them.

Milking is the best possible use for them. Their meat is almost fatless, which makes it attractive to some, but I'd rather eat native beef with its marbling of fat, and on other days, buffalo yoghurt and cheese. Buffalo milk is a little volatile – it needs to be very fresh when made into yoghurt or fresh cheese, or it will have an overripe flavour that can be off-putting. I am not a milk drinker, so turn it into a rich, creamy, white-as-chalk yoghurt and serve it with flower honey and ripe pears – a healthy breakfast, but I would not be at all ashamed to put it on the table as a hurried pudding after lunch. There's no need, if you are short of time, to arrange it on plates as in the recipe below. Instead, just let everyone d-i-y. The yoghurt can go, ice cold, into a large earthenware bowl with a ladle, the honey on the table and a bowl of pears.

Buying buffalo milk

Higher Alham Farm, near Shepton Mallet, produces milk, yoghurt and an excellent, not quite authentic, organic buffalo cheese to eat fresh with salads. Its products are available at Pimlico, Notting Hill, Stoke Newington and Archway farmers' markets in London. Mail order is available for a minimum quantity: www.buffalo-organics.co.uk; tel: 01749 880221.

Buffalo Milk Yoghurt with Lavender Honey and Pear Salad

To make the yoghurt, you will need four 250ml/9fl oz jars, spotlessly clean, and a warm place such as an airing cupboard. Automatic yoghurt makers are available from Lakeland Ltd (www.lakeland.co.uk; tel: 015394 88100).

You can, of course, buy the yoghurt, or use a good whole dairy milk brand that you are devoted to, but...

Serves 8

1 litre/1¾ pints fresh buffalo milk
4 tablespoons live yoghurt

For the lavender honey and pear salad:
6 Comice pears, peeled, quartered and sliced
juice of ½ lemon
2 heaped tablespoons lavender honey
a few lavender buds, if available

Warm the milk to boiling point, then leave it to cool to just above blood temperature – about 38°C/100°F. Stir in the live yoghurt and put it into jars. Seal and put in a warm place (about 29°C/84°F) for about 6 hours, until set.

Put the pears into a bowl, squeeze over the lemon juice, then pour over the honey. Gently stir, or turn the pears over so they get a good coating of the honey, which will thin as you do this. Add a little pinch of lavender buds. Eat the yoghurt with the pear salad spooned over.

CAULIFLOWER

Cauliflower with Lancashire Cheese

Leftovers
Crisped Cauliflower with Breadcrumbs
    and Garlic
Cauliflower Soup

I am an admirer of cauliflower but I am not sure about anyone else. It was astonishing to hear from a farmer, standing with him in a giant cauliflower patch near Preston, that the British are colour sensitive about the vegetable. Unless it is spotlessly white, no one will buy it. On the day of my visit to this mecca of cauli growing, the sun was out and the cauliflowers were swiftly turning yellow. The farmer told me he would grub the whole lot into the ground: it wasn't just the supermarkets who would be reluctant to buy them, the shoppers wouldn't touch them.

On that basis, I think we need some recipes for this vegetable that, when fresh, is less sulphurous, less aggressive, more… poetic than a cabbage. Mark Twain was right when he said that a cauliflower is a cabbage with a college education.

Cauliflower with Lancashire Cheese

The cheese sauce for this dish is a basic that you can pour over other leafy vegetables to make a filling supper – try it with Swiss chard, Brussels sprouts, curly kale, spinach, lettuce hearts and beetroot tops.

Serves 4–6

1 large cauliflower, broken into chunks
(use the leaves if they look fresh,
slicing them into thin strips)
a pinch of ground mace or a few
gratings of nutmeg

600ml/1 pint milk
1 bay leaf
40g/1½oz butter
40g/1½oz plain flour
200g/7oz Lancashire cheese, grated
sea salt and freshly ground black
pepper

Fill a large pan with water and bring it to the boil. Add a pinch of salt and the cauliflower and boil for about 7 minutes, until just tender but not soft. Meanwhile, put the spice, milk and bay leaf into a small pan and bring to the boil. Pour into a jug and set to one side. Melt the butter in the same pan and add the flour. Mix to a paste and cook over a low heat until the paste has a sandy texture. Gradually whisk in the hot milk (having removed the bay leaf), making sure there are no lumps. Bring the sauce to the boil, stirring all the time. Add the cheese and stir once more, then remove from the heat. Season with salt and pepper.

Put the cauliflower in a shallow ovenproof dish and pour the sauce over the top. Either brown it under the grill or bake for a few minutes in an oven preheated to 240°C/475°F/Gas Mark 9, until browned on top.

Kitchen note
You can make this dish without flour, whisking together 5 egg yolks and 600ml/ 1 pint single cream or crème fraîche. Bring very slowly up to the boil but do not let it bubble. Season with nutmeg, salt and pepper and add the Lancashire cheese. Pour the sauce over the cooked cauliflower and bake to brown the top. The result is more of a rich, baked custard.

Crisped Cauliflower with Breadcrumbs and Garlic

I like to fry previously boiled cauliflower with fresh breadcrumbs in a little oil, with a peeled garlic clove (to be removed later), then eat it with orecchiette, the little 'ears' of pasta that so effectively collect the broken, crisp pieces of cauliflower and crumbs. Grate some Parmesan cheese over the top.

Cauliflower Soup

Gently fry a chopped onion in butter or oil, then add the cooked cauliflower. Season with a little English mustard powder, cover with milk and stock (50/50) and bring to the boil. Liquidise and season, then serve hot with a little cream and chopped chives – or my favourite herb, chervil, if you can get it.

Glorious Rehash – A New Generation of Leftovers

Thin, melting slices of rare roast beef, eaten with a mustard dressing tinted with anchovies and capers; cockles in a hotpot of seafood broth, served with a garlic sauce; little cauliflower florets crisped in a pan with breadcrumbs and olive oil; the lightest shrimp shell and straw mushroom broth, made warmer still with needles of fresh ginger; a radiant, creamy squash soup, flavoured with melted, brandy-washed cheese; or perhaps a dish of rice spiked with allspice and green pistachios, cooked in a pan with shards of roast lamb...

A menu that sounds richly indulgent but which is a good deed: in all these dishes there is something that might otherwise have been thrown away. Leftovers – the skeletons, shells, skins and extra flesh of foods deserving of a better future. Landfill that became a tummy full.

If you pay more for the best raw materials, it makes sense to use up every little bit. When a cut of well-hung meat from a slow-reared, grass-fed animal costs between twice and four times as much as one that was reared indoors and forced to grow fast on an unnatural diet, spreading the cost becomes an economic necessity. But this is not the only reason to reduce waste. It is estimated that one-third of the food bought in the UK is thrown away, ending up in landfill where it rots, emitting methane, a major contributing factor to climate change. The value of this food is estimated at £8 billion yearly – sympathy wanes, in certain cases, with complaints about paying more for better food.

The case for eating leftovers has not historically been helped by gloomy offerings of unidentifiable rissoles, khaki-hued 'mystery' vegetable soups, or bubble and squeak. An occasional plate of fried, leftover greens and mash is bearable but taken weekly it is tedious. There are other ways: using the colour and fragrance of fresh herbs from a pot on the windowsill, trying interesting seasonings, adding piquant dressings, wrapping with good bread or thin, olive oil pastry. Abandon bubble and squeak, take those cooked sprouts or spring greens, shred them and fry them instead in butter with cooked rice or whole grains of wheat; add *ras al hanout*, a Moroccan spice mix, then perhaps some chopped celery and shredded cold cooked chicken, game or lamb; sprinkle with black onion seeds once piping hot, then serve with creamy Greek yoghurt and fresh coriander. Suddenly you have in front of you a feast, even if one grown from humble beginnings. As for the spare cooked potato, mix it with a little potato flour and beaten egg, then make it into little patties; fry them and eat with smoked haddock, fresh peppery watercress and soured cream. Two typical leftover Sunday lunch foods become two extra, economical meals.

Broth, or stock, is the tea of bones. How can a nation that is self-confessedly addicted to tea not feel the same about stock made from chicken carcasses, beef shins, fish bones or prawn shells? Like tea, stock warms the soul and revives flagging energy levels. It is impossible not to feel good after eating food made with stock. It is even time-economic: once in the pan, it bubbles along unassisted, ready to use in an hour, or to bottle and freeze. A risotto or soup made with real stock has reserves of natural, heavenly flavour that underpin the goodness in the other ingredients and cut the need for salt. Doctors should prescribe stock – and go some way to preventing heart trouble. Casting pearls before swine may seem all too easy, but eat the pig from the tips of its toes to the end of its ears and there will be money for gems.

CELERY

Green Celery, Crayfish and Potato Salad
Celery Soup
Celery Stock

Farmers and shops are dismissive of celery – you only have to watch the harvest to witness this, which I did one horrible wet day in Cambridgeshire. It is a magnificent-looking crop, tall and leafy, its big strong heart and root deep in the Fens. But as it is pulled out of the ground, the pickers immediately cut off all or most of the heart, then lop all but a few leaves from the top, leaving just 30cm/12 inches of stalk. I have a nasty suspicion that this execution, which is not practised in southern Europe where celery is sold in its gorgeous entirety, is carried out in order that the celery head will fit in the average carrier bag. It is true that no one is quite sure what to do with celery, except use it as a base for stews or stick it in a jug and put it out with the cheeseboard.

It's nice to emerge from a market with a mane of foliage flying out behind you, and tap into a vegetable that has a flavour I can only describe as important. Celery is as much a seasoning as a main ingredient. Even the leaves, where the flavour is at its most intense, are useful and should not be wasted.

Buying celery

The original 'Fenland' celery is still grown in deep furrows in the Fens, and is available from October to December in Waitrose. You can use ordinary celery in any of the following recipes, but look out for heads with leaves.

Green Celery, Crayfish and Potato Salad

Jane Grigson's salad of mussels, potatoes and celery inspired this rare, crayfish-packed version, which I made on my return from the Fens clutching a whole celery plant saved from the picker's knife. I fancied that freshwater crayfish roam the streams around the fields where the celery and potatoes grow, circling them. So, as it does with other things that share a landscape, like pork and apples, it seemed right that they ended up in the same bowl. The result is a fresh and unusual salad, the sweetness of the crayfish pitched against the sharp, savoury celery, with the potato in between, mopping up the dressing.

For information on buying crayfish, see page 159.

Serves 4 as a main course

600g/1lb 5oz new potatoes
280g/10oz celery sticks
200g/7oz shelled, cooked crayfish
4 tablespoons extra virgin olive oil
juice of 1 lemon
leaves from 2 sprigs of flat-leaf
parsley
sea salt and freshly ground black
pepper

Put the potatoes in a pan of water and bring to the boil. Cook until the point of a knife will slip in with just a little resistance. Remove from the heat, drain and immediately rinse with cold water to prevent further cooking. Allow to cool, then cut into slices 5mm/¼ inch thick. Put in a large bowl.

Pull any tough strings from the celery sticks and wash off any dirt. Slice them thinly across the grain, then rinse and pat dry.

Add the celery and crayfish to the bowl of potatoes and toss together with the oil, lemon juice, parsley, some freshly ground black pepper and a pinch of salt flakes. Use celery leaves for decoration.

Celery Soup

Celery has awkward bits – namely the strings that run up the length of the stalks. Removing some of them will make this a smoother, creamier soup. Using a mixture of stock and milk gives it a more velvety texture still. The important part is the stewing of the vegetables in butter or oil at the beginning, because it helps to extract the maximum flavour.

Serves 6

½ head of celery, with leaves
85g/3oz butter or 4 tablespoons
   olive oil
2 white onions, chopped
4 medium potatoes, peeled and cut
   into dice
600ml/1 pint chicken stock (see
   page 116)

600ml/1 pint whole milk
300ml/½ pint single cream
3 teaspoons pink peppercorns,
   crushed
sea salt and freshly ground black
   pepper
spare celery leaves, finely chopped,
   to garnish

Pull the strings from the celery, using a knife to lift them from the lower end, then pulling them away from the full length of the stalk. Throw away the strings and chop the rest of the celery, including the leaves, into 2cm/¾ inch pieces. Put them in a large pan with the butter or oil and the other vegetables and cook over a medium-low heat for about 10 minutes. Add the stock and milk, bring to the boil, then turn down to a slow simmer and cook for about 20 minutes, until the vegetables are tender. Remove from the heat, cool a little, then liquidise in small batches. You can, if you want a very smooth soup, pass the whole lot through a sieve after blending. All the above can be done in advance.

Shortly before you serve, reheat the soup with almost all the cream, but do not let it boil. Season to taste, ladle into bowls, then add a little cream to each, with a pinch of the pink pepper and a few celery leaves.

Celery Stock

If I have no meat stock, there's usually some celery lurking in the bottom of the fridge – bendy, no doubt. But chop it and put it, and especially the leaves, in a big pan with a tablespoon of butter. Cook over a medium heat for about 5 minutes then add about 1.7 litres/3 pints water and bring to the boil. Simmer – not too fast or the water will evaporate – for about 30 minutes. Part-liquidise it, then strain, pushing every bit of juice through the sieve. The stock will not have all the flavour of a slow-made meat stock but it will be useful for other soups, and better than using water. You will also have used up that bendy celery.

For another celery recipe, see Bacon and Potato Salad with Green Celery Leaf and Cider Vinegar on page 20.

CHEESE

Melted Cheese and Ale, to Eat with Bread

Pasta with Ricotta and Woody Herbs

Beetroot, Red Cabbage and Goat's Cheese Salad

Stinking Bishop Tart

Fried Fresh Goat's Cheese with Apples, Victoria Plums
   and Orange Blossom Honey

Flowerpot Cheesecake Decorated with Flowers

Cheese is a divided world, one that is 99 per cent industrially made and 1 per cent traditionally made by artisans on the farm with their own milk. The latter is always the most exciting to eat; one piece is a meal of greatness. But Randolph Hodgson of Neal's Yard, who has done so much for artisan and raw milk cheese, taught me not to be a snob about the block Cheddars, Cheshires and Wensleydales that take up so much space in the supermarket. They are good, cheap, healthy food, he said, and he is right. I do not subscribe to the paranoia that has had the Food Standards Agency label every cheese with a high-fat health warning. As long as you are not going to eat the whole block in one go, think of the protein and calcium, and remember that since we have been advised to eat low-fat dairy products, everyone has been getting fatter and fatter. Treat these cheeses as mainstays for daily life, then buy artisan cheeses for treats, eating them with fig cakes and quince paste, with green salads, bread, honey or toast.

Buying cheese

Neal's Yard Dairy is the place for the best British cheeses. It has a mail-order service but if you can visit their London shops, and taste as much as you can get away with, it is an education. Check the website for details: www.nealsyarddairy.co.uk, or try www.finecheese.co.uk.

Melted Cheese and Ale, to Eat with Bread

Like a fondue, but made with ale, the cheese becomes a runny, mustard-tinted dipping sauce for blanched purple sprouting broccoli and dry sticks of sourdough bread or flatbreads. A fondue set, or some other means of keeping the melted cheese warm on the table as you eat it, helps ensure it is nice and runny. Using a handmade farmhouse cheese gives a much better texture. Block Lancashire, made in factories and matured in plastic, tends to be too wet and rubbery for melting.

Add more mustard if you like it hot. Eat a big green salad after and follow it with fruit, to balance the richness of the dish.

Serves 4–6

150ml/¼ pint real ale
450g/1lb Mrs Kirkham's Lancashire
  cheese, grated
juice of ½ lemon
1 tablespoon English mustard
a dash of Tabasco sauce
a dash of Worcestershire sauce

Put the ale in a pan and bring to boiling point. Add the cheese and stir gently with a wooden spoon over a low heat until it melts. Add the lemon juice, mustard and sauces, then taste – add more of either, if desired. Serve hot, in a dish that has been warmed in the oven or in a fondue set, so the cheese does not thicken. Put a big dish of the dipping 'tools' beside it.

Pasta with Ricotta and Woody Herbs

No recipe needed here – just stir 250g/9oz fresh ricotta cheese into 4 helpings of cooked pasta (about 250g/9oz dry pasta). If you can find the original ewe's milk ricotta, so much the better. To finish, melt a little butter with a pinch of dried thyme (or a few leaves of fresh), plus a little fresh lemon thyme, marjoram or oregano, and drizzle it over, then scatter some grated fresh Parmesan cheese on top.

Beetroot, Red Cabbage and Goat's Cheese Salad

I originally paired up roast beetroot and raw red cabbage because the colours were good together, magenta on magenta, but I did not expect it to be so delicious. The red cabbage is the big surprise. Eaten raw, it is tender, with none of the sourness of uncooked white or green cabbage. Choose a goat's cheese with an ash rind – Dorstone, Chabis and Ragstone are perfect.

Serves 4

8 medium beetroot
2 tablespoons red wine vinegar
2 tablespoons olive oil
¼ small red cabbage, cut into thick slices, then shredded into 2cm/ ¾ inch pieces

200g/7oz goat's cheese with an ash rind, sliced and broken into bite-sized pieces
a little extra virgin olive oil
2 dried bird's eye chillies, crushed
sea salt

Preheat the oven to 175°C/350°F/Gas Mark 4. Put the whole beetroot, untrimmed and with a little stalk left on, in a roasting tin and add the vinegar and oil. Roll the beetroot round the tin to coat them with both, then cover with foil and bake for 45 minutes. Remove the foil and continue to bake for another 15 minutes, until burnished and tender. Allow to cool.

Divide the shredded cabbage between 4 plates. Slice the beetroot – there is no need to peel them – and pile them on top of the cabbage, then scatter over the goat's cheese. Pour a little oil on to each salad, scatter a pinch of the crushed chilli on top and finish with a little salt.

Stinking Bishop Tart

I used to make this with a good farmhouse Cheddar until I found, looking at monastic cheeses (those with rinds washed in liqueur, which originated in the monasteries of France and Germany), that Munster melts beautifully; but then Stinking Bishop replaced Munster in my affections. The name of this new British cheese is the name of the pear once used in the liquor that cheesemaker Charles Martell washes it in, not a friendly wink at the pious cheesemakers in the monasteries. The lovely surprise about smelly cheese is that it does not taste smelly and has volumes of flavour when hot. Be careful not to let anyone sell you one that has gone over the top, though – if it stinks of ammonia (a disinfectant), don't buy it.

If you cannot find Stinking Bishop or Munster, try St James, Celtic Promise, Criffel or Carola. See www.nealsyarddairy.co.uk or www.ijmellischeesemonger.co.uk.

Serves 4–6

115g/4oz cooked ham, diced (optional)
115g/4oz Stinking Bishop cheese, chopped into small dice (the rind removed only if crusty and dry)
2 eggs
2 egg yolks
300ml/½ pint single cream
a pinch of grated nutmeg
freshly ground black pepper

For the pastry:
225g/8oz plain flour, plus extra for dusting
a pinch of salt
85g/3oz chilled unsalted butter or lard, diced
1 egg yolk
2–3 tablespoons cold water

To make the pastry, put the flour and salt in a bowl and rub in the fat lightly but thoroughly with your fingertips until the mixture resembles breadcrumbs. Work in the egg yolk and enough cold water to form a dough (this can all be done in a food processor, if you prefer). Roll the pastry out on a lightly floured work surface and use to line a deep 20cm/8 inch tart tin. Prick the base randomly with a fork and chill for 15 minutes.

Preheat the oven to 190°C/375°F/Gas Mark 5. Cover the pastry with greaseproof paper and fill with dry rice or beans (this will prevent the pastry bubbling up). Bake for about 15 minutes, until the pastry is dry. You may want to take out the paper and rice or beans for the last 5 minutes of cooking so the base can dry out completely.

Scatter the ham over the pastry case, followed by the cheese. Mix together the eggs, yolks, cream, nutmeg and some pepper and pour this mixture over the ham and cheese. Bake the tart for 25–30 minutes at 190°C/375°F/Gas Mark 5, until risen and glossy brown.

Fried Fresh Goat's Cheese with Apples, Victoria Plums and Orange Blossom Honey

Autumn Saturday breakfast or light supper, and a treat if you can find a nice handmade goat's cheese, with a flavour-enhancing natural mould on its surface, like Dorstone (see Neal's Yard, page 95). Monika Linton, who imports Spanish food for her London company, Brindisa, introduced me to the method of dipping goat's cheese first in flour then in egg, on a trip to an exceptional goat's cheese dairy near Madrid, Monte Enebro. Small, fresh goat's cheese 'buttons' are also ideal – try Chabis. To buy Monte Enebro cheese, contact Brindisa: www.brindisa.com; tel: 020 8772 1600.

Serves 2

2 apples, cored and very thinly sliced
4–6 Victoria plums, pitted and
    quartered
a squeeze of orange juice
a few lemon balm or mint leaves, plus
    maybe a few rocket flowers if
    available

50g/1³/₄oz plain flour
2 eggs
2 slices of fresh goat's cheese, about
    1.5cm/²/₃ inch thick
150ml/¼ pint olive oil
3 tablespoons runny orange blossom
    honey

Mix the apples and plums with the orange juice and herb leaves and divide between 2 serving plates.

Spread the flour over a plate and beat the eggs together in a bowl. Cut each slice of cheese in half diagonally, then dip all 4 pieces in the flour. Turn to coat them on both sides, then submerge in the beaten egg. Heat the oil in a small frying pan until a drop of water sizzles when dropped in at arm's length. Put the goat's cheese slices quickly into the pan. Fry on both sides until golden and drain quickly on kitchen paper. Put 2 pieces on each plate, zigzag the honey over them and eat straight away. Toast and marmalade follows this nicely.

Flowerpot Cheesecake Decorated with Flowers

Without a doubt, this is the prettiest cheesecake for a spring feast, slightly sweet, rich yet light from the addition of egg white (which helps with the set). It is not baked, so eat with strawberries, and some sweet, nutty biscuits like those on page 311.

You will need a spotless middle-sized flowerpot (approximately 600ml/1 pint in capacity), lined with enough clean, damp muslin to overhang the edges.

Serves 4–6

300ml/½ pint double cream
225g/8oz full-fat cream cheese, or
   whole-milk ricotta cheese
55g/2oz caster sugar
2 egg whites

To serve:
grated zest of 1 lemon
various edible flower petals, such as
   pansies, marigolds and nasturtiums
   – gaudy windowbox colours are
   good
fresh berries, such as strawberries,
   redcurrants and white currants

Lightly whip the double cream until thickened. Push the cream cheese or ricotta through a sieve, then combine with the cream. Do not over mix. Stir in the sugar.

In a separate bowl, whisk the egg whites until they form stiff peaks. Fold them into the cheese mixture. Pile into the lined flowerpot and bring the muslin over the top to cover. Stand the flowerpot on a rack placed above a bowl in the fridge and leave overnight.

To serve, un-mould, sprinkle over the lemon zest and decorate with edible flowers, then eat with fresh berries.

Leftover cheese

Keep the rinds of hard cheeses when you have devoured all the 'flesh'; they can be chopped and added to smooth soups, where they will miraculously melt and add their flavour. This works well with the Pumpkin Soup on page 396.

CHESTNUTS

Hot Chestnut and Honey Soup
Potted Duck with Chestnuts

Sweet chestnuts are very important in European countries, where they
are yet another source of good, cheap nutrition. The flour is used in
pancakes, cakes and pasta, and the nuts feature in stuffings and fillings,
as they do here. In the UK we let chestnuts go; it is true our summers are
too unreliable for the trees always to crop well, but it is also due to the fact
that farmers have not concentrated on budding or grafting trees to produce
good-sized nuts over the years, as they have in France and Italy. It is
frustrating to see the low priority nuts are given as a food crop in the UK –
they are ignored as unimportant, while fields are filled with grain to feed
animals for our disproportionately meaty diet. We need chestnuts, hazelnuts
and walnuts again. Cobnuts are making a comeback (see page 134) – so we
know it is possible.

Buying chestnuts

I have never been able to buy British-sourced chestnuts but most sold
here hail from Europe, where the plant originated – so not a long journey
for a relatively lightweight food that can travel by road or boat. Merchant
Gourmet produces excellent peeled and vacuum-packed wild French
chestnuts all year round (www.merchant-gourmet.com; tel: 020 7635 4096).

Hot Chestnut and Honey Soup

I found a similar soup to this one in the Arndale Centre, Manchester, where a specialist and fresh food market is open every day. The chestnuts are the body, the part of the soup that does most of the warming and filling – as soups should – but they are not dominant in the sense that they make a thick, starchy soup. This one is more broth than ballast, and even elegant. The vegetables add a few layers of flavour, while the honey gives it some fruit. At Christmas it is a perfect candidate for using up all that turkey stock. I confess I never buy fresh chestnuts and peel them; it makes not a jot of difference to this soup and the process is hard work. Peeling chestnuts is a little like including whole wheat in a recipe for Victoria sponge and asking you to grind it yourself.

Serves 4

4 tablespoons extra virgin olive oil
2 onions, chopped
2 carrots, sliced
1 medium-sized turnip, peeled and
    cut into chunks
½ swede, peeled and cut into chunks

a large pinch of dried thyme
200g/7oz vacuum-packed sweet
    chestnuts
1.2 litres/2 pints meat stock (see
    pages 64, 116 and 238) or water
1 tablespoon honey – any kind
sea salt and freshly ground black
    pepper

Heat the oil in a large pan, add all the vegetables and cook gently until they begin to soften. Do not let them brown. Add the thyme and chestnuts, then pour in the stock or water. Bring to the boil, turn down to a simmer and cook until the vegetables are tender. Blend until smooth in a liquidiser, then add the honey. Stir well and season to taste. Serve very hot.

Potted Duck with Chestnuts

A lidded dish of potted meat – similar to a pâté – in the fridge will take care of all those hurried lunches and suppers when 'can't be bothered' is the thought overriding cooking dinner. It is a humble meal made of cheaper cuts, but a masterpiece to look at and full of dulcet meatiness: the pink layers of different textures, the studs of spice or nuts and fruit, and the flavours that set in deep after slow cooking and a day's storage. It is smart enough to serve for dinner, with a piquant chutney, pickles or fruit jelly, but it is honest and ordinary enough to stick a slice between 2 pieces of buttered bread.

There are various potted meats in this book (see pages 296, 325, 356 and 452) but this one concentrates on duck, working without pork, which is the usual mainstay of potted meats. This does mean it is more extravagant to make but if you use meat from duck legs, which are usually cheap (all the price is in the huge boneless breast), it will go a long way for relatively little. To make lighter work, ask the butcher to prepare the meat for you.

Serves 4

8 duck legs, skinned, the meat taken off the bone (reserve the skin and cut it into thin strips)
225g/8oz duck livers, very finely chopped
1 wineglass of dry sherry
30g/1oz softened butter
20 vacuum-packed cooked chestnuts, chopped
1 teaspoon green peppercorns
sea salt and freshly ground black pepper

Preheat the oven to 200°C/400°F/Gas Mark 6. Cut half the duck leg meat into strips and mince the rest (if you do not have a mincer, chop it into 5mm/¼ inch pieces). Put the mince and duck livers into a bowl with half the sherry, put the strips of duck in another bowl with the rest of the sherry and leave both to marinate for 1 hour.

Use the softened butter to grease a terrine dish, 750ml–1 litre/1¼–1¾ pints in capacity, and lay thin pieces of duck skin in a criss-cross pattern over the base. Put half the duck mince mixture into the terrine. Lay half the chestnuts on top, followed by the strips of marinated duck and the green peppercorns; add another layer of chestnuts, then finish with the remaining duck mince mixture. Cover with foil, place in a roasting tin containing 2cm/¾ inch of boiling water and bake for 1¼–1½ hours. When it is done, the meat will shrink away from the sides of the dish. Remove from the oven, place a weight on top (2 cans of tomatoes will do) and leave to cool, then refrigerate.

Serve sliced, with buttered toast, pickles, or green leaves dressed with walnut oil.

CHICKEN

Whole Poached Chicken, Leek and Bean Broth
  with Real Ale and Garlic Sauce
Dry-roast Chicken

Leftovers
Chicken Stock
Chicken Noodle Broth
Hot Chicken, Herb and Cream Soup
Cold Chicken, Mustard, Dill and Cucumber

Legs, thighs and wings
Coconut Chicken
Chicken Curry with Fresh Tomato and Ginger

Looking back at accounts of what was eaten over 1,000 years ago, the
period when Britain still had a diverse and eclectic kitchen, I am struck
by the relatively large quantity of chicken and other poultry that was
consumed. Discussing poultry in a modern-day setting, debating the
wrongs of the broiler house (indoor rearing systems) against the need
to feed millions, or arguing which is best, free range or organic, someone
will always say they rarely ate roast chicken as a child, only at Easter or
on special occasions. This is meant to illustrate the point that chickens are
now undervalued, and that we should return to eating only the rare, slow-
growing free-range organic bird.

   This is good advice, but again it does seem peculiar that in the
1,000-year-old diet, chicken was a regular meal – supposedly because in
an agrarian society everyone, whether rich or poor, kept lots of chickens.
Game birds were not the property of anyone but the landowner, and
poaching carried terrible penalties; cattle were valued mainly for their
milk, and beef eaten only for serious feasts; sheep were more precious for

their wool. So that left chickens, ducks, geese, rabbit and pork as the main protein.

Chickens, as we are now witnessing, can be reared free range on a large scale, as can pigs. Prices for free-range chickens in supermarkets are reasonable – especially if you use up the leftovers and make the bones into stock. It's not to say that these are the ideal, traditional free-range birds, but it is far better than keeping thousands of birds in a broiler house, competing for the smallest amount of space, weak and unable to support their body weight, which soars rapidly from being fed high-protein, high-energy foods.

So, is a chicken a meal for every day? A chicken breast is not – something must be done with the leg meat and remaining carcass, so the price of 'chicken fillets' is often the sum of the whole bird. I now make it a habit, when preparing a curry, to ask the butcher in advance if he will bone a whole bird, so I have a mixture of brown meat from the legs and wings and white meat from the breast. I also ask for the bones to make stock. Chicken leg meat is a good standard food to buy for everyday meals. Parents who know how difficult it is to please children will testify to the popularity of drumsticks and homemade breaded chicken.

Lastly, there is the specialist poultry, the rare breeds and the extra-slow-grown, traditionally reared birds – these are luxuries and their price dictates that. Instead of paying £11 for a 2kg/4½lb bird (the average price for a free-range bird), expect to pay up to £20 for the same weight organic traditional farmhouse bird.

Buying chicken

I do buy free-range and organic chicken from supermarkets but prefer to shop at butcher's shops and specialist food or farmers' markets for them. Label Anglais free-range chickens, French in style but reared in England, have been keeping my family happy for years. They have extra-long, strong legs and breast meat that has a good, well-exercised texture. Hard to beat. Tel: 01279 792460 or see www.labelanglais.co.uk for stockists.

Whole Poached Chicken, Leek and Bean Broth with Real Ale and Garlic Sauce

This is a circular recipe, where each week the stock is strained and retained, then another chicken poached in it to make a meal. If you can find a cockerel or a big mature chicken at a market, it is a good starting point for the process. The double chicken essence of this recipe, gained through poaching the bird in stock with a few humble vegetables that add all their scents and taste, is proof that the greatest recipes need very little. Such simplicity is a lesson to chefs who seem intent on adding *everything* to chicken on their menus. Better to trust the ingredients and use an age-old tried and tested technique. There will be no need to advertise – anyone can sense your good cooking the moment they are across the threshold, inhaling the wonderful smells of the simmer in the kitchen.

The garlic sauce that goes with this is optional – but is an exceptional, rich pool to dip bread into as you eat the chicken and the braised beans, sweetened with ale.

Serves 8

1 large, well-grown, mature chicken
chicken stock (see page 116) or water
   to cover
2 carrots, scraped
2 onions, halved, the skins left on for
   colour
2 celery sticks
2 bay leaves
2 sprigs of thyme
4 sprigs of parsley

For the garlic sauce:
2 egg yolks
1–2 garlic cloves, crushed to a paste
   with a little salt

300ml/½ pint olive oil or sunflower oil
a handful of parsley leaves, finely
   chopped
sea salt

To serve:
55g/2oz butter
1 wineglass of real ale
4 small leeks, sliced
2 cans of cannellini beans (drained
   weight 470g), or 200g/7oz haricot
   beans that have been soaked
   overnight and then cooked for 1–1½
   hours in boiling water

Put the chicken in a large pan and cover with chicken stock or water. Add the vegetables and herbs, bring to the boil, then turn down to a simmer and poach gently for about 1½ hours, until the meat is cooked and comes easily away from the bone.

Meanwhile, make the garlic sauce. Put the egg yolks in a bowl with the garlic, stir, then gradually whisk in the oil, bit by bit, until you have a smooth emulsion. Stir in the parsley leaves, then taste and add sea salt if necessary.

When the chicken is done, lift it out of the stock and cut away the meat. Put the meat in a separate pan with the butter, ale, about 600ml/1 pint of the cooking stock, plus the leeks and beans. Bring to the boil, season with salt and pepper and then serve with the garlic sauce; remember to put lots of bread on the table.

To make the dish go further:

Strain the remaining stock and discard the cooked vegetables. Put the stock back into the pan, add the chicken carcass, then cover with some extra water if necessary and simmer for about an hour. Strain again. You will have a store of very rich stock that will keep for a week in the fridge. Either use it in soups, risottos or stews, or poach another chicken in it next time.

Dry-roast Chicken

A revelation of a recipe for a whole chicken, similar to one by the American cook Thomas Keller. Because it uses no oil, a leap of faith is needed, but it works. I have never put this crisp roasted fowl on the table and not seen everyone eat every bit, including the flabby bits pulled from underneath. What's left is not so much a carcass as a skeleton. That is not to say, though, that the leftovers will not make great stock for other recipes, such as the soup on page 119. The theory goes that if you do not oil the chicken, there will be no steam in the oven and the skin will crisp all over. The first time you cook this bird, don't be nervous that it doesn't colour in the first 50 minutes. It will sit in the pan looking rather anaemic, then it all happens in the final minutes.

Serves 4–6

2–2.5kg/4½–5lb traditional free-range chicken
1 tablespoon fine sea salt
1 teaspoon thyme leaves (not the stalks)
1 teaspoon dried oregano
12 fennel seeds

Preheat the oven to 230°C/450°F/Gas Mark 8. Wash the chicken under the tap, then use paper towels to dry it thoroughly both inside and out. Take some string and truss the bird, tying the legs tightly to the breast and crossing them over at the tail cavity end. Sprinkle the salt all over the bird, including the underneath. Put it in a dry roasting tin, place in the oven and roast for 60–70 minutes. Don't be alarmed if, by the fiftieth minute, it looks as pale as a hungry vampire; it will turn to gold just in time. Take it out of the oven, sprinkle over the herbs, spoon the juices from the roasting tin over the bird and then allow it to rest in a warm place for 10–15 minutes.

Because you do not want too much steam in the oven while the chicken is cooking, serve it with a salad or with potatoes that have been sautéed on top of the stove, rather than with roast potatoes.

To 'carve', just untie the truss and cut the bird up with a pair of scissors. Take the legs and wings off, cutting through the joints. Snip 2 lines either side of the breast. Cut the backbone into 3 or 4 squares – underneath, there is more crisp skin, plus the parson's nose and the oysters.

Chicken leftovers

When you buy a chicken for roasting, you pay a lot for a traditionally reared bird. Now it is going to pay you back with good things that roll over throughout the days following the roast. It is a crime not to use every bit. Bones for stock, cold meat for salads, sandwiches and things ...

Chicken Stock

The bones of traditionally reared poultry are well calcified and make great, gelatinous stock. Use this recipe to make stock from other poultry and game birds too, such as pheasant and partridge. A raw carcass makes a pale, delicate stock; leftovers from the roast will make a darker, stronger-flavoured stock.

Makes about 1.5 litres/2½ pints

1 chicken carcass, either raw or from
   a roast bird
1 bay leaf
a pinch of dried thyme

6 black peppercorns
4 sprigs of parsley
2 onions, halved
2 celery sticks, roughly chopped
2 carrots, cut in half
1 leek, cut in half

Put everything in a large pan and cover with 1.7 litres/3 pints of water. Bring to the boil, skim away some of the rising foam, then allow to simmer very slowly for about 1–1½ hours. Strain, discarding the solids, and store the stock in the fridge.

Chicken Noodle Broth

Not really a Chinese recipe, because the egg 'noodles' we use are Italian, but a vital dish as the children love it.

Serves 6

1 large roast chicken carcass, chopped into 4 pieces
1 onion, halved but with the skin left on
1 celery stick, chopped in half
1 carrot, peeled and chopped in half

1.7 litres/3 pints water
225g/8oz egg vermicelli, or other soup pasta
a few chervil or tarragon leaves, or snipped chives
sea salt and freshly ground black pepper

Put the chicken carcass and vegetables in a large pan, cover with the water and bring to the boil. Skim off any foam from the surface, turn down to a simmer and cook for 1–1½ hours. Strain the broth through a sieve and set aside. If there is any lean meat clinging to the chicken, remove it and add to the broth. Taste the broth and add sea salt if necessary. Skim off surplus fat.

Just before you serve, heat the broth until it boils and add the vermicelli. Cool until the noodles are tender, then serve with the herbs scattered over. Freshly ground black pepper is essential.

Hot Chicken, Herb and Cream Soup

This is a rich one, and comes with strict rules. If you are going to make this chicken soup, make sure the stock is very full flavoured. If you are not happy that it is rich enough, don't go ahead. Also, the herbs must be very finely chopped, so that you can drink this soup straight from a cup.

Serves 4

2 pints/1.2 litres very rich fresh chicken stock (see page 116)
175ml/6fl oz double cream
leaves from 4 sprigs of chervil, very finely chopped
leaves from 4 sprigs of tarragon, very finely chopped
about 20 chives, very finely chopped
sea salt and freshly ground black pepper

Skim any fat off the surface of the stock, then strain the stock through a fine sieve into a clean pan. Heat to boiling point and stir in the cream. Bring almost to boiling point and add the herbs; taste and add salt if necessary. Finish with freshly ground black pepper, then pour into cups to serve.

Kitchen note
Chop any leftover chicken and add to the soup with some skinned broad beans. Serve in bowls, with plenty of bread. This also makes a good base soup to which you can add sliced mushrooms, wild or cultivated (see Mushrooms, page 262).

Cold Chicken, Mustard, Dill and Cucumber

Leftover chicken from the roast (see page 115), dressed with that powerful, winning mix of dill and mustard.

Serves 2–4

approximately 400g/14oz cold cooked
   chicken
1 cucumber, peeled, deseeded and
   sliced

For the dressing:
2 tablespoons Dijon mustard
1 teaspoon soft brown cane sugar
2 tablespoons white wine vinegar
300ml/½ pint olive oil
leaves and any soft stalks from
   6 sprigs of dill, chopped
sea salt and freshly ground black
   pepper

Mix all the ingredients for the dressing together and pour them over the chicken and cucumber. Mix well and serve.

Chicken legs, thighs and wings

The brown meat of chicken thighs and legs has a stronger flavour and more gelatinous texture than the breast meat, and makes a much better curry. It is possible to buy boned free-range and organic chicken leg and thigh meat in the supermarket but a charm offensive, and a little notice, should persuade your butcher to bone them for you. Boning chicken thighs is easy compared to the other joints and can be done in your own kitchen in a few minutes. Skin the thigh then cut a line through the flesh down the length of the bone. Work around the bone on both sides with a sharp knife, then lift the meat off the bone.

Coconut Chicken

As a contrast to the robustness of the chicken and tomato curry overleaf, here is a very light sauce with coconut and ordinary curry paste, to make in a few moments when you are pressed for time. Don't use cans of creamy coconut milk – the richness will ruin the dish.

Serves 4

250g/9oz desiccated coconut
1.2 litres/2 pints water
the raw brown and white meat from
 1 chicken, the skin discarded and
 the bones reserved for stock (ask
 your butcher to do all this for you,
 but give notice)
1–2 tablespoons sunflower oil
2 dessertspoons medium-hot Madras
 curry paste

4 onions, chopped
4cm/1½ inch piece of fresh ginger,
 grated or cut into very small
 matchsticks
4 garlic cloves, finely chopped
sea salt

To serve:
red chillies, deseeded and thinly
 sliced
coriander leaves

Put the desiccated coconut into a bowl, pour over the water and leave to steep for 10 minutes. Strain through a sieve, discarding the coconut, and set aside.

Cut the chicken meat into bite-sized pieces and set to one side. Heat the oil in a large pan, add the curry paste, onions, ginger and garlic and cook for a minute over a low heat. Add the coconut water, bring to the boil and skim off any fat from the surface. Drop in the chicken pieces and poach them in the liquid for 5–7 minutes, until cooked through. Taste the curry and add salt if necessary. Serve with red chillies and coriander leaves scattered over the top, accompanied by boiled basmati rice.

Chicken Curry with Fresh Tomato and Ginger

Prised from Bill Wagay, who has a tiny curry house in Bristol's St Nicholas Market, where he uses only locally produced chicken and tomatoes, this is a Vagar-style recipe from the Punjab and a great standard yet authentic curry to have up your sleeve. Its flavour is clean and fresh, thanks to the tomatoes, and the whole spices resonate in a way that ready-made powders and pastes cannot. Serve with basmati rice, toasted almonds and coriander leaves.

Serves 4

4 tablespoons sunflower oil
½ teaspoon ground cumin
½ teaspoon ground coriander
½ teaspoon garam masala
¼–½ teaspoon chilli powder
1 teaspoon fine sea salt
2cm/¾ inch piece of fresh ginger, grated

2 teaspoons black mustard seeds
1 cinnamon stick
4 garlic cloves, chopped
55g/2oz unsalted butter
8 or more skinned, boned chicken thighs, cut into bite-sized pieces
450g/1lb tomatoes, deseeded and chopped
1 teaspoon tomato purée
1 wineglass of water

Heat the oil in a large pan, add all the ground spices, plus the salt, ginger, mustard seeds, cinnamon stick and garlic, and fry until the seeds begin to crackle. Lower the heat and add the butter, followed by the meat. Stir over the heat for a minute, then add the tomatoes and tomato purée. Cover and cook for 5 minutes. Add the water and cook, uncovered, for a further 10 minutes.

CHICKPEAS

Squash and Chickpea Soup with Single
   Gloucester Cheese
Sprouted Chickpea Hummus
Blue Cheese and Gram Flour Biscuits

Chickpeas are grouped with beans, being economical to use, nothing but good for you and easy to cook with. But they are more than just worthy. I cannot eat canned green peas because the starch sticks to the roof of my mouth – my idea of hell is canned marrowfat peas (dyed with synthetic blue and yellow food colouring). Even the grander glass jars of French petits pois are a turn-off, because they have that same floury centre. In contrast, chickpeas have crisp, nutty kernels. They are good, substantial things to find in a pan of meat, herbs and spices, and they purée to a silky texture – think hummus. But they are peas only in name. In fact they are a tropical pulse – a lovely phrase that reflects their origins in Asia. I wish Britain had a tropical pulse, instead of a pea soup pulse, which sounds a bit grey, a bit stodgy.

Chickpeas share many good points with beans, and in India, where they are called 'gram', they are the most important pulse crop because of their high protein content. A gluten-free flour is made from roasted chickpeas and used to make batters and as a coating for fried vegetable pakoras.

If using whole chickpeas, I tend to buy them cooked and canned, because dried ones can take up to 12 hours to soak and 4 hours to cook.

Squash and Chickpea Soup with Single Gloucester Cheese

The chickpeas do not feature heavily here but they add substance. The Single Gloucester cheese is distinctively flavoured and responsible for the rich texture of this soup. Look for Smart's Single Gloucester.

Serves 4

6 tablespoons olive oil
2 medium white onions, chopped
1 small butternut squash, peeled, deseeded and cut into chunks
1.2 litres/2 pints chicken stock (see page 116) or water

1 can of chickpeas (drained weight, 225g), drained
1 garlic clove, chopped
1 courgette, cut into small dice
leaves from 2 sprigs of parsley
115g/4oz Single Gloucester cheese, grated

Heat 2 tablespoons of the oil in a large pan and add the onions. Cook over a low heat for a minute or two, until they become translucent, then add the squash and cook for a couple of minutes longer. Do not let the onions or the squash brown. Add the stock or water, bring to the boil, then turn the heat down to a simmer and cook until the squash is tender. Transfer to a liquidiser and blend until smooth, adding more stock or water if the soup is too thick. It should have the consistency of single cream.

Roughly mash the chickpeas in a bowl. Heat the remaining oil in a small pan and add the garlic, chickpeas, courgette and parsley. Cook until they are hot through and sizzling.

Pour the soup into 4 bowls. Add a spoonful of the chickpea mixture to each and then scatter over a handful of the cheese. Put the remaining cheese into a bowl and put it on the table with the soup.

Sprouted Chickpea Hummus

Hummus, the purée of chickpeas, garlic, sesame and lemon, is all too familiar but, in a new take on the appetiser, sprouted chickpeas produce an astonishing green-flecked mixture that makes the conventional type seem dull in comparison. You can grow sprouts at any time of year, using a jar or special kit placed near a window. Serve the hummus with Flatbreads (see page 232) and raw vegetables.

Makes a bowlful to serve about 6 for drinks

about 450g/1lb sprouted chickpeas
2 tablespoons tahini paste
juice of 1 lemon
2 garlic cloves, crushed to a paste
    with a pinch of salt

a little extra virgin olive oil
a few whole chickpea sprouts,
    coriander sprouts (grown the same
    way) or coriander leaves
sea salt and freshly ground black
    pepper

Put the chickpeas in a food processor with the tahini, lemon juice and garlic. Process to a thick paste, then transfer to a bowl. If the paste is very thick, mix in a little cold water until you have a texture that is soft enough to dip bread and vegetables into. Taste and add sea salt and freshly ground black pepper. Zigzag olive oil over the surface and throw over the spare sprouts or leaves.

Blue Cheese and Gram Flour Biscuits

I am devoted to gram flour, which is milled from roasted chickpeas. It can be used instead of wheat flour in cheese or other savoury biscuits, where the lack of elasticity provided by gluten does not matter.

In the past I have made biscuits with Cheddar or Parmesan, but these made with Stilton (a cheese that always needs using up quickly) have a lovely flaky texture and come out a subtle verdigris colour.

You can use a standard mass-market Stilton to make these biscuits but it is worth pointing out the two best cheeses available. The Colston Bassett dairy in Nottinghamshire makes the best conventional Stilton cheese and it is widely available; see www.colstonbassettdairy.com (tel: 01949 81322) for a local stockist. Stichelton is a blue cheese made with raw milk that I would describe as a Stilton, although the makers cannot as they are not a member of the Stilton Cheesemakers Association. It is available from Neal's Yard Dairy (www.nealsyarddairy.co.uk; tel: 020 7500 7653).

Makes about 20

85g/3oz gram (chickpea) flour, sifted, plus extra for dusting
70g/2½oz Stilton or other blue cheese, roughly grated
70g/2½oz unsalted butter, cut into cubes
½ teaspoon sea salt
a pinch of freshly ground black pepper
1 tablespoon very cold water
2 tablespoons walnuts, finely chopped

Put the flour, cheese, butter and seasoning into a bowl and mix well. Add the water and mix to make a sticky dough. Wrap in a plastic bag and chill in the fridge for 1 hour.

Preheat the oven to 190°C/375°F/Gas Mark 5. On a lightly floured work surface, roll the dough into a large circle, about 5mm/¼ inch thick. Cut out rounds and put them 2cm/¾ inch apart on a baking sheet lined with baking parchment. Scatter a few chopped walnuts on to each and bake for 15–20 minutes or until the biscuits are slightly puffed and lightly brown. Transfer to a wire rack and leave to cool. These biscuits will keep for about 5 days in an airtight container.

CHICORY

Creamed Chicory Soup with Pink Pepper, Parsley Oil
  and Soft-boiled Egg
Chicory and Goat's Cheese Puff Pastry Pie
Braised Chicory with Butter and Lemon Juice

Chicory, or Belgian endive (sometimes called Witloof chicory), is one
of those winter vegetables that can be forced to grow in the dark – like
Fenland celery (see page 90) and Wakefield rhubarb. I have a soft spot for
these vegetables. They remind me that we live in a country that has long,
dark, wet winters. Not for us early harvests of artichokes in February,
just a lot of roots and brassicas. We need to cope better at these times, and
introduce a little locally grown variety that will sprout in winter. Chicory
is one of the gems that will do this. It is not exactly cheap but, cooked in
butter for a long time, a dish of chicory is a rich one.

Buying chicory

Most chicory in our shops is grown in the Nord – the region of France
around Calais. Strictly speaking, this is just 20 miles from Kent, so more
local to people in the south of England than a Scottish raspberry. Some
farmers' markets sell a small amount of British-grown chicory.

Creamed Chicory Soup with Pink Pepper, Parsley Oil and Soft-boiled Egg

Light and thin, this is a delicate winter soup enriched with the addition of a poached egg. The flavour of the chicory is very delicate and quite out of the ordinary. Once this soup is in the bowl, with the contrasting parsley oil, the rich bomb of soft-boiled egg and the spice in the pepper, each spoonful will release a little parade of tastes – but without too much fuss.

It is very important that the chicory is properly braised before the liquid is added, because it can be startlingly bitter. A longer cooking time will release the sugars and prevent too much bitterness.

Serves 4

55g/2oz unsalted butter
2 onions, chopped
5 chicory heads, roughly chopped
   (discard the inner core)
600ml/1 pint whole milk
600ml/1 pint chicken stock (see
   page 116) or water

4 tablespoons double cream
2 teaspoons pink peppercorns
4 eggs
sea salt

For the parsley oil:
8 tender sprigs of parsley, chopped
4 tablespoons olive oil
a pinch of sea salt

Melt the butter in a pan, add the onions and chicory and cook gently for about 15 minutes, until the vegetables are translucent and soft. Add the milk and stock or water and bring to the boil. Turn down to a simmer and cook for 10 minutes. Liquidise with the cream until smooth and creamy, then taste for seasoning, adding salt if necessary.

Crush the pink peppercorns using a pestle and mortar or a pepper grinder, or by putting them in a strong plastic bag and bashing them with a rolling pin.

Prick the rounded end of each eggshell with a pin so it does not crack during cooking, then put them in a pan and cover with water. Bring to the boil and time for 4 minutes from boiling point. Leave under cold running water until they are cool enough to handle, then peel them, being careful to keep the eggs whole.

Blend the parsley, oil and salt in a pestle and mortar or whiz in a food processor to make a smooth, thick emulsion (if using a food processor, make extra and eat with pasta, fish and grilled meat).

Serve piping hot, putting an egg in each bowl and a zigzag of parsley oil across the top. Scatter some crushed pink pepper over each and serve with lots of bread.

Chicory and Goat's Cheese Puff Pastry Pie

A sandwich of two puff pastry rounds enclosing fresh goat's cheese, this has citrus flavours from the cheese and the toffee sweetness of braised chicory. You can eat it hot from the oven or lukewarm, and it can also be reheated. A pie to make for supper or lunch.

I rarely make puff pastry but buy it instead, trying to find a brand made with real butter. Most of the standard puff pastry sold in mainstream shops is made with vegetable oil but Dorset Pastry uses proper butter and natural ingredients. It is available from Waitrose, or contact them for other stockists and details of mail order: www.dorsetpastry.com; tel: 01305 854860.

Serves 8

6 chicory heads, halved lengthways
55g/2oz butter
600g/1lb 5oz puff pastry
flour for dusting

500g/1lb 2oz fresh goat's cheese, broken into chunks
leaves from 6 sprigs of basil
1 egg, mixed with a little milk, to glaze
sea salt and freshly ground black pepper

Preheat the oven to 200°C/400°F/Gas Mark 6.

Put the chicory heads in a casserole with the butter. Cook over a very low heat for about 4 minutes, until the chicory is quite soft and sweet tasting. Lift them out of the pan and allow to cool, leaving the buttery juice behind. Season with salt and pepper.

Divide the pastry in half and roll out each half on a lightly floured work surface into a round about 5mm/¼ inch thick. Set one round aside and put the other on a baking sheet. Lay the 12 chicory halves on top in a 'clock numbers' pattern. Spoon chunks of goat's cheese over the chicory, then roughly chop the basil and scatter it on top.

Paint the edges of the pastry with the egg wash. Cover with the second round of pastry and press the edges together to seal. Brush the whole surface with egg wash and then use a knife to score the surface in a wheel spokes pattern.

Bake for about 40 minutes, until the pastry is golden and the underside is crisp. Allow to cool slightly before slicing and serving.

Braised Chicory with Butter and Lemon Juice

A favourite way to eat chicory, and very good with roast lamb or chicken. It is also a very beautiful dish. The chicory, cut in half and cooked flat-side down in the butter, will be tinged with brown on the edges like a botanical drawing. This style of cooking also releases the sugar in the chicory. A good vegetable dish to eat with the grilled cheap cuts of beef on pages 47–55.

Serves 4

55g/2oz unsalted butter
4 chicory heads, halved lengthways

a few thyme leaves
juice of 1 lemon
sea salt and freshly ground black
    pepper

Melt the butter in a wide pan over a medium heat. Lay the chicory, cut-side down, in the pan, season with salt and pepper and add the thyme leaves. Cook for a few minutes, then add the lemon juice and cover the pan. Continue cooking over a low heat for about 20 minutes. Keep an eye on the chicory; they should brown underneath but not burn. Turn them carefully in the pan and cook for a further 5 minutes, until soft. Serve warm.

COBNUTS

Squirrel with Cobnuts and Walnuts

Pheasant Halves Stuffed with Cobnuts, Bread
   and Butter

Cobnut and Watercress Salad with Potato Bread

Cobnut Ice

Curses on the grey squirrel, which has made nut collection almost impossible in Britain. Walnut trees have grown here for 500 years but we must rely on France for a supply – the French are lucky not to have been invaded by these pests, which were brought to Britain from northeast America. Arguments over whether or not there should be a mass cull of grey squirrels are usually centred around the red squirrel, which has become rare since the grey invasion. What is not mentioned is the point that every country in the world relies heavily on a national nut for essential nutrition. In Europe, walnuts are prolific, and recent studies have shown that eating walnuts after a fatty meal benefits the arteries, reducing inflammation. But hey – why use the indigenous walnut supply to help save human health when you can have parks overrun with grey squirrels? In the real, natural world, the human position on the food chain is higher than that of the squirrel. We are meant to be culling these animals because if we don't they will gobble one of our essential sources of food.

    Native nuts are not totally lost to us. In Kent and other parts of the south of England there are professional cobnut growers who manage to keep the squirrels away long enough to see English seasonal nuts back in shops during the autumn season. Slightly longer in shape than the hazelnut, cobnuts are really filberts, an ancient plant that came to us from Southeast Asia. When fresh, their flesh is crunchy, with a sweet, milky flavour. Their scarcity makes them an exceptional meal, but the recipes that follow can be made substituting the easy-to-buy hazelnut and will be quite as good.

Buying cobnuts

Fresh cobnuts are available from some supermarkets from late August, but also via mail order through various members of the Kentish Cobnuts Association (www.kentishcobnutsassociation.co.uk). Ian Pitcairn can send cobnuts by post and is also a wet walnut supplier. Contact Orchard Farm, Boxted, Essex; tel: 01206 728629. Farnell Farm (which is a member of the KCA), will send fresh cobnuts in season, and dried ones until the supply runs out: www.farnellfarm.co.uk.

Squirrel with Cobnuts and Walnuts

I made this in an ill-advised photo shoot for *Loaded* magazine, which persuaded me to go on an expedition looking for road kill and bring back the spoils. I was fully clothed throughout, but the article appeared in the magazine's 'Biggest Breasts Ever' issue and I have spent every month since worrying that my mother would find it in a doctor's surgery.

Cut the filleted meat of one freshly killed squirrel into 2 x 1cm/¾ x ½ inch strips and season well with salt and pepper. Heat 3 tablespoons of olive oil in a pan, add a chopped onion and fry slowly until pale gold. Add the squirrel meat and fry until well cooked. Add 1 sour apple, cored and cut into thin slices, 1 tablespoon of cider vinegar and 1 tablespoon each of roughly chopped cobnuts and walnuts. Finish with chopped parsley, then eat with fried bread.

Pheasant Halves Stuffed with Cobnuts, Bread and Butter

A woodland recipe, all this needs to make it complete is the glowing embers of charcoal to cook it over, bought from Britain's new breed of charcoal burners. Unfortunately, by the time both pheasant and cobnuts come into season, enthusiasm for outdoor feasts has waned a little. But even if you cook it in the city, you can dream of wooded hills and the cluck of game birds. See Pheasant, page 305, for information on how to buy pheasant.

The quality of the butter is important here. Also, the cobnut season comes a little earlier than the pheasant one, so store shelled cobnuts in an airtight container in a cool, dark place to preserve them.

Serves 4

2 new-season pheasants, cut in half lengthways, then the backbone snipped out to tidy them up
115g/4oz shelled fresh Kentish cobnuts
115g/4oz fresh sourdough breadcrumbs
115g/4oz salted butter, softened
2 tablespoons chopped rocket or watercress leaves
olive oil for brushing
12 very thin rashers of smoked streaky bacon
sea salt and freshly ground black pepper

Preheat the oven to 240°C/475°F/Gas Mark 9. Wash the pheasants and dry them on kitchen paper. Pinch away any feathers the plucking machine missed.

Mix together the nuts, breadcrumbs, butter and rocket or watercress. Add a pinch of salt and a twist or two of black pepper. Slip your finger under the skin of one pheasant half, working from the wing end. Push in one quarter of the stuffing, right towards the top of the leg. Repeat with the remaining pheasant halves, then put them into an oiled roasting tin. Brush the birds with a little oil. Twist each piece of bacon as if it were old-fashioned candy, then lay them across the pheasants, here and there. Put the tin in the oven, and roast for 25 minutes, until the pheasants are golden brown and the skin is crisp. Remove and leave in a warm place to rest for 20 minutes. Serve with buttered egg pasta, mashed potato or gnocchi.

Cobnut and Watercress Salad with Potato Bread

Mix 115g/4oz chopped fresh cobnuts with the chopped leaves of 2 bunches of watercress, 2 chopped garlic cloves and 150ml/¼ pint olive oil. Season with salt and plenty of black pepper, then stir in the juice of ½ lemon. Serve with grilled meat – lamb, chicken or beef. Or, to make a stunning yet economical dish, make a batch of the Wild Yeast Bread on page 436 and roll it out into a large, flat disc. Score it 3 times across the centre with a knife, then slice a potato very thinly and press the slices on to the bread. Brush with olive oil and bake in an oven preheated to 230°C/450°F/Gas Mark 8. Serve with the cobnut and watercress salad.

Cobnut Ice

Very delicious and very easy to make – although it does need 3 clean bowls and whisks, so you may not forgive the extra washing up this creates. Whisking the eggs, both the whites and the yolks, introduces tiny air bubbles, which give the ice a slightly frothy texture as it melts. If the cobnut season is over, use hazelnuts or experiment with other nuts, such as pecans and pistachios.

Serves 8

4 tablespoons shelled Kentish
   cobnuts
1 heaped tablespoon light brown
   sugar
3 eggs, separated
4 tablespoons caster sugar
300ml/½ pint double cream
crystallised rose petals, to decorate
   (see page 378)

Chop the nuts until small – you can use a food processor for this but they must not be ground to a powder. Toast them in a dry frying pan until golden (if the nuts are fresh, this may take a few minutes). Shake the pan from time to time and do not let them burn. Once they are browned, sprinkle the brown sugar on top, remove from the heat and stir so they are thoroughly coated. Set to one side.

In a large bowl, whisk the egg yolks with the caster sugar until they increase in volume and become pale and fluffy. Whip the cream in a separate bowl until thick, then stir it into the egg yolks until the mixture is smooth. Fold in the nuts.

In a third bowl, whisk the egg whites to a stiff foam, using a clean whisk, and then carefully fold them into the mixture with a large metal spoon. Line a 23cm/9 inch long loaf tin with cling film, letting it overhang the sides, and pour the mixture into it. Cover with more cling film and freeze for at least 4 hours, until firm.

To serve, take the ice cream out of the freezer and lift it out of the tin using the cling film. Unwrap and cut into slices, putting one on each plate. Decorate with crystallised rose petals.

 Kitchen note
This ice melts quickly, so must be served as soon as it comes out of the freezer. However, you can make it hold its shape by adding a little gelatine: soak 2 gelatine leaves in cold water for about 5 minutes. Heat 100ml/3¹/₂fl oz of the cream in a small pan, then squeeze out excess water from the gelatine and add to the pan. Stir until dissolved. Allow this cream to cool to lukewarm before folding it into the mixture, just before the egg whites.

COCOA

Flourless Cocoa Cake

Let's skip the clichés about sex-drive enhancement – in its raw form, cocoa, or chocolate, is one of the great food-based preventative drugs. This is the science: cocoa powder contains calcium, copper, magnesium, phosphorus and potassium. It has more iron, gram for gram, than any vegetable, but more important is the polyphenol content, a groups of flavonoids with antioxidant properties; these nutrients promote vascular health, lower blood pressure, reduce blood clots and help to fight cancer. With this astonishing information, it seems that cocoa has a natural place as a food for every day, but there is one obvious snag – it tastes good only when sweetened. Sugar scarcely contains any nutrients and has a negative impact on health, but the good things in cocoa justify the occasional cake.

It is odd, I suppose, to include cocoa in a book with 'English' in the title but cocoa has withstood the test of time in terms of remaining a favourite food. Like bananas, citrus fruit and spices, it is an import so tied into our history that it is as English as a cup of tea. Er, no – that is an import, too. Strawberries? No, they originated in the Americas, along with potatoes, sweetcorn and much other adopted produce. This is the trouble with discussing British food. It has a baffling genetic makeup. The concept of British or English is a matter of interpretation. Ingredients migrate and settle; some, like strawberries, can be produced here, some, like cocoa, cannot. It must be added that importing cocoa has little environmental impact.

Buying cocoa

Buying organic or fairly traded cocoa is an ethical choice. This commodity, beset by scandals regarding pesticides and poor treatment of farmers, has become something that is hard to purchase with a clear conscience, although one brand, Green & Black's, is organic and Fairtrade, and available from major supermarkets.

The Fairtrade Foundation keeps a list of suppliers of cocoa, some of them organic; check the website, www.fairtrade.org.uk, for details. Look out also for Smilo, an especially delicious fair-traded, ecofriendly cocoa powder from Grenada that should arrive in British shops soon (www.grenadachocolate.com). Rococo Chocolates in London has a good reputation for buying Fairtrade raw materials; it sells cocoa powder, Grenada chocolate and many other fantasies. (www.rococochocolates.com; tel: 020 7352 5857).

Flourless Cocoa Cake

A cake to feel good about. It has a rather appetising, soggy look. I have been making this cake for 16 years, and since every new recipe book is greeted with an investigation into where the chocolate cake recipe was pinched from, I will come clean and say that it is based on one given in Rose Levy Beranbaum's *The Cake Bible* (William Morrow, 2001), a huge and forensic book on the subject. She calls it Queen Mother Cake, and says it was inspired by Maida Heatter's recipe. Maida Heatter was, I suspect, 'inspired' by someone else; so that is how chocolate cake recipe writing works. Frankly, when you have a good one, don't try to reinvent the wheel.

Beranbaum warns of the dip in the centre, too, but saying it adds interest. What it also does is provide a nice hollow in which to put something pretty: a flower or two or, at Easter, a few chocolate-filled, sugar-speckled eggs.

Serves 8–10

a little flour, for dusting
225g/8oz caster sugar
225g/8oz softened unsalted
 butter
6 eggs, separated
70g/2½oz cocoa powder mixed to
 a paste with a little hot water
200g/7oz ground almonds
½ teaspoon cream of tartar
icing sugar, for dusting

Preheat the oven to 180°C/350°F/Gas Mark 4. Butter a 20cm/8 inch springform cake tin and dust it lightly with flour.

Beat the sugar and butter together until pale and fluffy, then beat in the egg yolks one by one. Fold in the cocoa and ground almonds. In a separate bowl, whisk the egg whites to stiff peaks, adding the cream of tartar at the end. Fold them into the mixture, pour it into the tin and bake for about 40 minutes, until the sponge feels firm to the touch. Cool in the tin, then turn out and dust with icing sugar.

COURGETTES

Courgettes with Garlic Butter

Courgette Shavings with Olive Oil, Lemon, Pistachio,
   Basil and Chives

My family hates them, I like them. Cooked in a pan with butter and basil, courgettes are a wonderful vegetable to eat with pasta, chicken and lamb. I like to hollow out and stuff the round ones you sometimes see, using olive oil, cooked short grain rice and a Provençal herb mix, then bake them, letting their juices flavour the rice. Serve them covered in shavings of hard ewe's milk cheese.

    Courgette flowers are a rarity in shops but very good stirred into a hot rice dish. I rarely cook them at home; they are fiddly to stuff and a bore to deep-fry. It is a kitchen rule of mine only to shallow-fry – not because of health, safety or mess but because I cannot stand throwing the oil away afterwards. Tempura is for restaurants – sad to say.

Courgettes with Garlic Butter

Courgettes, butter and garlic is a magical trinity, extraordinarily appetising to smell and containing all the flavours of summer. Don't let the contents of the pan brown for this dish, only stew gently over a low heat until the courgettes are soft. It is important to buy good butter and I confess that it is somehow more successful with French lactic-culture butter (such as Président) because it melts to cream and there is less of the greasy separation you find with churned butter.

Eat these fragrant courgettes with roast or grilled meat or fish, or stir them into pasta and eat with a little grated hard cheese. I quite like a bowl of them on their own, too.

Serves 4

5 courgettes
55g/2oz unsalted butter
2 garlic cloves, chopped
about 5 basil leaves, torn
sea salt and freshly ground black
    pepper

If the courgettes are very fresh (look for pert little hairs on the stalk when you buy), there is no need to salt them before cooking to rid them of bitter juices, but perhaps it is good to have a record of how to do it. Cut the courgettes into dice and put them in a colander. Sprinkle them with ordinary table salt and leave for an hour. Water will seep out of them, which can be patted off with kitchen paper. They are then ready to use.

Melt the butter in a pan and add the garlic, diced courgettes and basil. Stew slowly for about 8–10 minutes, until the sharp edges of the courgettes begin to soften. Season and serve quickly, so they remain green and the flavours and aromas are still heady.

Courgette Shavings with Olive Oil, Lemon, Pistachio, Basil and Chives

An antidote to fried courgettes that goes well with Dry-roast Chicken (see page 115) or can be eaten as a starter with a little fresh cheese.

You will need very fresh courgettes for this recipe (choose ones with prickly hairs on their stalks). If you can find unusual varieties such as yellow, pale green or round courgettes, mix them. The dish will be even nicer.

To make a richer sauce, you could add 2 grated hardboiled egg yolks.

Serves 4

2–3 courgettes
extra virgin olive oil
sea salt
shavings of Parmesan cheese

For the dressing:
85g/3oz shelled pistachio nuts
a small bunch (about 55g/2oz) basil
a small bunch (about 55g/2oz) chives
150ml/¼ pint extra virgin olive oil
juice of ½ lemon

Pare the courgettes into very thin slices, using a mandolin or sharp potato peeler. Lay them on a plate, scatter over 2 pinches of salt and dress with a little olive oil, turning them over to coat them quickly. They will absorb the whole lot, but leave them a while and they will soften.

Blend the dressing ingredients in a food processor, adding salt to taste, then pour it over the courgettes and finish with shavings of Parmeson cheese.

CRAB

Potted Crab

Leftovers
Crab Broth
Crab with Spelt
Crab and Mustard Omelette

A big, boiled cock crab is a phenomenal feast, but one that need not cost the earth if you pick the meat from the shell yourself. Brown crabs, the type common in British waters, are not as scarce as lobsters; depending on where they are fished, they are still reasonably abundant and a seafood to eat with a clear conscience. But the crab to avoid is the 'dressed' version sold in supermarkets. They are expensive and the cooked meat has usually been pasteurised, which kills the flavour along with any bugs. If you buy freshly boiled crabs, cooked shortly after they have been taken out of the water and then kept refrigerated, there is no reason why they should be heat treated. Crabs are caught in pots, lowered into the sea far enough from the shore to find them (brown crabs like the water to be cold and do not come near the beach). The crabbers drop their pots, leave them for several hours or overnight, then come back to haul them to the surface. Again, depending on the waters, the season changes. I tend to buy crabs from the south coast because it is local to London, but they are no more delicious than those from Scottish waters or the Pembrokeshire coast. Size matters; go for the big, more mature crabs.

Buying crab

Be inquisitive when buying crab and ask where they were fished. If you have a good high-street fishmonger, keep him or her busy – small shops need all the help they can get with rising rents and the onslaught of chains. If you don't have a local fishmonger, you can buy crabs via courier from Matthew Stevens and Sons in St Ives (www.mstevensandson.co.uk; tel: 01736 799392). They sell cooked whole medium crabs, caught by local fishermen, serving one person, and dressed (non-pasteurised) brown and white hand-picked crab meat serving two. The ice-filled box will be with you the day after you order. It makes financial sense to order a little extra, or some of his beautifully fresh fish, and store it in the freezer for other meals.

Shore crabs

We sometimes see these small crabs (about 10cm/4 inches across the shell; pictured on page 150) when we are on holiday on the south coast. The crab fishermen bring them up with the brown crab and sell them boiled. You can spend a happy 10 minutes or so sucking meat out of their little claws and digging the rest out of their bodies. The meat is white, with a similar flavour to brown crab. Remove the dead man's fingers (feathery gills) before you do this. An unusual but delicious pre-supper snack.

Potted Crab

My favourite way to eat crab. The mace warms the flavour a little, the cayenne pepper a touch more. The crab is so rich that you need do nothing else to it except eat with salad leaves or toast.

Serves 4

2 whole medium-sized crabs or 350g/12oz mixed brown and white crab meat – or the meat from 2 dressed crabs
½ teaspoon ground mace
1–2 pinches of cayenne pepper, to taste
juice of ½ lemon
a few gratings of lemon zest
175g/6oz salted butter
a few chervil leaves or small parsley leaves, to garnish
½ red chilli, deseeded and thinly sliced (optional)
freshly ground black pepper
rye sourdough bread, for toast, or Three-minute Spelt Bread (see page 440), to serve

First pick the crabs: crack the claws and remove the white meat, then open up the whole carapace by snapping the little tab beneath the eyes and pulling it apart with your hands. Remove the dead man's fingers – the ghoulish, grey-green gills attached to the inner shell. Use a spoon to remove the brown meat and any red coral found on the inside of the main carapace. Crack apart the skeleton that holds the smaller legs and pull off the legs. Pick as much white meat as you can from inside the skeleton, then crack open the legs and pull out any meat you can get your hands on. I usually give up the will to live at this point, especially if the crabs are small.

Put the brown and white crab meat in a bowl, add the spices, lemon juice and zest and stir to combine. Season the mixture with a little freshly ground black pepper, then pack it into a shallow pot. The meat should be about 2.5cm/1 inch deep.

Melt the butter slowly in a pan, then tip it very slowly over the crab, taking care that the watery white sediment at the bottom is left behind. Scatter over the herb leaves. Press them down with your fingers to submerge them in the butter, then add the chilli if you are using it. Leave to set in the fridge; it will only take a few minutes.

Serve the potted crab, spooned from the bowl, with hot toast and a mustard and cress salad.

Leftover potted crab

Crab Broth

After you've picked the meat from the legs, brush the shells with vegetable oil and roast in a hot oven for about 20 minutes, until fragrant – do not let them burn. Transfer them to a saucepan and brew up with water, a wineglass of wine, a sliced fennel bulb, a sliced white onion, 1 chopped celery stick (including the leaves) and 1 chopped carrot. Simmer gently for 30 minutes, then strain through a sieve. Season with salt if necessary. Use in the recipe below, or make the lightest of clear soups and serve over Chinese egg noodles, with chilli and coriander scattered on top.

Crab with Spelt

For 2 people, gently fry 2 chopped shallots in a tablespoon of butter in a saucepan. Add 175g/6oz whole spelt, then cover with stock (crab, fish, vegetable, chicken or veal). Cook for about 20 minutes, until the spelt is tender, adding more stock if necessary. Taste and add salt, then spoon over some of the potted crab and swirl slightly with a spoon so the butter melts into the hot grains. Serve immediately, with a few leaves of parsley thrown over. The richness of this would overwhelm, if not for the vitality and goodness of the spelt.

Crab and Mustard Omelette

A never-forgotten dish eaten in a restaurant run by an Englishman, on a French beach. The heat of the mustard with the succulent crab is sensational. Buy the best eggs you can find so the omelette puffs nicely, from 'totally' free-range hens (see page 166) – this means they have access to plenty of pasture and their flavour is enhanced by pecking for grubs and among herbs and grasses.

Makes 1 omelette, serving 2 hungry people

350g/12oz picked brown and white crab meat
¼ teaspoon cayenne pepper
¼ teaspoon freshly ground white pepper
a squeeze of lemon juice

4–5 large eggs (the quantity depends on your hunger)
1 tablespoon English mustard – made from Colman's powder and water
3 tablespoons double cream
1 teaspoon unsalted butter
sea salt
2 sprigs of parsley, to serve

Loosely mix the crab with the seasoning and lemon juice. Don't make it into a mush. Beat the eggs with a large pinch of sea salt. Combine the mustard with the cream and set to one side.

Put the butter in a large, non-stick frying pan or omelette pan and heat until it foams. Pour in the egg mixture, then cook over a low heat – I do not think good omelettes should be heavily fried. Allow the omelette to set a little around the edges, then use a table knife to pull the edges into the centre in 4 places. The runny egg should overflow into the gap left by the moving knife. Continue to do this slowly until the omelette has thickened but there is still a very runny layer quivering on the surface. Spoon over half the crab meat, then drizzle the English mustard 'cream' over the top. Quickly flip over the omelette, folding it in 2 or 3. Hold a plate beside the pan and roll the omelette on to it, then stick the parsley sprigs on top.

CRAYFISH

Boiled Crayfish with Watercress and Egg Sauce

Leftovers
Crayfish-scented Broth with Trout and Rice

Wild river crayfish are getting rather trendy and turning up in London's East End restaurants – little pseudo lobsters revelling in being new on the scene. Time will tell if they are to become a classic British ingredient. These are the American signal crayfish – unwanted invaders of our rivers. Originally they were brought to UK crayfish farms to add some much needed robustness to the breed, which was succumbing to a plague affecting all Europe. Instead they killed most of the British crayfish, escaped and naturalised successfully. British wild crayfish are now a protected species and very rare.

The American ones do need eating, and many more could be trapped, caught and sold than are at present. The chef Mark Hix loves crayfish and campaigns for others to discover them. Last summer, on a dripping-wet evening that would please any river creature, he organised a feast at the Rivington Grill, London, where we dipped one meaty pink body after another into mayonnaise and sipped crayfish soup. A crayfish awareness feast – it sounds like an irresistibly silly evening, but Hix is at least making the important point that there is a need to look beyond prawns and lobster, to expand the menu and in doing so keep wildlife in British rivers healthy, too.

A heap of crayfish on a dish makes a table kingly; they cannot be described as subsistence food, although I suspect, like oysters, they once were. They tend to be expensive but they do award you a bonus, in the form of their shells, for making a crayfish-scented broth. You can also make proper, more substantial soup from the shells, but it involves crushing them. Unless you have a powerful food processor, this is not really practical for a domestic kitchen. That is what restaurants are for.

Wild crayfish may look like lobsters and be the size of prawns but they do not have the flavour of either. I would describe their flavour as similar to a chicken that has feasted on trout – very delicate. Do not confuse them with the crayfish you see in sandwiches and supermarket salads. Those are farmed, often in Norway but also in Spain and elsewhere in Europe. They are usually brought to this country already cooked and preserved in brine, and not surprisingly taste strongly of salt.

Buying crayfish

Ask at your local fishmonger's during the season (April to September). Freshly boiled, well-handled crayfish, fished out of the River Kennet in Wiltshire, are available by post from The Everleigh Farm Shop, near Marlborough (www.everleighfarmshop.co.uk; tel: 01264 850344).

Boiled Crayfish with Watercress and Egg Sauce

This reminds me of another crayfish feast: a lunch in Wiltshire, yards from the River Kennet. David Hammerson, owner of The Everleigh Farm Shop (see above), cooked them for us. Once again, we ate them the most practical way, with mayonnaise. I have simply added that other freshwater ingredient, watercress, to this recipe.

Live crayfish, incidentally, need to be boiled for 10 minutes in salted water, added live to the pan as soon as possible after being caught. You will find, however, that they are usually sold ready boiled.

Serves 4

16–20 freshly boiled crayfish

For the sauce:
4 eggs, boiled in their shells for
   8 minutes
3 egg yolks
1 teaspoon English mustard powder
   (add more if you are an English
   mustard fan)

300ml/½ pint sunflower oil
leaves and upper stalks from 1 bunch
   of watercress (about
   100–150g/3½–5½oz), very finely
   chopped
juice of ½ lemon
sea salt and freshly ground black
   pepper

Peel the hardboiled eggs, chop them finely and set to one side. Put the raw egg yolks in a bowl with the mustard and begin to whisk in the oil, adding it very slowly, until you have a thick, emulsified sauce. Once all the oil has been incorporated, add the watercress and lemon juice. Stir well, then fold in the hardboiled eggs and season to taste with salt and pepper.

Eat the crayfish by pulling the strip of meat out of the main body shell – there is a little meat in the claw, too. Use lobster picks and crackers or kitchen scissors to get at it. Put a bowl of the sauce on the table.

Crayfish leftovers

Crayfish-scented Broth with Trout and Rice

Prepare the broth as for Crab Broth (see page 155) and use to make an unusual freshwater fish dish. Gently fry 2 chopped shallots in butter, then add 100g/3½oz basmati rice and 2 crushed allspice berries. Pour over enough crayfish broth to cover, bring to the boil, then press a circle of greaseproof paper over the top and cook until the rice is just tender. Meanwhile, fry a trout in butter on both sides until just done. Peel off the skin and lift out the meat – remember to extract the meat from the cheeks of the trout – then break it up and scatter it over the rice. Throw some chopped dill over the top and serve immediately.

For another crayfish recipe, see Green Celery, Crayfish and Potato Salad on page 91.

CUCUMBER

Hot Spiced Cucumber

Chilled Cucumber Soup with Mint, Yoghurt
   and Green Chilli

Proper Cucumber Sandwiches

Easy to buy in any greengrocer's, cucumbers are usually British, economical and great in certain dishes. They now play quite a part in my everyday kitchen, either cooked on their own or in the soup recipe overleaf.

Hot Spiced Cucumber

I use either Southeast Asian panang curry paste or Thai yellow curry paste (both made by Mae Ploy) to make this bowl food. If there's a cucumber in the fridge, which there usually is even when all other vegetables have been used up, it's quick to make with other basic ingredients from my store cupboard. Have some plain boiled basmati or Thai jasmine rice ready. For 2 people, heat a dessertspoon of curry paste in a pan, add a 4cm/1½ inch piece of coconut cream (which comes in a block, like butter) and 300ml/½ pint of water. Cut half a cucumber in half lengthways, scoop out the seeds and slice the flesh into pieces 5mm/¼ inch thick. Add to the pan, bring the mixture to the boil and simmer for about 5 minutes, until the cucumber softens a little. Add salt to taste. Bash a few peanuts into gravel using the back of a knife or a mortar and pestle. Toast them in a separate pan and scatter over the top of the curry. Serve with the rice. If you have a red or green chilli – or some basil, coriander or mint leaves – slice the chilli and scatter it, with a few herb leaves, over each bowlful.

Chilled Cucumber Soup with Mint, Yoghurt and Green Chilli

So cool yet so out of fashion, chilled soups that are not gazpacho are rather welcome, not least because there's no taste of onion lurking in the mouth for hours after. This soup can be made well in advance and is good as a starter before a curry.

Serves 4

2 cucumbers
55g/2oz butter
1 litre/1¾ pints chicken stock
    (see page 116)
600ml/1 pint plain yoghurt

2 green chillies, deseeded and
    chopped
about 10 chives, finely chopped
leaves from 4 sprigs of chervil
    (optional)
nigella seeds (optional)
fine sea salt

Cut the cucumbers in half lengthways and scoop out the seeds. Slice, then put into a colander, sprinkle with fine salt and leave for about 1 hour to allow the bitter juices to run out. Pat dry with kitchen paper.

Melt the butter in a pan and add the sliced cucumber. Cook gently until translucent, then add the stock and bring to the boil. Switch off the heat, allow to cool completely, then place in a liquidiser with the yoghurt and chillies and blend until smooth. Chill until icy cold, then taste and adjust the seasoning.

When you are ready to eat, stir the soup and then serve with the herbs and nigella seeds scattered on the surface, if using.

Proper Cucumber Sandwiches

Just a reminder of how nice they are: peeled cucumber sliced thinly on a mandolin, salted in a colander for 1 hour as above to remove excess juice, patted dry, then packed in a generous layer between 2 slices of bread spread with yellow Cornish butter. Crusts cut off, if you wish.

DAMSONS

Damsons, Boiled Gingerbread and Lemon Cream
Damson Gin

Big boxes of damsons do find their way to cities in late summer. You will find them in markets and the few straggling greengrocer's shops that are left. They are a delicious northern, dark red, richly flavoured plum, but small, so annoyingly tricky to stone. The best tool is a cherry stoner – which pops the little pip out with reasonable accuracy. You will be swearing soon, however, which must be why I always find stones in jam gifted by friends who have a tree.

Buying damsons

Try farmers' markets, and always ask your local greengrocer, if you have one. To find a farmers' market, look at your local council website, or at www.farmersmarkets.net (for a nationwide list). London markets can be located at www.lfm.org.uk.

Damsons, Boiled Gingerbread and Lemon Cream

A trifle inspired by Grasmere in Cumbria, near the place where damsons grow so well. You could use the famous, heavenly spiced Grasmere gingerbread in this recipe – buy it direct from the bakery (www.grasmeregingerbread.co.uk; tel: 015394 35428). Or instead, here is a hybrid, a boiled spicy cake I featured in *The New English Kitchen* (Fourth Estate, 2005), which has become a favourite of my friends because we always have it at parties alongside the cheese. You will have some gingerbread left over after serving this dish but that's no bad thing. It keeps for ever. I forgot about some I had left over from a party where we served it with Cheddar cheese, and it was fine six months later, with not a spot of mould.

Serves 4

450g/1lb damsons
golden caster sugar, to taste
4 teaspoons damson gin (see
    opposite) or French plum liqueur
    (mirabelle or prune), or use
    ordinary gin
2 teaspoons dark muscovado sugar

For the gingerbread:
115g/4oz unsalted butter
115g/4oz soft brown sugar
2 tablespoons water
280g/10oz black treacle
1½ teaspoons ground ginger
2 eggs
175g/6oz plain flour
½ teaspoon bicarbonate of soda
55g/2oz ground almonds

For the lemon cream:
300ml/½ pint double cream
1 tablespoon icing sugar, sifted
grated zest of 1 unwaxed lemon
2 teaspoons lemon juice (optional)

First make the gingerbread. Preheat the oven to 150°C/300°F/Gas Mark 2. Put the butter, sugar, water and black treacle into a saucepan and bring to the boil. Boil for exactly 5 minutes, then set aside to cool until just hand hot. Beat in the ginger, then the eggs, one by one. Sift in the flour with the bicarbonate of soda and almonds and fold in well.

Use baking parchment to line a 23cm/9 inch shallow cake tin or a small baking tray about 25 x 17cm/10 x 7 inches. Turn the mixture into it and bake for 30–45 minutes, until a skewer inserted in the centre comes out clean. Remove from the oven and leave to cool on a wire rack.

Put the damsons in a pan and cook them to a pulp. Remove the stones, picking them out with your fingers, then add sugar to taste – it is good for this part of the pudding to be quite tart.

For the lemon cream, whip the cream into soft peaks and fold in the icing sugar, lemon zest and lemon juice (don't add the lemon juice if the cream is very thick or the mixture will become cakey).

Cut the gingerbread into 2cm/¾ inch squares and put a few in the bottom of 4 tumblers (flat-bottomed glasses are best for this recipe). Spoon in some cooked damsons and splash over a teaspoon of damson gin or liqueur. Spoon the lemon cream on top and finish with the dark muscovado sugar.

Damson Gin

To make 1 litre/1¾ pints, put 450g/1lb damsons in the freezer and leave overnight. The following day, defrost them and put them into two 75cl bottles. Top up with gin and put ½ vanilla pod into each bottle. Seal the bottles and leave for 4 months, agitating them from time to time. Strain and rebottle the gin.

You can make a demon damson sorbet with the gin-soaked damsons – but you will need to remove the stones first using a cherry pitter or a knife. Purée the damsons in a food processor, then combine with a mixture of 2 egg whites whisked until foamy with 175g/6oz caster sugar. Either churn in an ice-cream maker or freeze in a container for 1 hour, stir, then refreeze until solid. Take out of the freezer about 15 minutes before serving, to soften slightly.

Buying damson gin

Damson gin made in the Lythe Valley, Cumbria, is available from Strawberry Bank Liqueurs: www.damsongin.com; tel: 015395 68812.

EGGS

Eggs in Jelly with Tarragon

Poached Eggs with Rainbow Chard and Pink Pepper

Soft-boiled Eggs, Raw Vegetable Crudités, Mayonnaises
  (Basil, Nasturtium and Chilli)

Egg matters are much changed since I first began writing about food
12 years ago. Then, only a few supermarkets stocked free-range eggs and
none sold organic ones. If the battery-farm controversy has passed you by,
be aware that there are three types of egg: one from a hen that is caged in a
small space, one that is reared in a slightly roomier barn and one that roams
'free range'. There are various standards of free range, from systems where
the density of hens per square metre is still high (the maximum is 11 hens
per square metre in closed compounds) to the totally traditional system of
letting the hens roam around a farm, foraging freely. As long as I can
choose to buy an egg from a hen that is not caged, I am content, if not
pacified.

The system of caging hens has no justification, yet it will continue.
Cages are due to be improved, but really the only improved cage is no cage.
Unfortunately, cages will not be banned in Europe in the foreseeable future.
Far too many farmers are benefiting from this system of farming because
there is no legislation that insists caged hen's eggs must be labelled as such.
Consumers might avoid them if there was greater awareness of how the
eggs in the box were produced. These eggs have a big market in readymade
foods and are also widely used in restaurants, where menus do not have to
show that they have been used, either.

It is different in shops. Clearer labelling has seen shoppers demand more
and more free-range and organic eggs, and supermarkets report that sales
of free-range are rising constantly. It is quite clear what the public wants –
are they being listened to by those who govern animal welfare rules?
Supermarkets have promised change, but we wait to see.

One thing is certain: caging hens increases the risk of salmonella
infection that can be passed on to humans. Cramped and insanitary

conditions are a breeding ground for the disease. If the vast majority of caged hens were not vaccinated against the disease in this country as they are now, we would be rife with it again.

Free-range eggs are not an expensive food, bringing us to the lovelier aspect of eggs – eating them. If you like them, that is. For every five people I know that can look a soft-boiled or fried egg in the eye, I know one who can't. But if you love them and enjoy the many ways to cook with them, you are lucky. Eggs are singularly the most economical way to eat protein, and a vessel for extraordinary creativity. How many special meals have I cooked, when I would happily have rushed to buy something extravagant, then ended up making something with eggs for a few pence?

Buying eggs

There are plenty of opportunities to buy good eggs. Small, local food shops, including butcher's, delis and greengrocer's, often sell free-range or organic eggs. You can also buy eggs from farmers' markets or from local free-range or organic egg farms. Be circumspect. If you are able to meet the farmer, ask about the system they use. Maybe it is idealistic, but your curiosity might ignite theirs as to how they can improve the way they keep their hens. Farmers need to know that consumers mind. To find a farmers' market, look at your local council website or at www.farmersmarkets.net (for a nationwide list). London markets can be located at www.lfm.org.uk.

Organic egg farming systems are certified as welfare friendly – I tend to buy them when shopping in supermarkets. On the other hand, I am happy to buy non-organic eggs from a farm shop if I can see the birds in the field or farmyard.

Clarence Court Farm specialises in rare breeds and produces a range of eggs, including Old Cotswold Legbar, which are multicoloured, and Mabel Pearman's Burford Browns, my favourite, which have spectacular dark yellow yolks. They are available in Waitrose, or check www.clarencecourt.co.uk (tel: 01579 345718) to find a local stockist.

Eggs in Jelly with Tarragon

These are little moulds filled with a soft-boiled or poached egg and covered with chicken stock set to a jelly. They are not everyone's kind of dish but I love them, because they were always in my grandmother's fridge. Eating them is an exercise in texture: firm egg white, tender jelly and rich ooze of egg yolk – black pepper is essential.

You can poach the eggs, but unless they are very fresh you run the risk of the whites bolting around the pan. I am not a fan of putting vinegar in the boiling water to stop this because it ruins the flavour of the egg, so I soft-boil the eggs, cool them, then peel. If you prefer to poach them, try the cling-film method described on page 171.

Makes 8

8 eggs
leaves from 4 sprigs of tarragon

For the jelly:
1 litre/1¾ pints rich chicken stock (see
    page 116)
6 gelatine leaves
sea salt

To make the jelly, strain the chicken stock through a piece of muslin or a jelly bag. Taste it – if it needs salt, add it now. Soak the gelatine leaves in cold water for about 10 minutes. Heat the stock in a pan until it is the temperature of hot bath water.

Prick the rounded end of each egg with a pin so they will not crack, then put them in cold water. Bring to the boil and cook for 4 minutes. Run cold water into the pan, then peel the eggs very carefully, as they will be fragile and you do not want them to break. It is perhaps better to have some contingency and boil a spare one or two. Or use poached eggs if you wish, following the method on page 171.

Squeeze the water out of the soaked gelatine, add the gelatine to the hot stock and stir to dissolve. Pour a little jelly into the bottom of 8 ramekins or dariole moulds, add some tarragon leaves and leave in the fridge to set for 20 minutes. Remove from the fridge, put an egg into each one, then pour in enough jelly to cover the eggs completely. Shove a few more tarragon leaves down the side of each egg and leave in the fridge to set again.

To turn them out of the moulds, place each ramekin in hot water for about 30 seconds, dry the outside, then invert on to a serving plate. Eat with a little cress.

Poached Eggs with Rainbow Chard and Pink Pepper

Chard is a vegetable I am beginning to see a lot of. With its red, yellow and white stalks and big green leaves, it turns up in markets, greengrocer's shops and even supermarkets from mid-summer onwards. Infant leaves make good salad, while the large, mature leaves cook down to a nice, chewy spinach alternative. Chard is not as wasteful as spinach, losing less water in the cooking, but because of its sturdier texture it is slightly harder to use in recipes. It goes well with cream and cheese, and also with eggs, whose richness contrasts perfectly with the earnest mineral chard.

    This small supper dish is pretty, with its specks of pink pepper, and quick to make. The cling-film trick that helps keep the eggs in a neat pouch shape is one that can be used any time you need to poach an egg. You can, of course, use any other preferred method.

Serves 2

4 eggs
450g/1lb rainbow chard (you can use white chard if the multicoloured leaves are not available)

55g/2oz butter or 4 tablespoons olive oil
sea salt and freshly ground pink pepper (crush in a mortar and pestle)

First prepare the eggs. Have ready a bowl of cold water. Heat a small pan of water (about 4cm/1½ inches deep) to boiling point. Loosely line a teacup or ramekin with a sheet of cling film about 30cm/12 inches square. Crack an egg into it, then bring the edges of the cling film up and twist, sealing the egg inside. Repeat with the remaining eggs, then lower each into the pan and cook until the whites are firm but the yolks are soft – prod gently with the tip of a wooden spoon to see if the white is still wobbly. Remove the eggs, dip them in the bowl of cold water for a second, then take them out, carefully open the cling film and lift out the egg. You can do this well in advance, then reheat the eggs in warm water before you serve.

Wash the chard and cut it into ribbons about 3cm/1¼ inches wide. Bring a large pan of salted water to the boil, add the chard and cook for about 5 minutes, until the stalks are just tender. Drain and pat dry with kitchen towel.

Meanwhile, melt the butter or heat the oil in a pan. Swish the chard around in it and then divide between 2 plates. Place the poached eggs on top and scatter with the salt and pepper.

Soft-boiled Eggs, Raw Vegetable Crudités, Mayonnaises (Basil, Nasturtium and Chilli)

When the markets begin to brim with new-season, just-picked vegetables, it will surprise you how many are sweet and juicy enough to eat raw. Pile them on to the best-looking big dish you have, halve the soft-boiled eggs and balance the dishes of sauce beside.

Serves 6

12 medium eggs

For the nasturtium and chilli mayonnaise:
½ quantity of mayonnaise (see page 281)
10 nasturtium flowers, chopped, and/or petals from ordinary marigold flowers
2 red chillies, deseeded and chopped
10 pink peppercorns, crushed in a mortar and pestle
sea salt

For the basil mayonnaise:
½ quantity of mayonnaise (see page 281)

leaves from 4 sprigs of basil, torn or chopped into small pieces
freshly ground black pepper

Choose from the following vegetables:
small stems of purple sprouting broccoli
runner, yellow wax, purple heart and green French beans
rocket leaves and flowers
La Ratte potatoes, cooked and cut in half lengthways
small courgettes (yellow and green)
peas in the pod or mangetout
yellow tomatoes
small carrots, turnips and even parsnips – it is essential to choose the freshest of the latter

Mix together the ingredients for each mayonnaise, put them in small bowls and set aside.

Prick the rounded end of each egg with a pin to stop them cracking as they boil. Put them in cold water, bring to the boil and cook for 4 minutes, 5 if you like them harder boiled. When cooked, run the cold tap into the pan to cool the eggs, then peel them. Be careful – they are more delicate than hardboiled eggs. Break them in half – they look nice and tempting this way. Arrange all the vegetables and eggs on a dish, then place the bowls containing the sauces in among them.

ELDERFLOWER

Elderflower Fritters
Elderflower and Ginger Syllabub
Elderflower Syrup
Elderflower and Mead Marinade for Poultry

Wild things ... there are elderflower bushes in the park, and when they are in flower their branches sag over the fence. Their season runs roughly from the middle of May to the end of June but in recent years cold springs have caused delays. You can help yourself in a public park or (with care) from the hedgerows at the side of the road. They are not a wild flower whose proliferation causes much worry. Give the flowers a sniff before you use them; I have always been told that elderflower pollen is a cure for hayfever, and can also prevent an oncoming cold.

Elderflower Fritters

Once out of the pan, these fritters are a spectacle, like an exploding golden firework, and they taste deliciously exotic. Make the batter for the fritters just before you cook them, and eat them hot, with a little crème fraîche.

Serves 4

8 elderflower heads, each with
  1cm/½ inch of stalk
115g/4oz self-raising flour
carbonated water
sunflower oil for frying

To serve:
icing sugar
crème fraîche

Shake each elderflower head to remove any insects. Sift the flour into a bowl and stir in enough carbonated water to give a batter the consistency of single cream.

Heat approximately 1cm/½ inch depth of sunflower oil in a large frying pan until it sizzles when a drop of water is dropped in at arm's length. Working quickly, hold the stalk of a flower head and dip it into and then out of the batter. Lower it into the hot oil and fry until light golden, turning it to cook the other side. Remove from the pan, drain on kitchen paper and dust with icing sugar. Repeat with the remaining flower heads. Eat immediately, with a little crème fraîche.

Elderflower and Ginger Syllabub

I like to serve this fluffy pudding in delicate teacups. You can make it at any time of year using elderflower cordial, which can be bought in any supermarket. Given the choice, I buy Belvoir cordial, which has the strongest concentration – but most of them will give a syllabub the elderflower effect.

Serves 4

1 tablespoon elderflower cordial or syrup
2 tablespoons dry white wine
grated zest of ½ lemon
1 teaspoon lemon juice

2cm/¾ inch piece of fresh ginger, finely grated
400ml/14fl oz double cream
a few fresh elderflowers during the season, or a few gratings of fresh ginger, to serve

Mix together the cordial, wine, lemon zest, lemon juice and ginger. Leave to steep for at least an hour. Pour the double cream into a large bowl and add the cordial mixture. Whisk until it thickens to a sturdy (but not stiff) cream. Spoon into little teacups or glasses and keep in the fridge. Serve sprinkled with flowers or ginger.

 Kitchen note
The Pistachio Biscuits on page 311 are ideal for scooping up little mouthfuls of this syllabub.

Elderflower Syrup

This makes an intensely flavoured syrup to use diluted, as a drink, or neat in the recipe on page 175.

2 litres/3½ pints water
2kg/4½lb caster sugar
5 oranges, sliced
5 lemons, sliced
20 elderflower heads

Put the water, sugar, oranges and lemons in a large pan and bring to boiling point, stirring occasionally to dissolve the sugar. Add the elderflower heads, then remove from the heat and leave overnight. Strain through a muslin cloth and pour into bottles, ready to use. Store in the fridge.

Elderflower and Mead Marinade for Poultry

Not as sweet as it sounds, just a delicate, floral preparation for a jointed chicken to grill over charcoal in early summer or roast. I sometimes come across mead (a honey wine/liqueur) in farm shops or specialist food shops, but it can also be bought from the beekeeping monks at Buckfast Abbey (www.buckfast.org.uk; tel: 01364 645570).

Pull the flowers from 2 elderflower heads and mix with 2 wineglasses of mead and 1 tablespoon of ground coriander seeds. Joint a whole chicken, cut little slashes in the thicker, meatier places (breast and drumsticks) and put the pieces in a ceramic dish. Pour over the marinade and leave overnight. You could do this on a Saturday, to cook for Sunday lunch.

Preheat the oven to 200°C/400°F/Gas Mark 6, or preheat the grill. Roast or grill the chicken pieces for 35–45 minutes, basting them with the marinade, until the juices run clear when the meat is pricked with the point of a knife. Eat with Roasted Mixed Root Vegetables (page 369).

FAGGOTS

Faggots and Watercress

Fried Faggots with Caper and Parsley Sauce

Alternative sausages, filled with a mixture of the butcher's pork off-cuts and offal, plus breadcrumbs, onion and seasonings. The mixture is wrapped in caul – a lacy piece of fat – and braised. Not all butchers make great faggots – the devil is in the seasoning – but if they do, buy them. You will do them a favour – they need to use up as much of the carcass as possible – and there will be a good modest supper.

Buying faggots

Butchers specialising in offal are something of an endangered species, but if you are a fan and can make the detour, Cooper's family butcher shop in the Midlands will sell you faggots, chitterlings, polony and black pudding: Cooper's Family Butcher, 195 Walsall Road, Darlaston, Wednesbury WS10 9SW; tel: 0121 526 2181.

Faggots and Watercress

Serve this greened-up version of faggots with a dish of buttered mashed potato. If you have no meat stock, you can use cider or ale in the gravy. Eat with either English or French mustard.

Serves 4

2 smoked back bacon rashers, chopped into small pieces
1 tablespoon butter
2 shallots, chopped
2 carrots, sliced
600ml/1 pint meat stock (see pages 64, 116 and 238)
2 tablespoons olive oil or butter
4 faggots, cut in thick slices
leaves from 2 bunches of watercress
sea salt and freshly ground black pepper

Put the bacon, butter, shallots and carrots into a pan and cook over a high heat until the bacon and shallots brown. Pour over the stock, bring to the boil and simmer for about 15 minutes, until you have a light gravy. Season with salt and pepper. (If you prefer, you can thicken the gravy by adding a dessertspoon of flour to the vegetables just before adding the stock, which must then be stirred in bit by bit.)

Meanwhile, heat the oil or butter in a frying pan, add the faggot slices and fry for a few minutes on each side until lightly browned. Put them on 4 serving plates and scatter the chopped watercress over the top. Strain the gravy and pour it over everything – including some mashed potato.

Fried Faggots with Caper and Parsley Sauce

Cut 4 faggots into segments and gently fry them in butter until crisp. Serve with boiled new potatoes and a sauce made by whisking together 1 egg yolk, 1 tablespoon of rinsed, drained and chopped capers, 2 tablespoons of chopped parsley, 1 chopped shallot and 6 tablespoons of extra virgin olive oil. This quantity will serve 4.

FIGS

Breakfast Figs
Spiced Neck of Lamb with Figs
Baked Figs with Pear Purée

Prices for figs reach horrifying levels in late summer, considering the whole
of Europe is overloaded with a glut. We should have our own supply really,
but tend to have only dried figs in shops, nice as they can be. I notice that
fig trees grow contentedly in London. We sometimes gather a free harvest
from one whose branches hang over the street, and occasionally, in autumn,
I can get a discounted box from the Saturday street market. And then the
pudding on page 182 happens.

Breakfast Figs

Semi-dried Smyrna figs, sourced from the bumper crop in the Mediterranean and easy to buy in Middle Eastern shops or the dried fruit section of supermarkets, are too much of a good thing stewed on their own, but they can be stewed with apples to make a delicious and healthy breakfast purée. To prepare, trim 450g/1lb semi-dried figs of their hard stalks and cut each into 4 segments. Peel, core and slice 1kg/2¼lb Bramley apples. It will not matter that they are sour, the sweet figs will correct that. Put all in a heavy-bottomed pan with 600ml/1 pint water and bring to the boil, then turn down to a simmer and cook to a soft purée. Eat with Greek yoghurt and honey.

Spiced Neck of Lamb with Figs

A peppery, gingery stew using a relatively cheap cut of lamb and Smyrna figs. It is best made the previous day and reheated.

Serves 4

55g/2oz unsalted butter
2 white onions, grated
4 tablespoons chopped flat-leaf
  parsley, plus extra to serve
1 heaped teaspoon ground ginger
a pinch of cayenne pepper
½ teaspoon ground turmeric

1 teaspoon freshly ground black
  pepper
2–3 lamb neck fillets (about 700g/
  1lb 9oz in total), sliced into 2cm/
  ¾ inch chunks
12 semi-dried Smyrna figs, the stalks
  trimmed off, then sliced
sea salt

Melt the butter in a large pan and add the onions, parsley, spices and lamb. Stir over a low heat for a few minutes (nothing should brown), then cover with water. Bring to the boil, skimming off any foam, then turn down to a simmer and cook, covered, for 45 minutes. Add the figs and cook for a further 15 minutes, until the lamb is tender. Taste and season with salt. Scatter more chopped parsley on top and eat with boiled, cracked bulgar wheat.

Baked Figs with Pear Purée

Pears, figs and walnuts – an autumn trinity. A creamy, acidic blue cheese follows this well. Eat it with a green salad dressed with walnut oil, or buttered Oatcakes (see page 274).

Serves 4

8 ripe black or green figs, cut in half
acacia honey or other runny flower
    honey
a few walnuts, crushed and lightly
    toasted in a frying pan

For the pear purée:
5 Williams or other yellow pears,
    peeled, cored and cut into chunks
juice of ½ lemon

Preheat the oven to 230°C/450°F/Gas Mark 8 (or, if you have a grill, you can use this instead).

Put the pears in a pan with about 2cm/¾ inch of water and cook gently until just soft, then purée in a liquidiser until smooth. Add the lemon juice and leave to cool. The pear purée will darken to a rust colour as it cools.

Arrange the fig halves in an ovenproof dish in a single layer and spoon about ½ teaspoon of honey on to each. Bake in the oven (or place under a hot grill) for about 10 minutes, until the edges of the figs catch a little colour. Serve hot or cold, with the pear purée and the walnuts scattered on top.

GOOSE

Roast Goose with Apples and Blackberry Jelly

Leftovers
Cold Goose and Wild Rice
Cold Goose and Cucumber
Goose Fat

Food for serious feasts, geese are, like turkeys, only produced to be eaten in winter – it would not be economic for a farmer to rear them at any other time. A few farms, however, do rear geese for Michaelmas, the post-equinox period and the launch of the season for parties. The last few years have seen this to be a sunny time, when you can still eat a pavement lunch or throw a party in the garden. Not perhaps the best time to roast a giant bird, but a Michaelmas goose does not have to be prepared like a Christmas one. There are lighter, seasonal ways to cook it and enjoy its dark, savoury meat with its tender grain. There is a lot of fat on a goose, most of which needs to melt away during cooking (you can store it – see below). Pricking the goose before cooking helps this happen.

Goose is a grown-up meat. The flesh from the best birds is gamy and darkish in colour – a characteristic that does not endear it to children used to white poultry meat, but they can be consoled by the crispness of the goose-fat-roasted potatoes on the side.

Buying goose

Like other farmed poultry, geese should be slow grown with plenty of pasture for exercise and grazing. Unlike turkeys, they are not intensively reared. Try to buy from a local supplier – you can locate one by checking www.goose.cc. Or there is the home-delivery option. Judy Goodman is a very reliable supplier. Geese began as a hobby for her but she now rears over 4,000 a year, on the field of her family's farm in Worcestershire, where they also have a dairy and grow asparagus: www.goodmansgeese.co.uk; tel: 01299 896272.

Roast Goose with Apples and Blackberry Jelly

This is a Michaelmas recipe but could just as easily be served at Christmas – just keep a store of blackberry jelly to hand. Inspiration comes from the exciting story of the fight between the archangel Michael and the devil. The angel triumphed and the devil fell to earth, landing in a blackberry bush. Folklore says he peed on it in fury and frustration – and it is true, unaccountably, that blackberries look and taste terrible after the 29th September. Whether you believe all this is entirely up to you. Goose, blackberries and apple go well together anyway.

Make an extra store of this jelly. It is good with the potted meats on pages 296, 325, 356 and 452, and I like it on hot buttered toast for breakfast.

Serves 8–10 generously

6kg/13lb goose
1 head of garlic
10 dessert apples
10 tablespoons pumpkin seeds
10 tablespoons fresh sourdough
  breadcrumbs
juice of 2 lemons
4 tablespoons cider

sea salt and freshly ground black
  pepper

For the blackberry jelly:
2kg/4½lb apples – either windfalls
  or cooking apples, cut into
  quarters (there's no need to
  peel and core them)
1kg/2¼lb blackberries
preserving sugar

First make the blackberry jelly. Put the fruit in a large, heavy-bottomed pan with 900ml/1 ½ pints of water and cook, uncovered, over a very low heat for about 45 minutes, until very soft. Line a colander with muslin and set it over a dish, or set up a hanging jelly bag. Spoon the apply pulp into the bag and leave to drip through, but do not push the juice through or you will end up with cloudy jelly. Measure the juice that has dripped through the cloth. Put it in a large pan and for each 500ml/18fl oz juice add 1kg/2¼lb preserving sugar. Bring to the boil and simmer for about 15 minutes, until it reaches setting point. To test this, drizzle a spoonful of jelly on to a cold plate and leave for a couple of minutes; a skin should form on top. Pour into clean jam jars, seal and store. You can use the jelly within 24 hours of making, or it can be stored for about 3 months.

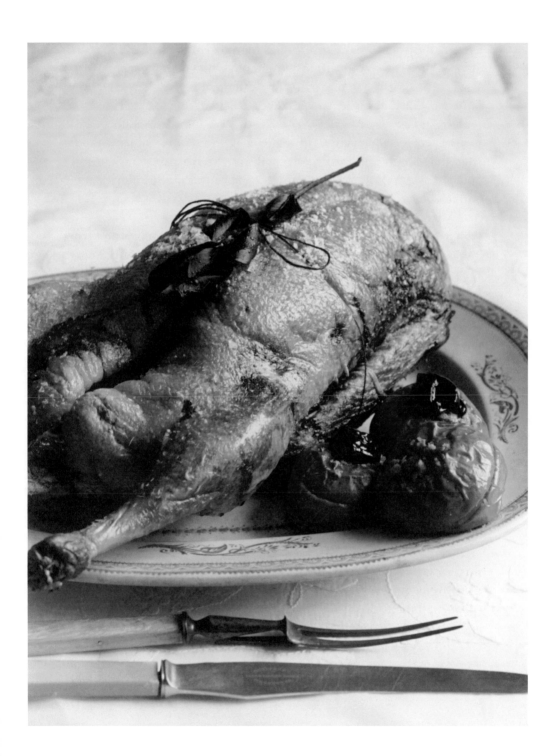

Preheat the oven to 200°C/400°F/Gas Mark 6. Pat the skin of the goose dry all over, then season the bird inside and out with salt and pepper. Place the whole head of garlic in the cavity. Prick the bird with a skewer all over the fatty parts, including the parson's nose, to help release the fat. Cover the legs with foil. Place on a rack set over a roasting tin and roast for about 2½ hours, basting occasionally. Halfway through cooking, pour off all rendered fat from the tin into a heatproof powl and store for roasting the potatoes. The goose is done if the juices in the thigh meat run clear when the leg is pierced with a skewer.

About 45 minutes before the goose is cooked, core the apples and score a line around the circumference of each with a sharp knife. Mix together the pumpkin seeds and breadcrumbs and use to stuff the cavities of the apples. Place them in a roasting tin with 4 tablespoons of the goose fat. Mix the lemon juice with the cider and spoon it over the apples. Roast for 45 minutes, in the same oven as the goose, until the apples are soft, burnished and slightly collapsed.

When the goose is done, remove from the oven and allow to rest for 20 minutes. Carve and serve with gravy, potatoes roasted in the goose fat (see opposite), and the apples, with the blackberry jelly on the side.

Gravy for goose

To make a gravy, tip the cooking fat from the roasting tin into a storage jar after removing the bird (reserve the fat for future roasts). Place the roasting tin over a medium heat. Add 3 wineglasses of wine and 1 of vermouth, bring to the boil, stirring and scraping the base of the tin with a wooden spoon, and then add 600ml/1 pint chicken stock. Bring to the boil again and add 1 heaped teaspoon of redcurrant jelly and some salt and pepper to taste.

Roast potatoes in goose fat

To roast potatoes in goose fat for 10 people, peel 3kg/6½lb floury potatoes and cut them into quarters. Parboil them for 5–7 minutes. Drain well, sprinkle with a dusting of plain flour and roast in a shallow tin in about 5mm/¼ inch of goose fat, putting them in the oven about an hour before you sit down to dinner. If you have only the oven capacity for the goose and no room for the potatoes, you can roast the goose and leave it to rest in a warm place for an hour while you cook the potatoes. Alternatively, shallow-fry your parboiled potatoes in goose fat on the hob, cutting them first into smaller pieces than you would for roast. This is also a good way to cook parsnips, but you will not need to parboil them first.

Goose leftovers

There is surprisingly little meat on a goose, no matter how enormous the bird, but if you have leftovers, try the following salads:

Cold Goose and Wild Rice

Combine the shredded cold meat with boiled wild rice, chopped parsley, toasted nibbed almonds, golden sultanas (soaked for about 1 hour in a little wine or sherry) and finely shredded radicchio or baby red chard leaves. Dress with oil, red wine vinegar, mustard and a little sugar.

Cold Goose and Cucumber

Peel ½ cucumber, cut it in half lengthways and scoop out the seeds with a teaspoon. Slice it into pieces 5mm/¼ inch thick and mix with shredded, leftover goose, a finely sliced shallot and a few sliced cornichons (baby gherkins). Make a dressing by mixing 1 tablespoon of sherry vinegar with 1 teaspoon of German mustard, 4 tablespoons of extra virgin olive oil and a pinch of salt (you could shake it all together in a jam jar with a tight-fitting lid). Pour the dressing over the goose mixture and mix well. Eat with other meaty offerings, such as salami and dry-cured ham, and a big green salad.

Goose Fat

If the goose was roasted in a moderately high oven (200°C/400°F/Gas Mark 6 or slightly less), the fat that ran from the meat will still have the necessary properties for using again to roast potatoes or to brush on other meats before roasting. If the fat was overheated, it will develop 'free-flowing fatty acids' – meaning it will soak into the potatoes and they will not crisp up well. Sieve goose fat before putting it in storage jars; it will keep in the fridge for 2–3 months.

GOOSEBERRIES

Gooseberry Sauce for Duck

Gooseberry Fool

Northern berries, needing little sun, are the most delicious in the world. Gooseberries may not be the prettiest of the collection, which includes redcurrants, blackcurrants, blueberries and purplish-blue raspberries, but they have the most unusual flavour and I rather enjoy the 'spawn' texture of the flesh inside. When the British ones turn up in markets and greengrocer's shops, snap them up. There is plenty of variety among the gooseberry family, and some of them are enigmatically named. 'Careless' are green with pale green veins, 'Early Sulphur' have a pink tinge, and Whinham's Industry – presumably the result of a hard-working plant breeder – are mottled with red. Green gooseberries are not necessarily more sour than those tinged with red. But if you see a punnet of red gooseberries, pause before putting them in the pot and try one raw. Some varieties, especially the large red-green types, are sweet enough to put on the table and nibble or serve on a plate with smoked and cured meats.

Buying gooseberries

Look out for British gooseberries in greengrocer's shops during the summer season. The first ripen at the end of June and they will pop up in the shops until the end of July. Frozen gooseberries, which are often British, are sometimes available in supermarkets and, since gooseberries are usually served cooked, it will not matter that these are slightly mushy when defrosted.

Gooseberry Sauce for Duck

The French traditionally eat gooseberries with fat-rich foods such as mackerel, but I have always thought this was to cover the flavour of stale fish oils. These days mackerel are much fresher when they reach the shops (see Mackerel, page 255) and they are better suited to piquant seasoning such as red chilli or radish. Free-range duck, however, needs an astringent to cut the fat, and a sweet and sour gooseberry sauce does the job.

This is not a dish that goes well with 'two veg'; better to eat a salad after or, if you are having a feast, make a rich starter such as the Potato and Fresh Cheese in an Olive Oil Pastry Pie on page 339, or the Chicory and Goat's Cheese Puff Pastry Pie on page 131.

Serves 4

4 duck legs
fine sea salt
3 tablespoons water
115g/4oz caster sugar
450g/1lb gooseberries, topped and
    tailed

Score the skin of the duck legs in a crisscross pattern with a sharp knife, trying not to pierce the flesh. Put them in a non-metallic container, then rub them with about 3 tablespoons of fine salt. Leave in the fridge for 24 hours, turning them occasionally; watery liquid will seep out. An hour before you serve the duck, drain off the liquid and pat the legs dry with a towel. Preheat the oven to 230°C/450°F/Gas Mark 8. Place a cast-iron casserole over a high heat, add the legs and briefly brown them all over. Transfer to the oven to roast for 45 minutes.

Meanwhile, make the sauce. Put the water in a small, heavy-bottomed pan and add the sugar. Heat slowly, allowing the sugar more or less to dissolve before the mixture boils. Boil for a short time on a high heat – the mixture will become syrupy. Add the gooseberries and turn off the heat. Very gently swish the gooseberries around in the hot syrup so they become coated but do not break up. To serve, put a duck leg on each plate and spoon some sauce around it.

Gooseberry Fool

Eat this pudding with the Pistachio Biscuits on page 311.

Serves 4

300g/10½oz fresh gooseberries,
 topped and tailed
golden caster sugar
150ml/¼ pint double cream

Put the gooseberries in a pan with a couple of tablespoons of water and cook gently until just soft. Remove from the heat, leave to cool and then chill. Sweeten with sugar to taste.

Whip the cream until thick, then fold it into the gooseberries. Serve in little glasses.

The Local Table

The French call it terroir – we say local. Eating local is a case of looking at your feet, noting the ground you walk on and understanding what that habitat will yield for your stomach – or, put more delicately, your table. That ground could be tarmac or paving stones; but it could be pasture, moorland, hillside, forest or coastal headland. There may be water nearby, fresh or salty; or a street of supermarkets. You could be shopping in an area without any specialist shops and variety, or spoilt for choice in the centre of a city. It is not that easy to be a local cook. The boundaries are basic – where you are is what you eat.

The more that we learn about the wider cost of distributing food over long distances, the faster the local movement has grown. We may look at some organic produce and wonder if it is right to buy it when it has travelled a long distance to reach shop shelves, but with local there are no negatives. I'd much rather buy the fresher, free-range egg from the non-organic smallholder down the road than an egg freighted all the way from Poland, stamped with an organic logo. There is the added incentive that buying local food supports British farmers. Not all deserve it, but the threat of hill farms returning to scrub within a decade or Dartmoor turning into a giant golf course is too real to ignore.

To be able to buy a fish landed at the nearest port, or meat from the farm you pass every day on your way to work, feels good – when it is possible. At the moment, the food supply is more or less centralised. Shops do not like to store large quantities, and rely on regular deliveries. Remember the fuel crisis in 2000, when distribution ground to a halt? A separate crisis, the slow but inevitable depletion of fuel, is forcing the food industry to rethink – partly because it has politicians on its back now, and not just a few consumers. Ways are being found to better localise the supply. This is sea change, not something relished by retailers who have efficiency down to a tee, but inevitable all the same.

Local makes me cheerful. It is not just economy of energy, there are other effects. Various experiments show that spending money with local suppliers gives that region's economy a substantial lift. The impact is very visible in some places, where a muscular concentration of good food shopping attracts a devoted following and has local-authority support. In a remarkably short space of time, a town centre can go from drab to fabulous. Clone Britain, the concept where the high street in one market town has matching branches of the same chains in a mall 30 miles away, is a reality. But no one wants clone towns – not even the chain retailers, who often want to move on to a high street because it has great shops or a vibrant Saturday market. If incoming shops are responsible for the closure of the popular shops they came to join, their endeavour ultimately fails. More satisfying would be proper regional distinctions in the chain stores and a change in planning law that reserves a proportion of space for community shops – supported by the all-important landlords. Examples of this do exist, but are all too rare.

Distinctive is something I know we want to have back. It has only been lost a short time. Without local specialities, we are gastronomically embarrassed, unconfident. And, in very small pinches, distinctiveness is returning, but this time with a new set of clothes. Cheese and pickle may still be a typical dish on the table, but woodpigeon with fresh figs could be too, the fruit growing, once again, in English gardens. With distinction rejuvenated and restored, back comes the pride.

So, what shall we have for supper?

GROUSE

Roast Grouse
Grouse with Heather Honey Toast

Leftovers
Grouse Stock with Oat Groats and Bacon

I fear our children may one day live in a world without grouse, the genuinely indigenous birds that are found on high moorland. That is not to say that going without eating them is the end of the world, simply that if the moor landscape cannot support grouse there is something wrong with that environment and the way it is managed. And not to know grouse is not to taste its rare flavour, which has notes of freshwater fish combined with powerful elements of well-hung beef. There is no other meat like it – but it is under threat. The numbers have been declining for a long time; grouse thrive on heather but also, conversely, on the interference of humans. Unless the farmer or landowner maintains the heather in the right way, keeping it long when the grouse want to nest, short when they need to feed up, they will abandon the hill.

The sport of grouse shooting is the only incentive for landowners to work hard at managing what is essentially a wilderness that only hill-bred sheep and some very hardy beef cattle can be reared on. Dressed and ready for the oven, grouse are very expensive to buy – about £18–20 per brace (pair). Prices are governed mainly by availability. Old grouse and later-season birds are cheaper. Ask for young grouse if you plan to roast them. But think of it this way: enthusiastic sportsmen pay a fortune for a day's grouse shooting, so the real cost of the bird you eat has been heavily subsidised! A grouse is a peculiar kind of bargain, then.

Buying grouse

The season for grouse runs from 12th August to 10th December but it is inadvisable to buy grouse for roasting after the end of October. Instead it is better to slow cook the grouse whole in a braise. Butchers with game licences often have a good supply, and some fishmongers are also licensed to sell game, but make sure they are reputable. Grouse are expensive and you deserve the best. They should not be full of shot, or the meat bruised. You can buy grouse via mail order – Yorkshire Game is a very reliable supplier sourcing grouse from its own moor in Scotland and from selected shoots in both Scotland and the north of England (www.blackface.co.uk; tel: 01387 730326).

Roast Grouse

Make sure to buy only young birds for roasting. If on the feather, a good sign of youth is baby, fluffy feathers on the inside of their wings. Avoid grouse that have been trussed and 'barded' with bacon – it can disguise bruising and the salt in the bacon 'cooks' the surface of the breast, drying it out. A good supplier will send an oven-ready grouse with the feet still on – leave them on for roasting and serve them that way, if you like. You will need 1 bird per person. Season them before cooking and rub them with butter. Roast in an oven preheated to 220°C/425°F/Gas Mark 7 for 20 minutes – the flesh will be pink (which is really the only way to eat grouse). Rest the birds in a warm place for 10–15 minutes, covered with foil, before serving with either fried breadcrumbs (see page 292) or bread sauce (see page 306).

Grouse with Heather Honey Toast

Grouse eat heather, and heather honey shows off the flavour of grouse nicely. There is a rightness about matching ingredients in this way that is hard to explain, but it is a fact that foods that inhabit the same environment taste good together, too.

There are plenty of grouse devotees who do not want their favourite game bird served any way other than hot with bread sauce; one of my chef friends told me – without having tasted it – that the grouse and honey idea was an aberration. But on a trip to Dumfries earlier this year I made it for Percy Weatherall and family, proprietors of Yorkshire Game (see above). They have been involved in grouse shooting, and especially in eating it, for decades. The whole family, old and young, adored it.

Serve 4 as a starter or something to eat with drinks

1 loaf of oaten soda bread
softened butter
heather honey

the meat cut from 2 cold roast grouse – the breast sliced, the leg meat pulled off the bone
a few red or white currants, or blueberries cut in half (optional)
sea salt and freshly ground black pepper

Preheat the oven to 200°C/400°F/Gas Mark 6. Cut 8 or more slices of bread, then cut each slice in half diagonally. Butter them on both sides, place on a baking sheet and bake for 8–10 minutes, until pale golden and crisp.

Brush each piece of toast with honey and put on a plate. Divide the grouse meat among the toasts, grind a little black pepper on to each one and scatter over a few salt crystals. Add the currants or blueberries, if you have them, and serve. The grouse toasts can be kept waiting a while.

Grouse Stock with Oat Groats and Bacon

A soup that uses up every scrap of your extravagant feast.

Serves 4

a walnut-sized piece of butter
115g/4oz smoked back bacon, cut into
   1cm/½ inch pieces
1 shallot or small onion, finely
   chopped
1 celery stick, de-stringed and very
   finely sliced
85g/3oz oat groats

For the stock:
2 grouse carcasses
2 carrots, roughly chopped
1 celery stick, roughly chopped
1.2 litres/2 pints water
sea salt and freshly ground black
   pepper

To make the stock, put the grouse carcasses, carrots, celery and water in a pan and bring to the boil. Skim off any foam that rises to the surface and simmer for 1 hour. Strain through a cloth or a fine sieve, then taste and season with salt and pepper. The stock will be a dark grey brown.

To finish the soup, melt the butter in a pan and gently fry the bacon, shallot and celery in it for about 2 minutes. Add the oats, followed by the grouse stock, and bring to the boil. Turn down the heat and simmer for 20–30 minutes, until the oats are tender. Serve in bowls, with hearty bread.

GURNARD

Gurnard with Sweet and Sour Violet Aubergine and Celery

Fish offcuts

Fish Stock

Cockle, Potato and Garlic Hotpot

Not only one of my favourite fish to look at but also one worth discovering as an unfamiliar non-quota type – 'non-quota' means that there is no limit on the number that fishermen can land. Quota fish include most commonly eaten species, such as cod, haddock and monkfish, whose numbers have been greatly reduced over the years by overfishing. Quotas are a conservation measure brought in by the EU as part of the Common Fisheries Policy to save fish stocks. It is a controversial rule. If a boat lands more than its quota, it has to chuck them back into the water, where they will certainly die. But quotas are the least worst solution to the problem.

It is a mystery why gurnard are not more popular. A gurnard's head has a sculpted, handsome brow, tinged with rose, and, if the fish is a good size, there are two fat fillets of pale flesh that can compete with cod in their big-flake texture and gentle taste. If small, they are too bony but it is always better to buy a bigger fish in any case. A large fish is mature, and will have been able to breed. Fishermen may not catch a species below a certain size but it still surprises me how weeny some fish on the slab can be. (Most offensive is the sight of cod no larger than a man's foot.) A small dead fish on the fishmonger's counter is useless, however. You could choose to eat it – or send a strong message to the fish trade and tell the fishmonger why you do not want it.

I see gurnard in greater number every time I shop for fish. They have finally been recognised by the ever-influential TV chefs as a treat, although back in 2005 I was writing about unfamiliar species such as gurnard in *The New English Kitchen* (Fourth Estate, 2005) and the *Telegraph* magazine (I had to say that). If you cannot buy gurnard regularly, Matthew Stevens will send out whole ones or the fillets and bones needed for the recipes below. He is a fishmonger whom I constantly refer to in this book simply because he is the best supplier I have found who can deliver proven sustainably caught fish to your door. Last time I bought gurnard from him (in 2007) I paid £3.25 per kilo – so not much. Gurnard freezes beautifully. One last point: a gurnard's skin is very thick, making these fish difficult to fillet unless you have exceptionally sharp knives.

Gurnard with Sweet and Sour Violet Aubergine and Celery

Devotees of Sicilian food will recognise the aubergine mixture in this dish as caponata, a delicious, sweet-sour vegetable braise that I much prefer to ratatouille. I have used violet aubergine, which sounds like the doomed heroine of a gothic novel but is a pretty vegetable, now growing with success in the UK and turning up at some farmers' markets. I have seen it in Waitrose during the summer, too.

Celery also plays a major part in this dish, which has so many parallels with old English food. Gurnard likes to share a plate with a full-bodied chum, and these vegetables are it.

Try to buy a good red wine vinegar for the vegetable mixture, such as Maille. I have seen Cabernet Sauvignon red wine vinegar in Spanish food shops and supermarkets, and this would work well here. Do not use balsamic vinegar; it will kill this dish dead.

Serves 4

2 large gurnard, each weighing
   over 500g/1lb 2oz, filleted to make
   4 fillets (reserve the bones to make
   stock – see below)
2 tablespoons olive oil
1 lemon, quartered

For the sweet and sour violet
aubergine and celery:
1 violet aubergine
4 tablespoons olive oil

6 small shallots, chopped
4 garlic cloves, sliced
2 celery stalks, finely sliced
½ fennel bulb, finely chopped
2 tablespoons pine nuts
3 tablespoons good-quality red wine
   vinegar
3 tablespoons passata (or 1 heaped
   teaspoon tomato purée mixed with
   1½ teaspoons water)
leaves from 1 sprig of flat-leaf parsley
sea salt and freshly ground black
   pepper

Cut the aubergine into 1cm/½ inch dice and put them in a colander. Sprinkle with salt and leave for 30 minutes, then pat dry with a towel.

Heat the oil in a pan, add the shallots and garlic and fry gently for a minute. Add the aubergine, celery and fennel and cook until soft and lightly browned. Do not turn the heat up too high. Add the pine nuts and stir for another minute, then pour over the red wine vinegar, add the passata and season. Stir well, turn off the heat and leave to marinate for half an hour so the flavours can develop. Season to taste and scatter the parsley leaves over the top.

Meanwhile, cook the fish, brushing the fillets on both sides with the olive oil, then cooking in a frying pan for 3–4 minutes.

Serve the fish over the vegetables, with a lemon quarter on each plate.

Fish Stock

Gurnard bones and heads make a well-flavoured fish stock. Fillet the fish (or ask your fishmonger to do this) and put the bones in a pan with a tablespoon of olive oil, a sliced onion, celery stick and carrot, 4 chopped tomatoes and 6 fennel seeds. Cook over a medium heat for about 3 minutes, then cover with water, bring to the boil and simmer for 30 minutes. Skim off any fat from the surface and then strain. Use for the stew below or for any other dish requiring fish stock.

Cockle, Potato and Garlic Hotpot

Make this from any leftover fish, plus the gurnard stock above.

Serves 4

2 tablespoons olive oil
2 celery sticks, de-stringed and finely sliced
1 wineglass of white wine
16–20 Charlotte potatoes (according to appetite)
600ml/1 pint fish stock (see page 202)

1kg/2¼lb cockles, rinsed in several changes of water to remove any sand
leftover gurnard flesh, picked from the carcass, if available

For the sauce:
4 garlic cloves, crushed to a paste with a little salt
150ml/¼ pint mayonnaise (see page 281)

Mix together the garlic and mayonnaise for the sauce, then thin with a tablespoon of cold water to give a dropping consistency. Set aside.

Heat the oil in a large casserole, add the celery and cook for a minute. Add the wine and the potatoes, cover with the stock and bring to the boil. Put on the lid and simmer for about 15–20 minutes, until the potatoes are just cooked. Add the cockles, cover with the lid again and allow to steam over a fairly high heat for a few minutes until the cockles open wide. Discard any that do not open.

Throw in the gurnard flesh, if available, then divide between 4 bowls. Stir a tablespoon of the garlic sauce into each bowl and put plenty of crusty white bread on the table.

HADDOCK

Spiced Haddock Pasties
Baked Haddock Soup
Raw Haddock with Apples

Leftovers
Creamy Haddock Cakes

Haddock is a fish that has swum precariously away from the endangered list. The Marine Conservation Society, while not advocating an all-out haddock fest, says stocks from the North Sea, the west coast of Scotland, Norway and Barents Sea are currently healthy. They are less happy about Icelandic and Faroese stocks, and say haddock caught in the Rockall area should be avoided. See www.fishonline.org for the latest information. The best plan when shopping is to ask your fishmonger, who should be able to tell you the source of the fish. Having said this, there has been criticism of their economy with the truth when revealing location. For this reason, I find it easier to buy from fishmongers who get their fish from short-trip boats, because the fish is fresher when it is landed than haddock from a trawler that may spend over a week at sea. Haddock spawn in spring, so it is best to avoid eating them at this time.

Smoked haddock is a favourite reliable buy. If the supply of fresh fish is limited, undyed (so not the colour of a cyclist's safety jacket) smoked haddock from a sustainable source is a supper I keep returning to. Good in fish pies and fishcakes, or just simmered in milk, then eaten with a poached egg and a crumbled slice of smoked bacon, it is a British (often a Scottish) ingredient for which I have enormous affection. Finest of all is Finnan haddock, which is juicy through being left on the bone. Otherwise seek out Arbroath smokies, which are very nearly just as good.

Buying haddock

A growing number of fishmongers deliver nationwide. I suggest buying haddock (and also other fish) from The Whitby Catch (1 Pier Road, Whitby, North Yorkshire; www.thewhitbycatch.co.uk; tel: 01947 6013130). It is a co-operative of fishermen with small boats and its own shop on the town's pier. Buy extra fish to freeze, as it will justify the carriage charge. Fresh haddock and undyed smoked haddock, both sustainably sourced, are available in Waitrose and Marks & Spencer. In the port of Mallaig, on the west coast of Scotland, Andy Race sells beautiful fresh haddock and also smokes it expertly in his own kilns (he makes a great kipper, too). Mail-order service available: www.andyrace.co.uk; tel: 01687 462626.

Spiced Haddock Pasties

Makes 4

450g/1lb fresh haddock fillet
1 tablespoon butter
1 red chilli, deseeded and chopped
leaves from 4 sprigs of coriander
leaves from 2 sprigs of mint, chopped
leaves from 2 sprigs of parsley,
    chopped
½ garlic clove, crushed with a little salt
juice of 1 lemon
½ teaspoon ground cumin
1 egg, lightly beaten

a few cumin seeds
sea salt and freshly ground black
    pepper

For the pastry:
225g/8oz plain flour
a pinch of salt
a pinch of cayenne pepper
a pinch of smoked paprika
140g/5oz softened unsalted butter,
    diced
2 egg yolks
2–3 tablespoons cold water

First, make the pastry. Put the flour in a bowl and stir in the salt and
spices. Add the butter and rub it into the flour with your fingertips.
Add the egg yolks and enough cold water to form a dough. Knead for
a minute, wrap in cling film and chill for 1 hour. Remove from the fridge
half an hour before you want to use it.

Meanwhile, preheat the oven to 200°C/400°F/Gas Mark 6. Wrap the
haddock in a piece of foil with the butter on top and bake for about
10 minutes, until it feels firm to the touch through the foil. Remove
from the oven and allow to cool.

Flake the fish, discarding the skin and any bones, and mix it with the chilli,
herbs, garlic, lemon juice and ground cumin. Season with salt and pepper.

Roll out the pastry on a lightly floured surface and cut out 4 rounds, 18cm/
7 inches in diameter. Place a little pile of the fish mixture to the right of the
centre of each round, leaving the edges free. Paint a little beaten egg round
the edge, then fold the pasty in half and pinch the edges together to seal. Paint
the whole surface with beaten egg and throw on a few cumin seeds. Place on a
baking tray lined with baking parchment and bake at 200°C/400°F/Gas Mark
6 for 20–25 minutes, until the pastry is crisp and golden. Eat hot.

Baked Haddock Soup

Not so much a soup but a little pot of creamy broth, packed with haddock, North Atlantic prawns, small pieces of potato and chives, topped with cheese and baked for a few minutes, until the haddock is just cooked. So rich that just a small amount will make a supper – or a substantial supper when there is a lot of wine to be consumed.

Serves 6

8–12 small salad potatoes
450g/1lb undyed smoked haddock fillet, skinned and cut into bite-sized chunks
175g/6oz peeled North Atlantic prawns
2 tablespoons chopped chives

300ml/½ pint milk
2 egg yolks
300ml/½ pint double cream
2 tablespoons grated aged Cheddar, such as Isle of Mull, Lincolnshire Poacher or other good mature Cheddar
sea salt and freshly ground black pepper

Boil the potatoes in their skins until tender, then drain and leave to cool. Slice into rounds.

Preheat the oven to 230°C/450°F/Gas Mark 8. Divide the haddock between 6 large ramekins about 9cm/3½ inches in diameter, followed by the prawns and chives. Lay a few slices of potato on top.

Bring the milk to the boil. Put the egg yolks into a bowl and gradually whisk in the hot milk, then whisk in the cream. Season with pepper and a little salt. Pour this mixture over the haddock pots until they are quite full. Scatter over the cheese and bake for about 10–15 minutes, until the haddock is cooked. The soups need be very lightly browned; a few tanned spots is fine. Eat very hot, with plenty of bread.

Raw Haddock with Apples

Very good smoked haddock makes an excellent tartare (thin slices of raw meat or fish). The dressing is apple and shallot. I buy Irish wheaten soda bread to eat with this, but other seeded grainy loaves will do.

Serves 4

450g/1lb undyed smoked haddock fillet, skinned and cut into 1cm/½ inch dice
3 Russet or Cox's apples, cored and thinly sliced
2 shallots, sliced

5 tablespoons extra virgin olive oil
10 chives, chopped
4 sprigs of chervil, if available
5 tablespoons soured cream
4 lemon wedges
sea salt and freshly ground black pepper

Arrange the haddock on a large serving dish with the apple and shallots. Just mix it all roughly, it looks prettier that way. Drizzle over the olive oil and scatter the herbs randomly. Season with a few salt crystals and grind over some black pepper. Put a bowl of soured cream on the table, plus a dish of lemon wedges. Serve with brown soda bread and butter.

Creamy Haddock Cakes

If you have bought too much smoked haddock, make these utterly delicious fishcakes. It is essential to chill the mixture thoroughly, or they will be very hard to handle at the breadcrumb stage.

Makes 4 cakes, serving 2 hungry people

225g/8oz smoked haddock
150ml/ ¼ pint whole milk
1 tablespoon butter
1 tablespoon plain flour
2 tablespoons cooked mashed
   potato

a little olive oil for frying
sea salt and freshly ground black
   pepper

For coating (each on a separate plate or bowl):
4 tablespoons plain flour
1 egg, lightly beaten
5 tablespoons dried breadcrumbs

Put the haddock in a small pan, cover with the milk and bring to a simmer. Cook for just a minute or two until firm, then remove from the pan and flake the flesh, discarding the skin and any bones. Set to one side. Strain the milk.

Melt the butter in a small pan, add the flour and cook, stirring, for 1 minute. Whisk in the milk a little at a time and bring to the boil, stirring constantly. When the sauce boils and thickens, remove from the heat and stir in the haddock and mashed potato. Season to taste and leave to cool, then place in the fridge until firm.

To shape into cakes, divide the mixture into 4 and roll into patties. Dip each one first in flour, then in beaten egg, coating them thoroughly. Finally, roll them in the breadcrumbs. To cook, fry gently in olive oil, browning on both sides. Serve with peas.

HAM AND GAMMON

Ham and Peas Dressed with Mayonnaise, Capers
   and Chives
Gammon and Lentil Broth

I am fussy about all the pork I buy, both fresh and cured. There is no sensible economic reason to buy cheap gammon, the term given to raw ham. It is usually injected with polyphosphates that encourage the water they are mixed with to stay in the gammon. Once cooked, this runs away and the gammon, now a ham, loses body weight. Equally a gammon that comes from a pig grown fast on high-protein cereals will also lose weight during cooking, because a fast-grown, intensively reared pig has a higher water content in its flesh. The combination of these two issues results in a very uneconomical ham indeed. At all costs avoid 're-formed meat' or 're-formed ham'. This is chopped bits of ham, fat and gristle, shaped in a hammy oval mould (comical if it were not so tragic) with the help of gelatine and an awful lot of salt.

I buy good-quality British gammon hocks (the lower part of the leg) on the bone, from the small butcher's shop across the road. He and his cousin are Portuguese and survive there against the odds. Their cheap cuts are increasingly popular with locals and they do a good line in mutton, too. Next to them, a branch of a bookmaker's has opened. This was the inspired doing of the council when the beloved old-fashioned greengrocer's on the precinct closed down. We would have liked another of those, perhaps even a hairdresser's or a café to cheer up the community; instead we got the bookies and its desperate crowd of hangers-on. Urban regeneration, backwards. I want a greengrocer across the road again. Our butcher wants a greengrocer next door to his shop so we can buy the vegetables to eat with his meat.

But a piece of gammon is a nice thing to make do with while we dream. For a few pounds I can make a big pot of cooked ham and pulses ready to dip into any time. I'll just have to go further afield for parsley to add to it at the last minute.

Buying ham and gammon

Gammon made with meat from slow-grown pigs, which has been carefully dry cured and matured, costs more but is ultimately better value. Avoid imported gammon (raw ham) or ham (cooked gammon) – welfare and feed systems for pigs in exporting countries, commonly Denmark and Holland, do not measure up to even intensive pig farms in the UK. Naturally reared gammon and ham from British farms are a good choice. Hock is a cheap cut from the shin end of the front leg; collar the shoulder. All other gammon is raw cured leg. Buy from a local butcher and ask where it is sourced. On balance the British butchery trade is good at sourcing local, free-range meat. Many butcher's shops in city and rural locations are listed on www.bigbarn.co.uk. The archive of my *Daily Telegraph* 'Shop Local' columns can be found at www.roseprince.co.uk, detailing butchers who stock local meat.

You can buy British air-dried ham from Sillfield Farm (www.sillfield.co.uk; tel: 015395 67609), or from a new producer, who makes the best coppa (cured shoulder packed into an ox skin and air dried) I have yet to try: Best Butchers, near Milton Keynes; tel: 01908 375275 for mail order.

Ham and Peas Dressed with Mayonnaise, Capers and Chives

There are various ways to prepare this slightly retro salad. If the peas are just picked – and I mean *this morning* – and the pods are small and juicy (the best test is to eat one raw), boil them whole for a minute and add to the salad in their natural state. If they are very fresh, pod them – but cook them according to their freshness.

Serves 4

450g/1lb very fresh peas in the pod
225g/8oz cooked ham, cut into dice
½ quantity of mayonnaise (see page 281)

2 tablespoons capers, rinsed in cold water, squeezed dry, then chopped
2 tablespoons chopped chives
sea salt and freshly ground black pepper

Pod the peas. Bring a pan of water to the boil and add a teaspoon of salt. If the peas are very fresh and sweet, rather than starchy, when tasted raw, add them to the boiling water, bring it back to the boil and drain immediately. Refresh in cold water. Allow the peas to cool, then mix gently with all the other ingredients.

 Kitchen note
Substitute broad beans, or even frozen peas. I buy frozen broad beans in winter, defrost them and pop the green inner part of the bean out of the grey skin. Time consuming but worth it for the economy and essentially for the joy of green beans in January.

Gammon and Lentil Broth

This is a good basic recipe that will provide a pot of food to take from and heat in just a few minutes. It will keep for several days in the fridge. Have a bunch of parsley standing in a jar of water nearby, adding a little to each hot bowl of soup.

Serves 4

2 raw smoked hocks, about 1.5kg/3¼lb in total (use 'green' or unsmoked for a paler-flavoured soup)
55g/2oz butter or 4 tablespoons olive oil
2 garlic cloves, chopped
4 onions, chopped
2 large carrots, scraped and cut into dice
1 celery stick, diced

6 fennel seeds
12 coriander seeds
2 sprigs of thyme, or a large pinch of dried thyme
1 bay leaf
400g/14oz green lentils
sea salt and freshly ground black pepper

To serve:
leaves from 4 sprigs of parsley
extra virgin olive oil

Soak the hocks in cold water for at least 5 hours or overnight to remove excess salt, changing the water twice. Heat the butter or oil in a large pan and add the garlic, vegetables, spices and herbs. Cook for about 5 minutes, until the vegetables are translucent but not browned. Add the hocks and cover with water. Bring to the boil, skim any foam from the surface and then leave to bubble slowly for about 1½ hours. Add the lentils and continue to cook for another ½–1 hour, by which time the meat should be falling off the bone. Lift out the hocks, remove the skin and pull the meat off the bone. Cut the meat into dice and return it to the pot. Skim off any fat. Taste and season if necessary – you are unlikely to need much salt.

To serve, chop up plenty of parsley and put it on the table in a separate bowl, with a bottle of extra virgin olive oil. Add parsley and shake over a little oil just before eating the broth.

 Kitchen note
Substitute white beans or other beans for the lentils. To make life easier, buy canned beans and drain them, adding them in the last half hour of cooking.

HONEY

Greengage and Almond Tart with Honey Sauce
Honeycomb Cream with Hazelnut Meringue
    and Raspberries

It has never been more urgent to keep an eye out for locally produced honey. The honey you buy supports beekeepers, a profession that is dwindling by the moment. Sickness in the bee population, the high cost of keeping the bees healthy, the threat of genetically modified crops, and the use of pesticides by farmers are driving more and more beekeepers to give up. This isn't like the grubbing up of apple orchards in the 1970s – sad to say, we are able to exist without apple farming. A healthy bee population (both wild and kept) is essential for the pollination of many food plants, and we cannot afford to discourage beekeeping. It is said that one mouthful of food in every three could not exist without bees. Keep this in mind as you drizzle delicious honey, which, depending on where the bees have been working, will be flavoured with heathers, spring flowers, wild flowers, exotics. One cheering development in the last few years is London honey. Thanks to the eclecticism of London gardens, a number of beekeepers in the city are selling honeys with some very interesting tastes.

Buying honey

Buy honey as you go, from local producers as you travel around. Farmers' markets are usually a good source but specialist food shops, farm shops, village shops, even roadside honesty stalls are also worth investigating. It is shocking that supermarkets have yet to see the sense in promoting local honey farms. And many other independent city shops, while obviously the places where much local honey could be sold, pay little attention to the necessity of buying it. Keep your eyes peeled and ask your local high-street shops to find a source of honey gathered nearby.

Greengage and Almond Tart with Honey Sauce

Once this lovely tart comes out of the oven, it gets a drench of hot honey and lemon sauce, which soaks into the almond cake around the greengages.

Serves 10

225g/8oz unsalted butter
225g/8oz golden caster sugar
225g/8oz ground almonds
3 eggs, lightly beaten
5 greengages, pitted and quartered

For the sweet pastry:
55g/2oz icing sugar

250g/9oz plain flour, plus extra for dusting
a pinch of salt
125g/4½oz softened unsalted butter
1 large egg yolk
1–1½ tablespoons double cream

For the honey sauce:
225g/8oz honey
juice of 2 lemons

Make the sweet pastry with cool hands, mixing all the ingredients together to form a smooth paste. Or you can use a food processor, which is quicker: put the icing sugar, flour and salt in the processor and whiz for a few seconds, then add the butter with the egg yolk and enough double cream to form a paste when the mixture is whizzed briefly. Do not overwork it. Place on a well-floured board and lightly work into a ball, then wrap in cling film or greaseproof paper and chill for about 30 minutes.

Dust the worktop with flour and roll out the pastry to about 5mm/¼ inch thick. It will be very soft. Lift it by wrapping it around the rolling pin, then use to line a 28cm/11 inch tart tin. Don't worry if it tears; just patch it up with spare pieces of pastry. Chill for half an hour.

Preheat the oven to 175°C/350°F/Gas Mark 4. Prick the base of the pastry case randomly with a fork, cover the base and sides with greaseproof paper and fill with dry rice or beans (this will prevent the pastry bubbling up). Bake for about 15–20 minutes, until the edges are crisp and the base of the pastry dry. You may want to lift away the paper and beans for the last 5 minutes of cooking so the base can dry out. Remove the pastry case from the oven and leave to cool.

Meanwhile, make the almond mixture. Melt the butter and sugar together over a low heat, stirring with a spoon or whisk, then cook for 2–3 minutes, until the mixture has a golden fudge consistency. Remove from the heat, add the ground almonds and the beaten eggs and stir until well combined.

Turn the oven up to 190°C/375°F/Gas Mark 5. Pour the almond mixture into the pastry case, then drop the greengage quarters on to it so they are evenly spaced. Bake for 15–20 minutes, until the almond mixture is just firm and slightly puffed.

For the honey sauce, warm the honey with the lemon juice and pour over the tart as you serve.

Kitchen note
You could substitute Victoria plums for the greengages, or pitted damsons and other plums. In winter, when we are plumless, you can use fat Agen prunes that have been previously soaked or are sold semi-dried.

Honeycomb Cream with Hazelnut Meringue and Raspberries

An unusual fool with chunks of honeycomb, raspberries and crisp pieces of nutty meringue. Just a little in a glass is enough for pudding but you can also serve it with shortbread.

Serves 6

2 egg whites
115g/4oz icing sugar, sifted
85g/3oz hazelnuts, chopped, toasted
   in a dry pan and cooled
400ml/14fl oz double cream
115g/4oz cut honeycomb
4 tablespoons raspberries

Preheat the oven to 150°C/300°F/Gas Mark 2 and line 2 baking sheets with baking parchment.

Put the egg whites and icing sugar in a large bowl and beat with an electric whisk until stiff peaks of white foam are formed. This will take about 9 minutes, so a tabletop food mixer is best, although you can use a handheld mixer. Fold the nuts into the meringue. Drop small dessertspoonfuls of the mixture on to the baking parchment, 5cm/2 inches apart. You should fit approximately 9 on each sheet. Bake for 30 minutes, until very pale brown and slightly cracked. Allow the meringues to cool on the trays, then lift them off the baking parchment.

Whip the cream to soft peaks. Cut the honeycomb into chunks and fold it roughly into the cream. Serve spooned over the meringues, with the raspberries scattered on top.

JOHN DORY

Spiced John Dory

Fried John Dory with Brown Butter, Parsley
   and Hazelnuts

One of my favourite fish to look at, John Dory (or St Peter's fish) has
muscular steaks of boneless, gently flavoured flesh on either side of its
knobbly skeleton. It is a non-quota by-catch fish, meaning that while
numbers of popular white fish such as cod are governed by conservation
rules, John Dory numbers are not under threat. They are not a target fish,
so tend to come up in nets when fishermen are hunting for other species.
At present, many are exported because they do not fit the narrow consumer
remit of favourite species such as cod, which are so recognisable on menus.
Snap John Dory up when you see it; this is a white-fleshed fish whose
flavour matches the delicate elegance of the overfished types that now need
protection.

Buying John Dory

Any good fishmonger ought to be able to pick up some John Dory for you
if you ask in advance. It is rarely available in supermarkets, presumably
because no one is quite sure what to do with it. John Dory is a pricy fish,
so this is a small but phenomenal feast.

Spiced John Dory

A clever recipe that could be adapted to wild sea bass, grey or red mullet or gurnard (see page 199) – all of them round fish with a good chunk of meat on each side.

Serves 4

leaves from 6 sprigs of mint
leaves from 6 sprigs of coriander
4cm/1½ inch piece of fresh ginger,
    peeled, then chopped
2 green chillies, halved, deseeded
    and chopped

4 large (200g/7oz) John Dory fillets, or
    a greater number of smaller ones
    (keep the bones and use them to
    make stock – see page 202)
extra virgin olive oil for frying

Put the mint, coriander, ginger and chillies into a food processor and process until very finely chopped. Spread over both sides of the fish fillets and leave to infuse in the fridge for half an hour.

Pour enough olive oil into a non-stick frying pan to cover the base and fry the fish for about 2 minutes on each side, until golden and firm to the touch. Serve with a rice pilaf, or Spiced Rice with Cauliflower, Coconut, Cloves and Ginger (see page 365).

 Kitchen note
Instead of frying the fish, you could bake it in an oven preheated to 220°C/425°F/Gas Mark 7 for about 10 minutes.

Fried John Dory with Brown Butter, Parsley and Hazelnuts

John Dory is such a fierce, fighting little fish, it will face up to any sauce. In the ocean it is very aggressive, and its fitness translates when you match it with potent ingredients. The sauce here is brown and nutty, and eating this dish is a nice contrast between the clean whiteness of the fish and the earthy, lemony character of the sauce, which is green with parsley.

Serves 2

2 tablespoons unskinned hazelnuts
115g/4oz unsalted butter
1 John Dory, weighing about 750g/
    1lb 10oz, or 2 smaller fish – or 4 fillets,
    weighing about 115g/4oz each
4 sprigs of curly parsley, finely
    chopped
juice of 1 lemon
sea salt and freshly ground black
    pepper

Toast the hazelnuts in a dry frying pan until the skins darken. Allow to cool a little, then rub the skins off in a tea towel. Chop roughly.

Warm 2 plates in a low oven. Melt a walnut-sized bit of the butter in a frying pan into which the fish will fit comfortably. Season the fish lightly, then lower it into the hot fat. Cook over a medium heat for about 4 minutes per side, until it feels firm to the touch; fillets will obviously take less time.

Meanwhile, heat the remaining butter in a separate pan until it changes colour to a light hazelnut brown. Add the hazelnuts, parsley and lemon juice, stir and serve with the fish. In spring, some of the new-season young broad beans will go well with it.

LAMB AND MUTTON

The cheap cuts

Curried Lamb and Brown Lentil Broth

Lamb Braised with Thyme and Rosemary, Served
    with Egg Pasta

Skewered Spiced Mutton

Flatbreads

The prime cuts

Barbecued Somerset Salt-marsh Mutton

Lamb Shoulder Steak with Broad Beans, Shallots
    and Mint

Lamb with Tomatoes and Garlic, Finished with
    Spring Vegetables

Leg of Mutton Slow-roasted with Woody Herbs,
    Butter and Hay

Leftovers

Shepherd's Pie

Pistachio and Lamb Rice

Lamb Stock

The parallels drawn between sheep of a certain age and women of a certain
age have done nothing for either. I have a friend who describes passing the
mirror on her way out in the evening as her 'mutton check'. Well, I have
never seen her look anything but the business but for how long now have
we lived with the lie that mutton is not just older but somehow lesser?
Thanks to the jokes, mutton would do anything to reverse the years, yet it

is all so wrong somehow. Talking of the woolly variety, it is time to say that mutton should not want to be anything else and lamb, while delicate and occasionally beautiful, lacks all the character that age brings. The campaign to return mutton to the table is gaining strength with some seriously persuasive arguments. Not to eat mutton is to ignore the landscape. When they are well managed, older sheep that graze the hill country of Britain do it a great favour. If it wasn't for those sheep, some hardy beef cattle and a small amount of game, this country, which covers vast areas of Wales, the English moors and fells and the Scottish highlands, would look a mess. The farms on it would cease to exist and even the people who buy them in order to run, say, a rural IT business would soon get sick of the pervading giant weeds, and grumble about their country walks being ruined by overgrown grass and paths that are impossible to navigate.

The meat we call lamb is from animals that are three to six months old, many bred by farmers on the lower country. They are usually reared on pasture, which is a wholesome way to do it; sometimes they are moved from one area to another to find new grazing, in order to speed up their progress to a weight appropriate for slaughter. The mutton animals, on the other hand, will be at least two years old; ewes that have outlived their usefulness producing lambs. They were traditionally exported live to Europe for slaughter and the kitchens of people who appreciate their stronger flavour. That is what needs to be reclaimed here. Aversion to mutton may well say something about the way food is valued only for how convenient it is to prepare and eat, not for the wider impact of what we choose to eat. Mutton is less predictable than lamb. It is not the case that you can treat it in the same way, no matter what the pro-mutton campaigners say. Most cuts need slow cooking, although steaks can be cut from the legs to put on a grill with success, particularly if the animal has been slaughtered during the warmer months and has eaten plenty of grass, which gives it a perfect 'finish'. Salt-marsh mutton is good for grilling purposes, because the sheep, while older, graze by the warmth of the sea for most of the year.

The answer lies in a happy balance of eating both types, old and young, in harmony. A young lamb occasionally – I cannot ever feel quite comfortable with the idea of a sheep having just three months of life – and mutton, wether, hogget or shearling (all names for older sheep) at other times. You can't lose.

Buying lamb and mutton

Always ask high-street butchers if they have any local lamb or mutton, and buy into it if they do. This is probably the most economical source. Farmers' markets and farm shops will have lamb and often mutton, while some supermarkets in hill districts where their conscience has been pricked will sell meat from animals that have not travelled the usual distances. www.bigbarn.co.uk will highlight your nearest producer or butcher, even in cities.

Buying 'boxes' containing a whole or half butchered lamb or sheep by post is another option. Blackface.co.uk sells supreme five-year-old mutton that has been fattened on lowland grass for its final summer – kind to beast and our palates, because the meat is astonishingly tender (www.blackface.co.uk; tel: 01387 730326). Sheepdrove Organic Farm in Berkshire grazes its sheep on the Downs (www.sheepdrove.com; tel: 01488 674747).

Somerset salt-marsh mutton, grazed on the salty grass of Bridgewater Bay, is available by mail order and more than worth tracking down: www.thoroughlywildmeat.co.uk; tel: 01963 824788 or 07770 392041.

Farmer Sharp, a co-operative from Cumbria, sells mutton and wether at Borough Market, London SE1, and also via mail order: www.farmersharp.co.uk; tel: 01229 588299. Recommended for slow cooking.

For economical cuts of lamb to cook on the grill, plus other good lamb, go to Jack O'Shea Family Butcher (11 Montpelier Street, London SW7 1EX; www.jackosheas.com; tel: 020 7581 7771). They do not do mail order but are worth seeking out for their special skill in cutting cheap cuts for the grill.

The cheap cuts

The following recipes are economical dishes for every day.

Curried Lamb and Brown Lentil Broth

An easy soup that is a meal in itself. Serve it with the Thin Breads on page 439 or simply buy pitta bread, brush with a little melted butter and toast in the oven.

Serves 4 generously

55g/2oz butter
4–8 good-sized lamb chops
2 onions, chopped
200g/7oz small brown lentils
1 heaped tablespoon medium curry powder
½ teaspoon cayenne pepper (optional)

2 tablespoons passata (puréed tomatoes)
1 litre/1¾ pints lamb or other stock (see pages 64, 116, 238)
sea salt and freshly ground black pepper
mint leaves, whole-milk yoghurt and nigella seeds, to serve

Melt half the butter in a large casserole, add the chops and brown on both sides. Add the remaining butter and the onions, turn down the heat and cook, stirring occasionally, until the onions are softened. Try not to let them burn. Add the lentils, then the curry powder and the cayenne pepper, if using, and stir to coat the contents of the pan. Add the passata and stock, bring to the boil, then turn down to a simmer and cook for about 45 minutes, until the lentils and lamb are tender. Season to taste. Serve with mint leaves, and yoghurt with a few nigella seeds scattered over.

Lamb Braised with Thyme and Rosemary, Served with Egg Pasta

A hearty, full-flavoured and rich-textured braise, using diced shoulder or neck of lamb, to eat with pasta.

Serves 8 generously

olive oil or butter
6 garlic cloves, chopped
3 onions, finely chopped
1 celery stick, finely chopped
2kg/4½ lb lamb shoulder or neck fillet, diced into 2cm/¾ inch pieces
2 sprigs of thyme, or 1 teaspoon dried thyme
2 sprigs of rosemary, or 1 teaspoon dried rosemary

1 teacup of passata (puréed tomatoes)
2 wineglasses of white wine
sea salt and freshly ground black pepper

To serve:
750g/1lb 10oz dried egg tagliatelle
a few leaves of fresh thyme and rosemary, if available, or some roughly chopped flat-leaf parsley

Heat the oil or butter in a large casserole, add the garlic and fry until pale gold. Remove from the pan and add the onions and celery. Cook until soft and slightly coloured, then remove with a slotted spoon. Brown the lamb dice quickly over a high heat, then return the vegetables to the pan with the herbs, passata and wine. Boil for 1 minute, then add enough water to cover and simmer for 1–1½ hours, until the lamb is tender. Season to taste with sea salt and black pepper.

Meanwhile, bring a large pan of water to the boil and add a tablespoon of sea salt. Cook the tagliatelle until *al dente* (just tender, with a slight 'bite' in the centre), then drain. Serve immediately, with the sauce and a scattering of herbs. Do not serve with cheese.

Skewered Spiced Mutton

Mutton is one good British, eco-friendly meat that is easier to buy in cities than in the countryside, thanks to the Asian communities and their sometimes great restaurants. It tends not to be well hung, however, so benefits from being seasoned with spices. This is a recipe for the famous skewered minced mutton served at the Lahore in Umberston Street, London, an East End institution and favourite family restaurant. The owner, Mohammed Siddique, kindly gave me his recipe. Spiked with ground masala spices, green chilli and coriander, the skewers are served with cucumber salad, flatbread and a yoghurt chutney. It is a meal with qualities that make a drive through the area almost impossible without the tiniest momentary stop-off. Even having the recipe does not stop the lure of the place, a truly democratic, intercultural restaurant where everybody who loves spicy food – Muslim, Jewish, Christian, Hindu and atheist – goes out to eat.

Serves 4–6

1kg/2¼lb minced raw mutton, including some fat
2 green chillies, deseeded and chopped
a large handful of coriander, chopped
a large handful of mint, chopped
1 tablespoon yoghurt
2 teaspoons grated fresh ginger
1 tablespoon ground masala
1 garlic clove, chopped

Combine all the ingredients, making sure that the herbs and spices are evenly spread through the meat. Wrap the mixture around skewers, then barbecue or grill on a high heat. Serve with flatbreads (see opposite), and plain yoghurt with chopped mint and coriander.

Flatbreads

The roti bread at the Lahore is delicious and simple to make – but difficult to make well, particularly if you don't have a tandoor oven. Here is a variation on the Lahore version that you should be able to cook at home.

Makes 8–10

750g/1lb 10oz chapatti flour, plus extra for dusting

2 tablespoons sunflower oil or melted butter

1 teaspoon salt

500ml/18fl oz water

Put the flour in a bowl and add the oil or butter and salt. Gradually mix in the water until you have a smooth, workable dough. Stop adding water if it becomes sticky. Wrap the dough in cling film and chill for an hour, then roll out or stretch pieces on a floured work surface to make thin, round flatbreads. Cook on an oiled flat griddle or heavy-bottomed frying pan over a high heat for about 3 minutes, turning occasionally, until puffed and light.

The prime cuts

These are the more expensive cuts to eat for treats, and include the rack (tiny cutlets attached in one joint) and leg. Use up any leftovers – especially of roast leg of lamb – to make the high cost of these joints go further.

Barbecued Somerset Salt-marsh Mutton

Grilled mutton? Never. Actually, yes – when it comes from the warm salt marshes of Bridgewater Bay. Far from needing to be stewed until submissively chewable, this meat can be thrown on a barbecue and grilled. (Do buy from a trusted supplier, however – see shopping information above.) No recipe is really needed here, but do be patient while building the fire. Leave the charcoal to burn right down until the embers are grey – it would be a shame to burn this valuable meat. Ask for leg steaks, cut about 2cm/¾ inch thick. Rub the meat with olive oil and dried rosemary first, then cook for about 4 minutes on each side. Serve with Cobnut and Watercress Salad (see page 138).

Lamb Shoulder Steak with Broad Beans, Shallots and Mint

The French call this cut a *pavé*. It is a single muscle, found close to the H-bone (hip) at the top of a leg of lamb – a relatively economical cut that can be grilled whole, then sliced.

Use the inner green 'kernels' of frozen broad beans, if fresh are out of season. They are a useful winter vegetable.

Serves 4

1 tablespoon olive oil
2 tablespoons unsalted butter
4 lamb shoulder steaks
4 shallots, roughly chopped
8–10 tablespoons shelled broad
 beans (or use frozen, if you wish)

approximately 150ml/¼ pint rich
 meat stock, preferably lamb (see
 page 238)
leaves from 2 small sprigs of mint
sea salt and freshly ground black
 pepper

Set a heavy-bottomed sauté pan over a medium-high heat, add the olive oil and half the butter and brown the lamb on all sides. Continue to cook for a few minutes, turning the meat on every side. The lamb will cook quickly and should be served pink. Overall it should take about 5–7 minutes to cook. Remove from the pan and leave in a warm place to rest for about 10 minutes.

About 5 minutes before serving, melt the remaining butter in the sauté pan. Add the shallots and cook for a minute, then add the broad beans and enough stock just to cover. Bring to the boil and cook for about 2 minutes. Add the fresh mint leaves at the end and season with salt and pepper.

Slice the lamb (the meat is very tender, so can be sliced quite thick) and divide between 4 warm plates. Spoon the beans around the slices and serve.

Kitchen note
Use canned drained butterbeans or flageolets in this dish, if you wish.

Lamb with Tomatoes and Garlic, Finished with Spring Vegetables

My favourite lamb stew to make in summer with the new season's green, purple and yellow beans, podded fresh peas, young carrots and fennel. This is a braise that needs a trip to a farmers' market for some original produce.

Serve 6

55g/2oz dripping
1.5kg/3¼lb lamb shoulder meat, cut into 4cm/1½ inch chunks (alternatively, use neck fillet, which has less flavour)
2 garlic cloves, chopped
2 onions, finely chopped
1 wineglass of white wine
1 bay leaf
a sprig of thyme

6 tomatoes, skinned, deseeded and chopped
1.5 litres/2¾ pints lamb stock (see page 238)
1kg/2¼lb mixed fresh vegetables, as many varieties as you like (see above)
sea salt and freshly ground black pepper
fresh chervil, mint and parsley, to serve

Heat the fat in a deep casserole until it begins to smoke, then brown the meat in it in batches, setting it to one side as it is done. Turn down the heat, add the garlic and onions and cook, stirring, for a minute. Pour in the wine, scrape the bottom of the pan clean with a wooden spatula and return the meat to the pan with the bay leaf, thyme and tomatoes. Cover with a good depth of lamb stock (remember that the vegetables will be added later and will need room). Bring to the boil, then turn down to a simmer and cook for about 1½ hours, until the meat is just tender. Turn off the heat. Taste and add salt if necessary, then add freshly ground black pepper. About 15 minutes before you serve, bring the casserole to a simmer again, add carrots and fennel and cook for 7 minutes. Add French and runner beans and cook for 4 minutes, then add broad beans and peas. Cook for about 3 minutes, then serve, with the herbs scattered over the top. Eat with buttered boiled new potatoes.

Leg of Mutton Slow-roasted with Woody Herbs, Butter and Hay

Silvy Weatherall cooked this precious piece of five-year-old mutton, reared by her husband, Ben (chief of Blackface.co.uk – see Buying Lamb and Mutton on page 228), on his farm in the hills of Lanarkshire. It was Easter lunch for the family and revealed that, in an insulated cladding of herbs and grasses, older meat can be cooked in a short time yet be tender and juicy, with a hint of pinkness in its tight-grained flesh. Make sure it has a good rest before carving.

Serves 12

375g/13oz softened unsalted butter
3 heads of garlic, cloves separated, peeled and crushed
4 sprigs of rosemary
a bunch of thyme
a few sprigs each of marjoram and oregano, or a few lavender stalks

1 whole leg of mutton, weighing approximately 3.5kg/7½lb, the hock bone severed so that it fits in a roasting tin
4 handfuls of hay (the pet shop will provide if you have no other supply)
600ml/1 pint lamb stock (see page 238)
sea salt and freshly ground black pepper

Preheat the oven to 230°C/450°F/Gas Mark 8. Combine the butter with about 3 pinches of freshly ground black pepper and the crushed garlic. Chop half the herbs finely and add to the butter mixture, then slather it all over the joint. Line a roasting tin with aluminium foil, then make a bed of half the hay and half the remaining herbs in it. Lay the mutton on top and cover with the rest of the hay and herbs. Season with salt, bring the foil around and pinch it together to seal.

Bake in the oven for about 2½ hours (a large leg may need 20 minutes more), turning the temperature down to 175°C/350°F/Gas Mark 4 after 20 minutes. Remove from the oven and leave to rest in a warm place for about 30 minutes.

Lift from the roasting tin, open the foil and tip the juices back into the tin. Close the foil and seal; leave the meat in a warm place to rest for at least 20 minutes. Skim the fat from the juices – there will be quite a lot of it. Pick out any stray pieces of stalk and hay from the tin and set over the heat. Add the stock and bring to the boil, stirring. Simmer for a few minutes, adjust the seasoning and then pour the gravy into a warm jug. Serve slices of the roast mutton with the gravy and some vegetables.

 Kitchen note
Capers go well with mutton. You could add 2 tablespoons of chopped capers to the gravy in the final stages.

Lamb leftovers

Shepherd's Pie

There are few better uses for leftover lamb. This is a quick version. Mince the cold lamb, omitting the fat, and set to one side. If you have about 450g/1lb minced cold lamb, fry 2 chopped onions, 2 chopped carrots, 1 chopped celery stick and 2 chopped garlic cloves in a little vegetable oil until softened. Add the meat, with a heaped tablespoon of tomato purée, 600ml/1 pint lamb or other meat stock, or vegetable stock, and cook for about ¾–1 hour, until the meat is tender. Add Worcestershire sauce to your taste, then transfer to an ovenproof dish and top with mashed potato. 'Distress' the top with a fork, dot with butter and bake in a moderately hot oven until crisp on the surface, bubbling underneath. Serve with extra Worcestershire sauce and ketchup.

Pistachio and Lamb Rice

See page 312, under Pistachio Nuts, for a quick lamb leftovers dish.

Lamb stock

Roast a few lamb or mutton bones (available from the butcher) until coloured, then put them in a deep saucepan with an onion, a carrot and a celery stick. Cover with water, simmer for 1–1½ hours and then strain.

LANGOUSTINES

Langoustine Tartare with Hot Olive Oil
Langoustine Cocktail

Leftovers
Langoustine Stock
Langoustine Soup with Lemon Grass and Coconut

Having been a luxury for a long time, the Scottish langoustine, also known as a Dublin Bay prawn, suddenly finds itself on the threshold of being an everyday food. Well, nearly. At the time of writing, Young's Bluecrest expects the Marine Stewardship Council (MSC) to certify its Hebridean langoustine fishery as sustainable. Some smaller fisheries, notably the Loch Torridon one, already have MSC certification, but the size and scale of Young's means that the certification will make sustainable more affordable – not quite cheap as chips, but certainly cheaper than before. However, Young's has achieved something other than tackling the sustainability issue and operating boats that have less impact on the marine environment – it is bidding to triumph over the langoustine's great weakness.

Langoustines must be cooked as soon as possible or their white flesh deteriorates, becoming soft inside the shell even when cooked. The British have never been too fussed over the standard of the 'prawns', as they are known by Scottish fishermen; very few of any quality make it past a few top chefs, who serve them in their restaurants. Until recently, no decent ones have been available in shops, and the majority of good-quality langoustines were road- or sea-freighted to France and Spain, often in seawater tanks to keep them lively. It has always seemed peculiar to me that you can eat a better Scottish langoustine in a Madrid tapas bar than you can in Mallaig on the west coast of Scotland, where thousands of them are landed every day. But Young's has installed state-of-the-art equipment on its boats, so the langoustines will be cooked and blast frozen to preserve their muscled insides.

In the meantime, other fishermen have been working out how to get langoustines to the city, fresh as can be – Jimmy Buchan, for example, who operates the *Amity*, a boat that makes short trips out to catch the 'prawns', carefully trawling for them without damaging stocks or taking a by-catch of other fish, and returning in time to send them high speed to the city. *Amity* langoustines are in short supply, but I suspect that Buchan will have inspired others and we will see a lot more of them.

Not all langoustines are trawled, however. There are still a few fishermen who catch them from small boats in creels – baited baskets left on the floor of sea lochs to attract the prawns. This is the most traditional, low-tech, sustainable catch method, sadly in decline.

Buying langoustines

Jimmy Buchan's *Amity* langoustines are available from Fish Shop, Kensington Place, 201 Kensington Church Street, London W8 7LX; tel: 020 7243 6626. Also from Cape Clear, 119 Shepherds Bush Road, London W6 7LP; tel: 020 7751 1609, or via home delivery (London only) from Pittenweem Fisheries (www.pittenweem-fisheries.com; tel: 01784 421596). Outside London, The Whitby Catch sells creel-caught langoustines by mail order (www.thewhitbycatch.co.uk; tel: 01947 6013130). It is a cooperative of fishermen with small boats and its own shop on the town pier.

Young's expects the MSC-accredited langoustines to be available in major supermarkets late in 2008.

Langoustine Tartare with Hot Olive Oil

A dish that can be made only with the freshest raw langoustines, so save it for that Scottish seaside holiday and hunt down some friendly fishermen. Raw langoustine meat has a fragile, sweet, marine flavour. In this dish the langoustines are poached for a moment to make peeling easy, but the meat is still raw in the centre. It is a very special, if occasional, plate of food.

Serves 4

1 egg cup of salt
12 large live langoustines
5 tablespoons extra virgin olive oil
juice of ½ lemon
about ½ teaspoon sea salt

Have a large bowl of iced water ready, to one side. Bring 2 litres/3½ pints of water to the boil in a pan and add the salt. Quickly add the live langoustines to the boiling water and blanch for just 10 seconds. Remove and plunge into the iced water. This helps the meat to detach from the outer shell. Separate the tails from the body, gently pulling the head section in order not to lose any of the tail meat. Use small scissors to cut along the underside of the tail, from top to bottom. Open out each langoustine and remove the meat in one piece. Flatten each piece with the back of a knife and arrange neatly on a large, flat dish.

To serve, heat the olive oil in a small pan, almost to smoking point, then pour it over the langoustines. Squeeze over the lemon juice and scatter the salt crystals on top. Serve with the Courgette Shavings on page 149.

Langoustine Cocktail

A happy time can be passed shelling a pile of langoustines and eating them with freshly made mayonnaise (see page 281), but another fine way to enjoy a boiled langoustine is in a cocktail.

Serves 4

5–8 cooked langoustines per person, depending on size
a few Cos lettuce leaves, shredded

For the sauce:
200ml/7fl oz double cream
2 level tablespoons grated horseradish
2 tablespoons tomato purée
1 teaspoon Worcestershire sauce, or more to taste
1 teaspoon malt vinegar
a pinch of caster sugar

Peel the langoustines by prising apart the soft scales on their underbelly, then carefully lifting away the shell. Put a few shreds of crisp, green Cos lettuce in 4 individual bowls or glasses and put the langoustines on top. Lightly whip the cream. Fold all the remaining sauce ingredients into the cream and spoon the sauce over the langoustines.

Langoustine leftovers

Langoustine Stock

This can be made as for Shrimp Shell Broth but without the ale (see page 347).

Langoustine Soup with Lemon Grass and Coconut

For 2 people, heat 400ml/14fl oz langoustine stock and add a little chopped or grated lemon grass, a teaspoon of Panang curry paste and a 2cm/¾ inch piece cut from a block of coconut cream. Stir the soup as the coconut cream melts, then taste and season with either Thai fish sauce or salt. A light broth to eat very hot – I recommend adding a little chopped red chilli.

LEMONS

Water Pudding
Leg of Hogget with Lemon

I remember Jif 'lemon'... We kids would squirt it down our throats during lunch hour, then spend the afternoon lessons enjoying terrific gastric cramp believing we were losing tons of weight. Living in a country that has plastic lemons is fairly embarrassing. It is doubly ridiculous when you know that real lemons store well. Waxed ones last for ages; even when their skins become dry, the juice inside is still usable. Synthetic lemon juice is just not on, and you can leave preserved or pasteurised in the shop, too. Honour real lemons. They are as at home and essential in a British kitchen as those other émigrés, cocoa, anchovies and olive oil. Show some respect.

Recently I wondered whether I could cook without lemons and was horrified by the idea. It would be the cooking equivalent of having no electric light. It was time to make a list of ways to use lemon – to live without the following would be hard. Lemon is my second salt.

With olive oil To dress salad leaves. I like red wine vinegar or tarragon vinegar for a vinaigrette but, more often than not, it is lemon that I add to a green salad.

With fish Impossible to imagine being without a lemon. Crab would be inedibly rich, sole tasteless, mackerel too oily.

With fried food That habit of squeezing lemon over breadcrumbed fish or escalopes of meat is a good one that dispels any grease.

With the cabbage family Lemon butter transforms any brassica: cabbage, cauliflower, purple sprouting broccoli or spring greens.

On grilled or roast meat Copious amounts of lemon juice on hogget or lamb give it an entirely different character (see Leg of Hogget with Lemon, p.248) and I cannot eat calf's liver without it.

To flavour cakes and puddings I am not a fan of chocolate, so many of the sweet things I make will have lemon zest in there somewhere.

To prevent fruit discolouring Lemon has frequently saved the pears in my fruit salad, the apples for the tart.

Buying lemons

Unwaxed lemons are ever so slightly nicer to use because you get only the oils on the outside and not the wax used to preserve them. I still use waxed lemons, though, for general-purpose cooking, but if I need the zest I try to remember to scrub them first.

Water Pudding

This honestly is an amazing pudding. It has the qualities of a soufflé, but keeps its shape. It is the lightest lemon pudding, too, being made with water rather than milk or cream. When cooked, it separates into two decks: below is a velvet-smooth, yellow curd, above a light, puffy crust. It takes an hour to cook but must be put in the oven as soon as it is made. If serving it at dinner, I suggest making it – it is easy and quick – about half an hour before you sit down to the main course. It keeps for a while, being nicest when lukewarm.

The recipe was given to me by Bill Brogan of St John's College, Cambridge, who runs one of the best kitchens in England. In charge of food for every student, fellow and guest, he goes to extraordinary lengths to find interesting things to feed them, whether in the canteen or at the high table. He found this historic recipe, and it has become a favourite at the college.

Serves 6

150ml/¼ pint warm (just above hand-hot) water
100g/3½oz caster sugar

juice and grated zest of 1 unwaxed lemon (this is an instance where unwaxed lemon makes a real difference to the flavour)
100g/3½oz very soft unsalted butter, plus a little extra for greasing
4 eggs, separated

Preheat the oven to 150°C/300°F/Gas Mark 2. Pour boiling water into a roasting tin so it is 2cm/¾ inches deep and place it in the oven. Butter 6 small ramekins.

Combine the water with the sugar, lemon juice and zest and butter, then whisk by hand. The butter should break down into small, floating globules. Lightly beat the egg yolks and stir them into the mixture.

Put the egg whites in a separate bowl and whisk until stiff. Fold them into the egg and lemon mixture, then pour into the ramekins. Place the ramekins in the roasting tin of hot water and bake for 1 hour. Serve immediately, or lukewarm.

Leg of Hogget with Lemon

Hoggets are two-year-old castrated sheep. They have a lighter taste than mutton and are gradually making a comeback as an English dish after years of export to the Mediterranean, where stronger-flavoured meat is appreciated. Hence the use of lemons in this recipe.

Serves 4–6

1 shoulder of hogget, lamb or mutton, weighing 1.5–2.5kg/3¼–5½lb
4–6 garlic cloves, cut into slivers
100g/3½oz butter, or 5 tablespoons olive oil
2 lemons
2 carrots, finely chopped
2 onions, finely chopped
2 celery sticks, finely chopped
a pinch of dried thyme
2 sprigs of rosemary
2 wineglasses of white wine
2 wineglasses of water
2 tomatoes, chopped
sea salt and freshly ground black pepper

Preheat the oven to 230°C/450°F/Gas Mark 8.

Use the point of a knife to make incisions about 2cm/¾ inch deep at 2.5cm/ 1 inch intervals all over the surface fat of the meat. Insert a piece of garlic into each one, then rub the shoulder with half the butter or oil. Cut the lemons in half, squeeze out the juice (set to one side), then slice the lemons thinly and put slices all over the surface of the meat. Season the meat with salt and pepper. Put any remaining garlic and the vegetables into a heavy-bottomed roasting tin with the remaining butter or oil and place it over the heat. 'Stir-fry' for about 2 minutes, then spread the vegetables evenly over the base. Add the thyme, place the joint on top, then pour over the lemon juice. Place the rosemary on top of the shoulder. Transfer the tin to the oven and roast for 20 minutes.

Remove the roasting tin from the oven. Use a spoon to remove excess fat from the tin. Pour in the white wine and water, then add the tomatoes. Replace in the oven, turn the heat down to 175°C/350°F/Gas Mark 4 and cook for about 1½ hours, until the meat is quite well done. Place the joint on a warm serving dish, cover with foil and leave to rest in a warm place for 20 minutes. Strain the cooking liquid through a sieve for an instant gravy. Taste and add salt if necessary, then season with black pepper.

LENTILS

A Lentil Store
Brown Lentils with Red Wine, Carrots and Thyme
Lentils and Rice

Shying away from vegetables and pulses is an art form amongst children. I find the money argument helps. I once knew a man who used to go into a three-star restaurant in London and order a plate of braised green lentils and a £600 bottle of wine. Maybe it was the spark of something but it seemed a totally sensible balance of home economy. He spent less on one thing so he could spend more on another. In this extreme example is the spine of a philosophy. Eating a quantity of low-cost, low-environmental-impact foods allows a foray into something more extravagant – a prime cut of beef, a fish sent from the coast, a creamy pudding to finish it all off. I don't, in case it appears that way, pay my children to eat their vegetables and pulses. I argue instead that if they want to eat chicken breasts, there will be other meals dedicated to jacket potatoes, pasta and lentils.

Like peas, lentils are legumes – crops that not only yield highly nutritious vegetables at minimum environmental cost but also return nitrogen to the soil, enriching it for the next crop. Like cattle, they fertilise, and they are a sort of livestock of vegetables, a replacement for meat that is affordable. No surprise, then, that for a long time those who ate lots of such a worthwhile ingredient were mocked, and still are to an extent: as the unreconstructed bearded ones, wearers of Birkenstock sandals and probably stop-the-war protestors. They sound like sensible people to me. But this is Britain, where we cannot extract ourselves from the ways in which what we eat divides us.

It is said that lentils could grow here – but how could we contemplate something so sensible when we have covered East Anglia in peas? Imagine the excitement of an oncoming lentil season… I fantasise. But the lentils we import – at relatively low fuel cost, since they are dried – are class food plants and keep us happy; diverse in taste, texture and appearance. Red lentils are best in spicy dals; brown lentils are earthy and therefore good with buttered leaves such as spinach and chard, which sharpen up their

taste a little. The small Umbrian brown lentils are my favourites. They have bite, stay tidily in shape once cooked and have a beautiful verdant flavour. Green lentils can be large, and rather vulnerable to overcooking, becoming floury, but the little green lentils, the mottled Puy type from hilly France, are another grand lentil, good enough to serve as a dish in their own right.

I tend to cook quantities of these, storing them in the fridge to dip into during the week. They are easy to find in most supermarkets and wholefood shops.

Hearing of all these varieties, you will not be surprised to learn that lentils share similarities with beans in terms of their importance as a diverse food crop and their impact on the places where they grow. A dip into that section will reveal more detail (see page 31).

Two vital points about lentils

First, they do not need soaking, so are as much a convenience food as pasta; secondly, they should not be overcooked. Mistime them and they change from an elegant vegetable to tiresome ballast. The following technique should prevent any lentil disasters. Do be aware, though, that the cooking time for lentils can vary greatly, depending on how recently they were harvested. I find that I always check for doneness slightly in advance of the possibility.

A Lentil Store

With some cooked lentils in the fridge, I can have a salad ready in a minute, just by adding herbs and leaves or chopped raw vegetables. Or I can make a spicy dish to eat with rice or have a side vegetable to serve with a piece of grilled meat.

Makes 8 servings

5 garlic cloves, peeled
2 bay leaves
400g/14oz Puy lentils
olive oil
sea salt and freshly ground black
   pepper

Put the garlic, bay leaves and lentils in a pan and cover well with water. Bring to the boil and simmer for about 25 minutes. Check if the lentils are ready; the skin should be firmly intact and the insides just tender. If there is any 'bite' on the inside, they are not ready – in which case you need to return the pan to the heat, cook for another 5 minutes and test again.

When you are satisfied they are perfectly cooked, remove the pan from the heat and tip the contents quickly into another vessel – a ceramic bowl is ideal; the idea is to cool the lentils quickly and stop any further cooking. I advise against transferring them to your storage container. If it is plastic, it may insulate the lentils and keep them too hot. When the lentils have cooled to lukewarm, splash over a little olive oil and stir lightly to moisten the skins of the lentils. Season with salt and pepper. Now transfer the store to a container and put on the lid. The lentils should keep in the fridge for about 6 days.

Brown Lentils with Red Wine, Carrots and Thyme

The most basic, rich and meaty lentil dish – it goes with everything, but especially roasts, grilled chops, roasted vegetables or fried whole fish such as sea bass. This type of lentil cooks in approximately 25–35 minutes; it all depends how long they have been in dry storage. Lentils that are very old will take longer to cook. It is a fact that the oldest pulses tend to be exported to the UK, because we really don't care about them in the same way that they are revered in southern Europe, where these foods are an important aspect of the diet.

Serves 6

400g/14oz brown Italian lentils
4 garlic cloves, crushed
½ bottle of red wine
12 small carrots, trimmed and
    scrubbed
2 sprigs of thyme
4 tablespoons extra virgin olive oil
sea salt and freshly ground black
    pepper

Put the lentils, garlic and wine into a pan, add enough water to cover by 1cm/½ inch, then add the carrots and thyme. Bring to the boil, cover the pan and cook for 25–30 minutes, until the lentils are just done. Their skins and centres should be soft to the bite but they must still hold together. As soon as you are happy that they are perfectly cooked, remove from the heat and add the oil. I sometimes transfer them to a bowl so that they do not continue to cook even though away from the heat. Season to taste and serve.

Lentils and Rice

An idea copied from India, where it is a daily staple. I have used red lentils here but the recipe is interchangeable with other pulses and beans. Red lentils are known as masoor dal. They are hulled and will fall apart during cooking to make a purée.

Grinding your own whole spices will give the lentils a more complex, multilayered taste.

Serves 6–8

1.2 litres/2 pints water
250g/9oz red lentils
2 onions, chopped
1 butternut squash, peeled, deseeded
    and finely chopped or grated
3 garlic cloves, chopped
2 green chillies, chopped
3cm/1¼ inch piece of fresh ginger,
    peeled
1 teaspoon ground coriander
1 teaspoon ground cumin
½ teaspoon red chilli powder

juice of 1 lemon
200g/7oz basmati rice, rinsed in
    cold water
sea salt

To serve:
2 tablespoons butter
1 small onion, chopped
2 garlic cloves, chopped
1 teaspoon cumin seeds, ground
½ teaspoon nigella seeds
4–6 sprigs of fresh coriander,
    including the roots, if attached,
    chopped

Put the water in a large pan and bring to the boil. Add the lentils, bring back to the boil, then add the vegetables, spices and some salt. Cook for about half an hour, until the lentils are soft, then add the lemon juice.

While the lentils are cooking, cook the rice. Put it in a saucepan and add enough water to come 2cm/¾ inch above the top. Add a pinch of salt and bring to the boil. Cook at a medium-fast boil for 5 minutes, then cover the pan and turn down the heat. Cook for 5 more minutes, then turn off the heat and leave to steam for 5 minutes.

To serve the lentils and rice, heat the butter in a separate pan, add the onion, garlic, cumin seeds and nigella seeds and cook for 2 minutes over a medium-high heat. Then add the coriander and stir once before tipping the mixture on top of the lentils. Take the pan to the table and serve with the rice.

MACKEREL

Grilled Mackerel
Cured Mackerel

A positive development in the last few years has been the availability of very fresh line-caught mackerel in supermarkets, fished out of Cornish waters, where the fishery (fishing business) is certified as sustainable. The achievement is a collective one. There are the 'ideas' people, who showed fishermen how to put fish straight from hook into slush ice (seawater and ice), which chills it in moments rather than the hours it takes for fish to cool on ordinary ice. This way the fish is biologically as fresh as if it had just been caught. There are also the mediators between supermarket and fishing boat, who make sure that good-quality fish like this is worth a premium, paid to the fishing boats. Andrew Mallinson of Marks & Spencer is one such person, a marine scientist who advises both fishermen and his employers, and has won awards for the way he has changed the quality of fish in this supermarket chain. It is possible to buy mackerel in supermarkets (see below) that is a mere day and a half out of the water and not a week. The outcome of this inspired work is that mackerel is not just a fish to eat with peace of mind because the numbers are at safe levels, but also that this fish, once loathed because it was often sold stale anywhere but where it was landed, is now back in our affection.

Buying mackerel

Line-caught mackerel is available in Marks & Spencer, Waitrose, Sainsbury, Asda and Tesco. Fishmongers should be able to source it for you, too – it has Marine Stewardship Council (MSC) certification and the logo should be visible on the box. Alternatively, the Cornish fishmonger Matthew Stevens will send it to you, fresh as anything, packed in ice, via courier: www.mstevensandson.co.uk; tel: 01736 799392.

Grilled Mackerel

It is not how you cook it but how you buy it. Track down the freshest mackerel, wash and pat dry. Brush with olive oil and grill for a few minutes on each side, preferably outside over charcoal. Mackerel flesh is buff coloured and translucent before cooking; once grilled it turns white, and the meat is succulent and firm. The flavour of a very fresh mackerel, like all the best fish, is very delicate.

As to what to eat with it, many old recipe books suggest stewed fruit, but I suspect these sauces were created to hide the taste of stale fish oil in less than fresh fish. Much better to eat it with a fresh sauce of cucumber, red chilli, spring onion, lime flesh and juice, and a little very good olive oil. If you still want fruit, try it with pomegranate seeds or even small dice of melon.

Kitchen note
Mackerel is also very good served with the Radish and Horseradish Sauce on p.358 (pictured left).

Cured Mackerel

A salt and sugar cure, flavoured with herbs, is spread on to the raw fish, preserving it but not cooking it. You can slice the cured mackerel, just like smoked salmon, and serve with salad leaves, soured cream or brown bread and butter. Use it also to fill the Airy Buns on page 443.

This recipe is not suitable for small mackerel.

Serve 4–6

2 large mackerel, filleted
40g/1½oz coarse sea salt
30g/1oz caster sugar
½ teaspoon pink peppercorns, crushed in a mortar and pestle or grinder
a few sprigs of dill

To serve:
soured cream
sliced shallot
lemon wedges
dill

Lay 2 of the mackerel fillets skin-side down in a shallow dish. Mix the salt, sugar and peppercorns together. Sprinkle the mixture evenly over the flesh, then scatter over the dill sprigs. 'Sandwich' the other 2 fillets on top, skin-side uppermost. Cover loosely with cling film and lay a board or flat plate on top. Put a weight on the board (a can of beans is fine) and leave in the fridge for 24 hours to cure. Turn the fish over after half a day.

To serve, remove the fillets from the dish and pick off the dill. Pat the fillets dry with kitchen paper. Pull out any pin bones sticking up through the flesh, otherwise it will be hard to slice the fish. Using a sharp knife, cut slices on the diagonal, working towards the tail. Serve with soured cream, sliced shallot, lemon wedges and more dill.

MEGRIM SOLES

Fried Megrim Sole

These are the secret fish of Cornwall. Thousands of tonnes of them are netted in the southwest each year, yet they are never available in the shops. The reason is twofold – one explanation being that the British only regularly eat five species of fish out of a choice of several thousand. It is true. There are 29,000 known species of fish in the world (both sea and freshwater), 7,000 of which are used by humans. Of these, 350 types can be farmed, 200 are used as bait, and 3,000 go into aquariums. Of the edible fish, over 2,000 are palatable.

Secondly, megrims, like mackerel, are better when very fresh – unlike the more popular Dover or lemon sole, which have a bit of shelf life, endearing them to fish merchants. But the sweet flesh of megrims is too good to miss. French and Spanish fish merchants have been shipping it out of Newlyn in Cornwall for years to their customers who appreciate it. It is also a fish whose numbers are at safe levels.

Once fish was a food to fast on, to consume when meat eating was banned by spiritual leaders for reasons that protected and maintained the food supply. Had every day been a meat-eating day, there would not have been enough to go around. Now it is the beleaguered fish supply that is in sore need of preservation. Sure, there are plenty of mussels and North Atlantic prawns in the sea to feast on, but the best and freshest fish now come at a premium price and are no longer a dish for every day.

Buying megrims

Fishmongers with access to fish from the southwest short-trip boats will be able to find megrims. They may need persuasion, however, because they will have to buy a whole box, and convince all their customers to eat this unfamiliar thing. You can buy megrims packed on ice via courier from St Ives fishmonger Matthew Stevens and Sons: www.mstevensandson.co.uk; tel: 01736 799392.

Fried Megrim Sole

An average-sized megrim serves one generously. Treat it as you would Dover or lemon sole: simply season the gutted fish with salt and pepper, then heat a tablespoon of unsalted butter in a frying pan, add the fish and fry it for about 3–4 minutes on either side, until the flesh flakes away from the bone when pierced with a knife.

Serve with a little lemon and butter whisked together over a low heat with some parsley. A more complicated sauce than this would be a distraction.

 Kitchen note
Megrim fillets can be cooked in the same way. If you want to make them look a little more spectacular, scatter a little grated lemon zest over them and brush with melted butter. Roll each fillet into a loose hoop and secure with a wooden toothpick. Pack them into an ovenproof dish and bake in an oven preheated to 200°C/400°F/Gas Mark 6 for about 10 minutes. Serve with a sauce made by whisking together olive oil, lemon juice, basil and parsley. A dish of sliced fennel, braised for 30 minutes with a little water and butter (or the Braised Chicory with Butter and Lemon Juice on page 132), together with some boiled new potatoes, would go perfectly.

MUSHROOMS

Any-mushroom Soup
Mushroom Salad with Lemon, Parsley and Prawns
Mushrooms on Toast
Guinea Fowl Stuffed with Mushrooms, Groats
    and Herbs

At last, at last, exotic mushrooms have been developed for cultivation on a scale that allows everyone to have access to them; an everyday food has just got much more interesting. Some supermarkets sell cultivated species of formerly wild mushrooms. The trend began with oyster mushrooms, which are still grown on logs in mushroom farms – a curious sight, this simulated forest – but the varieties are now expanding all the time. The less familiar (for now) varieties of Japanese mushroom have been a revelation. With their big, fat, meaty stalks, king oyster mushrooms cook like ceps, the precious European wild fungi, and have a lovely flavour of cashew. Namiko and enoki, both from Japan, are also interesting mushrooms. Mushroom farming in the UK has embraced diversity in a way that should inspire other market gardeners.

I am wary about buying wild mushrooms unless they are European and in season. Ones that you might expect to have originated from the south of France or Italy may well have been flown in from South Africa, China or Turkey. They may not be very fresh, or could be from a source that is being exploited – over-picking is a problem in the world of wild fungi.

You need to be especially circumspect, too, about buying luxury fungi such as truffles. The rule is this: there are two truffles with both aroma and flavour enough to justify their staggering price – the black *Melanosporum* from Périgord in France (accept no other black species) and the white Alba truffle from Italy. Both are semi-cultivated – the trees whose roots they grow on can be 'infected' with the truffle spore and planted in a grove of others, helping the truffle farmer have more control of his or her harvest. These systems have done little to reduce the price, I notice. Just one golf-ball-sized black truffle can cost about £40, but it does have an astonishing allure in both aroma and flavour. Let your face hover over a dish of eggs or hand-cut pasta scented with grated truffle and you'll know what it is to be a honeybee in a flower garden.

Certain dried mushrooms are invaluable to me: Italian porcini, a fragrant wild mushroom that holds much of its fresh flavour, and morels, which are better fresh, it is true, but so expensive I am happy to settle for second best.

Buying mushrooms

More and more varieties of mushroom are now stocked by supermarkets, but I would recommend buying them by post. Being light, they are ideally suited to it. John Dorian, who grows mushrooms on a farm near Liverpool, can send them anywhere, and doesn't charge postage for dried mushrooms. He specialises in Japanese mushrooms and gives great advice. His company is Smithy Mushrooms, at 229 Smithy Lane, Scarisbrick, Ormskirk L40 8HL (www.smithymushrooms.co.uk; tel: 01704 840982).

Sporeboys (www.sporeboys.com; tel: 07711 328548) is a London-based company run by David Robinson and Andrew Gellatly, who sell fresh exotic mushrooms in London markets (contact them for locations) and will send dried mushrooms by post.

Any-mushroom Soup

After several attempts to make a mushroom soup with an ingredient other than mushrooms and bread, I gave up. Few broths are better than a smooth mushroom soup, touched up at the end of cooking with some cream. Use any mushroom, discovering the enchantment of all the new types that are becoming available. Try a mix of king oyster, chestnut and porcini and you will almost feel the forest under your feet as you eat...

Serves 4

3 tablespoons butter
4 medium onions, peeled and
    chopped
100g/3½oz dried porcini mushrooms,
    soaked in boiling-hot water for
    15 minutes
225g/8oz fresh chestnut or Paris
    brown mushrooms, roughly
    chopped
225g/8oz fresh king oyster (eryngii)
    mushrooms, roughly chopped

1.2 litres/2 pints chicken stock (see
    page 116) or water
1 slice of light rye, sourdough or
    brown bread, cut into dice
sea salt and freshly ground black
    pepper

To serve:
4 tablespoons double cream
extra virgin olive oil or melted butter
chopped flat-leaf parsley or chervil,
    if available

Melt the butter in a pan and add the onions. Cook without colouring for 6 minutes or so. Drain the porcini, reserving the soaking liquid, and chop. Add the porcini and chopped fresh mushrooms to the pan, turn with a spoon to coat them in the butter and then add the stock or water, the mushroom soaking liquid and the bread. Bring to the boil, turn down to a simmer and cook for 15–20 minutes. Blend in a liquidiser until smooth.

To serve, reheat gently and season to taste. Ladle into bowls, add a little cream to each, then drizzle over a little extra virgin olive oil or melted butter. Throw over some chopped parsley or chervil and freshly ground black pepper.

Mushroom Salad with Lemon, Parsley and Prawns

Another long-forgotten salad, and a very good one – everything lies in leaving the mushrooms to macerate with the lemon and oil for a while so the grassy flavour of the olive oil and the sharpness of the citrus is thoroughly absorbed. The process seems to 'cook' the mushrooms slightly. It is easier to use ready-peeled prawns, but if you can find time to peel cooked shell-on North Atlantic prawns, they are just a bit nicer.

Serves 4–6

450g/1lb small white mushrooms,
   cleaned and halved, or sliced
   if large
4 tablespoons lemon juice
125ml/4fl oz olive oil
450g/1lb peeled North Atlantic prawns
leaves from 10 young sprigs of
   flat-leaf parsley, chopped
sea salt and freshly ground black
   pepper

Dress the mushrooms with the lemon juice, olive oil, a couple of pinches of sea salt and some black pepper and leave for half an hour. Add the prawns and parsley and mix lightly. Put a big bowl of the salad on the table.

Mushrooms on Toast

An ideal supper dish that can be grand or humble, depending on the mushrooms you use. For 2 people, butter or brush with oil 4 slices of sourdough bread (or the Wild Yeast Bread on page 436) and toast them in a flat, heavy-bottomed pan or in the oven until crisp and golden. Meanwhile, fry about 350g/12oz roughly chopped mushrooms in butter or olive oil until soft and browned in places. Mix with plenty of parsley or chervil, or even watercress leaves, and pile on to one slice of the toast per person – place the other on top. Tabasco and Worcestershire sauce on the table.

Guinea Fowl Stuffed with Mushrooms, Groats and Herbs

If you have a very understanding butcher, this is a recipe that takes only a little time to make but will be a truly extraordinary feast. The issue is taking the central carcass out of the guinea fowl while leaving it whole. Boning the legs and wings is not necessary, thankfully. A butcher should be able to do the boning for you but if you do it yourself, a good sharp knife will make the job a little easier. The stuffing is good and earthy, like all things mushroom.

Serves 8

2 guinea fowl, the central carcass bone removed (see below)
2 carrots, roughly chopped
1 onion, halved
200g/7oz spelt groats – or use durum wheat, farro or buckwheat
55g/2oz butter
2 garlic cloves, chopped
grated zest of ½ lemon
200g/7oz wild mushrooms, such as fairy rings, chanterelles or girolles, washed and left to dry on a towel

600g/1lb 5oz Paris brown or chestnut mushrooms, chopped into small dice
leaves from 4 sprigs of thyme, chopped
leaves from 1 small sprig of rosemary, chopped
4 tablespoons chopped parsley
2 tablespoons sherry, plus a glass of sherry for the gravy
butter or dripping, for basting
sea salt and freshly ground black pepper

First, take the carcass out of each guinea fowl, if your butcher hasn't done so: turn the bird on its breastbone and make an incision down the backbone. Begin to fillet the meat away from the right-hand side of the backbone, making sure you do not puncture the skin. Scrape at the backbone with the knife, pulling the meat away from it. As you reach the joints where the wing and the leg are attached to the central carcass, use the point of the knife to sever the joints. This can be tricky but a sharp knife or kitchen scissors will help. Repeat, working from the left-hand side of the backbone.

Work the knife around one breast side of the carcass, opening out the guinea fowl as you do so. Be very careful as you reach the centre point of the breastbone that you do not puncture the skin. Repeat, working from the other side. Very carefully sever the whole length of the breastbone from the meat and skin, but try not to pierce the skin, then lift out the carcass.

Before making the stuffing, quickly fry the carcasses in a pan to brown them slightly, then add the carrots and onion. Cover with water, bring to the boil and simmer for about an hour, so that when the stuffed guinea fowl come out of the oven, there will be stock for making the gravy.

Cook the groats in boiling water for about 25–35 minutes, until soft to the bite, then drain. Melt the butter in a separate pan and add the garlic, lemon zest, mushrooms and herbs. Cook until soft, then add the groats and sherry. Season to taste and leave to cool.

Preheat the oven to 200°C/400°F/Gas Mark 6. Lay the boned birds out on the worktop, skin-side down. Put half the stuffing on each bird, bring up the sides of the meat around it and wind string around the whole thing, legs and wings too, trussing it. Tie the string in a tight knot.

Brush the guinea fowl with butter or dripping, then put in a roasting tin – they must not be too close to each other or the leg meat will not cook.

Roast for 1 hour, basting with the fat in the tin from time to time, until the juices in the thigh meat run clear when the leg is pierced with a skewer.

Remove the birds from the tin and set aside in a warm place to rest, covered with some foil. Meanwhile, place the roasting tin over the heat on the hob and pour in a glass of sherry. Scrape at the sweet, caramelised bits in the bottom of the tin with a wooden spoon, then add 600ml/1 pint of the stock made from the carcass. Cook, stirring, until the liquid reduces a little and tastes rich, like a gravy. Let the gravy simmer very slowly until it is needed, then season to taste.

To serve the guinea fowl, cut off the legs and wings and put one of either on each person's plate. Cut 4 thick slices of each stuffed bird and put each on a plate beside the leg or wing. Serve with the gravy.

 Kitchen note
Serve the guinea fowl with roasted beetroot, parsnip, carrot and turnips – left whole if they are not too large (see page 369). They can be roasted in the same oven as the meat and will take the same amount of time. A mixture of mashed potato and mashed celeriac also goes well.

Buying guinea fowl

Guinea fowl are chickens in character, game birds in flavour, making them reliable in the pan but with an interesting, savoury gaminess. I always see corn-fed guinea fowl in supermarkets and often in butcher's shops. These won't be free range unless the label or butcher explicitly says so, and most are imported from France. Do not take the words 'corn fed' as a guarantee of quality – it means they will not have been able to forage on grass, which produces a healthy, happy bird that is also healthier to eat. English guinea fowl, reared in free-range systems, are available by mail order from Ellel Free Range Poultry (www.ellelfreerangepoultry.co.uk; tel: 01524 751200) – subject to availability, as they rear them mainly in spring and summer – or from Freebird, a free-range poultry farm in Devon (www.free-bird.co.uk; tel: 01271 815601).

OATS

Bircher Muesli

Haggis and Vegetables that are not 'Tatties
and Neeps'

Oatcakes

Split Mealy Pudding, Scrambled Eggs and Cress

When it is freezing, I like getting up that extra 15 minutes early to make the children porridge before school. Later in the morning, once they have left the house, I imagine their bodies chugging like small, well-cared-for engines, powered on oats. It's a thought that is never there when they catch the bus after a round of white toast. I have great trust in the nourishment side of oats, and I like their salty, husky taste, but I have to confess I eat very little porridge – it is a texture I can't cope with. Oats can be milled in different ways for other uses, however; the various grades of oatmeal make them very adaptable to other recipes that do not end up with the porridge problem. The most exciting oatmeal recipes are those you do not have to make yourself, like haggis and mealy pudding. By the time you buy the raw materials for your dinner, a trusty Scottish butcher will have done most of the hard work. All you have to do is heat, fry and put it with something good.

Buying oatmeal and oatmeal things

For good oatmeal, seek out traditionally milled types. The Oatmeal of Alford, milled near Aberdeen, comes in four grades – rough, fine, medium and pinhead – and is especially good for making oatcakes, or toasting, then stirring into whipped cream and raspberries. Buy online at www.oatmealofalford.com or phone 01561 377356. For breakfast, I prefer rolled oats, which are easier to buy – organic types are widely available in supermarkets.

Good haggis and mealy pudding (sometimes called white pudding) are available by mail order from Rory Macdonald, a traditional Scottish butcher in Perthshire, who makes his own (www.macdonald-bros.co.uk; tel: 01796 472047).

Oat groats

Oat groats are the whole grain with part of the husk removed. I buy them packed by Infinity Foods, whose grains are available in many healthfood shops and organic supermarkets; see www.infinityfoods.co.uk for stockists. Oat groats can be substituted for barley and spelt groats (see pages 22 and 446). The basic preparation is the same. To cook, put them in a pan and cover with water. Bring to the boil and simmer for 15–20 minutes, until they are just tender. They are good dressed with butter or olive oil and a little lemon juice and parsley, with grilled vegetables, roast root vegetables and all types of roast or grilled meat.

Bircher Muesli

Bircher muesli is my essential breakfast soup. I make this with pressed apple juice instead of milk so it is not 100 per cent authentic, but otherwise it is close to what the doctor ordered. Use a combination of oatmeal – pinhead and rolled – for an interesting texture.

Serves 2

100g/3½oz oatmeal
100ml/3½fl oz milk (or apple juice)
100ml/3½fl oz yoghurt
1 tablespoon runny honey

100ml/3½fl oz freshly squeezed orange juice
1 tablespoon hazelnuts, toasted in a dry frying pan and then chopped
1 dessert apple, quartered, cored and thinly sliced

Preheat the oven to 190°C/375°F/Gas Mark 5. Spread the oatmeal out on a baking tray, place in the oven and toast for 20 minutes. Leave to cool. (The oatmeal can be toasted well in advance and stored in an airtight jar.) Combine the milk or apple juice, yoghurt, honey and orange juice until smooth. Add the oatmeal and leave to soak for up to an hour. Stir in the hazelnuts and apple.

Haggis and Vegetables that are not 'Tatties and Neeps'

It is not because I do not like haggis that I deviate from cooking it with its usual mates, potatoes and turnips, but because I do. It deserves to be eaten with better vegetables than a mash made from enormous, floury roots. I love haggis with a big pile of boiled young vegetables: carrots, peas, beans and smaller turnips, all dressed with butter, parsley, salt and pepper. And some good beef stock spiked with whisky to keep everything juicy.

To cook haggis, bring a large pan of water to the boil with a good splash of whisky, drop in the haggis, gently so as not to splash, and simmer for 10–15 minutes. Lift out the haggis, cut an opening with a knife and spoon out the contents.

Oatcakes

For eating with cheese, or just carrying around, which I do when I am travelling and don't want to get caught out by a bad sandwich. Made with butter and eggs, these oatcakes are richer than the ones available everywhere, and a great treat with cheese.

Makes about 35

225g/8oz fine oatmeal, plus extra for
   dusting
a small pinch of baking powder
115g/4oz softened butter, diced
1 egg
1 egg yolk
a few green pumpkin seeds
   (optional)

Preheat the oven to 175°C/350°F/Gas Mark 4.

Put the oatmeal and baking powder in a large bowl. Rub in the butter, stir in the egg and egg yolk and mix to a dough. Dust a work surface with fine oatmeal and roll the dough out to about 5mm/¼ inch thick. It can be sticky, which is good for the richness of the oatcakes but makes it tricky to handle. As long as there is plenty of oatmeal under the dough, you can roll or use fingers to press it out until you have the right thickness.

Use a cutter to cut out 4cm/1½ inch rounds, lift them carefully with a palette knife or fine spatula and place on a baking sheet lined with baking parchment. Shape the surplus dough into a ball and repeat the rolling process until you have used up every scrap. For some of the oatcakes, dip a pumpkin seed in a bowl of water and stick it on the surface, just for decoration. Bake for about 8 minutes, until pale golden.

Split Mealy Pudding, Scrambled Eggs and Cress

Mealy pudding consists of a natural sausage skin, about 30cm/12 inches long, filled with oatmeal and meat juices. Sliced and fried, it is ready to be put on a plate with some creamy scrambled eggs. The cress greens it all up a little, but just a little. Serve with brown toast.

Serves 4

1 tablespoon olive oil
4 mealy puddings, sliced into 2cm/
    ¾ inch chunks
9 eggs, lightly beaten
55g/2oz unsalted butter
2 tablespoons double cream
2 punnets of mustard and cress
sea salt

Heat the oil in a large frying pan and fry the mealy puddings over a gentle heat until golden on both sides. While they cook, scramble the eggs. Season the beaten eggs with salt, then melt the butter in a saucepan. Pour in the eggs and cook over a low heat, stirring with a wooden spoon, until the egg begins to thicken on the base of the pan. Scrape at the base with the spoon and continue to cook until the egg is thick and creamy. Do not allow it to get too solid – before this happens, remove from the heat, add the cream and stir. The mealy pudding should be ready by now. Serve it on warmed plates with a pool of scrambled egg, and the toast, mustard and cress on the side.

 Kitchen note
To make this an even more substantial supper, serve with a little poached smoked Finnan haddock, or some strips of smoked streaky bacon – or both – for a big fry-up.

OLIVE OIL

Little Lemon and Olive Oil Cakes
Raisin, Currant and Sultana Pie in Olive Oil Pastry
Mayonnaise

It may take some convincing that olive oil is an English or British food, but with few 'good-fat' alternatives to cook with or use in a raw state, it can join lemons, spices, pulses, lentils and bananas as an ingredient that we cannot do without. It may well one day actually become an English food. With the climate changing and summers predicted to get warmer, a smallholder in Devon, Mark Diacono, planted a grove of 120 trees on a 17-acre plot in 2006, and hopes to have a harvest within seven years.

Try to choose an oil that is healthy, whole and tastes good. Cold-pressed olive oil – or extra virgin – is widely available, and economic enough to use daily. The special, single-estate extra virgin oils are treats to use more occasionally. I am reluctant to use refined vegetable oils, with the exception of sunflower oil, for the following reasons:

If the last few years spent investigating food have left a lasting impression on me, it is that the world eats too much bad fat. For 'bad fat', read any that is not in its natural state – i.e. simply separated from the seed or whole food from which it is extracted. Many oils are extracted with the help of acids, heat, bleach and steam – processes that extract the maximum amount of oil, remove inconvenient components like free-flowing fatty acids that can lower the smoking temperature, or deodorise it to remove any smell (and flavour). Processing oils in this way can create transfats, especially in rapeseed oil, which is usually sold as 'vegetable oil'.

Transfats are toxic molecules that interfere with cell metabolism. So concerned are the authorities in the USA about their links to serious health problems, such as heart disease, cancer and low-nutrient-quality breast milk, that they have insisted transfat content be shown on labels. In the UK, however, the Food Standards Agency has dragged its feet on the issue. It concedes that transfats have no known nutritional benefit but does not admit the health problems specified above, and is yet to tackle the food industry on the subject.

So, to the quest for good fats to cook with or eat raw. Extra virgin olive oil, which is made by pressing olives with no use of heat at all, is one. Cold pressing keeps the acidity in the oil low, at no more than 8 per cent – anything above this and it cannot be labelled 'extra virgin'. Cook with it over moderate temperatures for shorter periods of time and you will be eating a fat that has the lowest impact.

I imagine that the first concern for most of us when starting to use olive oil as more than just a drizzle is the cost. Top-quality oil is expensive, but good basic extra virgin olive oil can be bought at a decent price via mail order (see below). Supermarkets' extra virgin oils are also more affordable than specialist ones. I suggest having a bottle of your favourite to hand, no matter the cost, for using raw, and a supply of bargain extra virgin on the side.

Olive oil need not be confined to frying and salads. Travels in Italy have taught me that it is a great baking ingredient and can make wonderful pastry, biscuits and cakes.

Buying extra virgin olive oil

Elanthy is a great budget extra virgin oil from southern Greece: low acidity and green, yet light enough to use when frying and for making mayonnaise. It is available by mail order from www.elanthy.com; tel: 0800 169 6252.

Charles Carey, at www.oilmerchant.co.uk (tel: 020 8740 1335), has a list of the very best single-estate olive oils. Brindisa keeps a close eye on who is producing the best oils in Spain. Contact them for stockists (www.brindisa.com; tel: 020 8772 1600). Olives et Al is a Dorset importer of good olives and excellent oils: www.olivesetal.co.uk; tel: 01258 474300.

A note about cold-pressed rapeseed oils and others

New to shops are a few varieties of golden-coloured cold-pressed rapeseed oils made from seeds grown in England and pressed on the farms where they are grown. These oils are very high in essential fatty acids (such as omega-3) – nutrients that are damaged during normal refining. They are designed for cooking and pouring on to salads. I am not convinced that they can replace the fruit flavours of good olive oil, but I urge you to try them for yourself and use them in the recipes below – except mayonnaise, which is always best with olive or a mixture of olive and sunflower oil.

Rapeseed oil, sometimes called canola, is the most common base for shop-bought 'vegetable' oil and is always heavily refined, so these cold-pressed oils are a healthy departure. It was suggested to me, by an East Anglian farmer, that if plant breeders (not to be confused with the biotech industry that is currently imposing the folly of genetically modified crops on Europe) developed a more suitable seed for cold pressing, we may one day soon have some very delicious British oils available, with flavours comparable to olive oil. There are other good British-grown seed oils to try – hemp and linseed, for example. The following brands are the ones to seek out: Mellow Yellow, for rapeseed oil (www.farrington-oils.co.uk; tel: 01933 622809); Hillfarm Oils, for cold-pressed linseed (www.hillfarmoils.com); River Cottage, for hempseed oil (www.rivercottage.net).

Little Lemon and Olive Oil Cakes

Little buns that can be eaten fresh from the oven or kept in a tin. They dry out quite quickly, but in a way that I like – rather like those hard Italian biscuits with nuts. Talking of which, you can add pine nuts to these with great success.

If you don't want to ice them, you can just dust the cakes with sifted icing sugar.

Makes 10

150ml/¼ pint extra virgin olive oil
200g/7oz golden caster sugar
2 eggs
350g/12oz Italian '00' flour
1 teaspoon ground cinnamon
1½ teaspoons bicarbonate of soda
½ teaspoon cream of tartar
½ teaspoon sea salt
grated zest of 3 lemons

For the icing:
3 tablespoons icing sugar
a little lemon juice

Preheat the oven to 160°C/325°F/Gas Mark 3. Beat the oil and sugar together until homogenised. Add the eggs one at a time and beat until the volume increases a little. Sift together the flour, cinnamon, bicarbonate of soda, cream of tartar and salt and add them gradually to the egg, oil and sugar mixture, folding them in with a metal spoon. Finally, add the lemon zest. Spoon the mixture into paper cake cases and bake for 20–25 minutes. The cakes are done when a wooden toothpick inserted in the centre comes out dry. Leave to cool on a wire rack.

To make the icing, put the icing sugar into a bowl and stir in enough lemon juice to make an icing that will coat the back of the spoon lightly. Spoon a little icing over each bun. Decorate with cheerful yellow mimosa flowers, if you have any. You could also give these as presents, individually wrapped in aluminium foil and tied with a ribbon.

Raisin, Currant and Sultana Pie in Olive Oil Pastry

A different Christmas 'mince pie', with olive oil replacing the lard or butter in the pastry.

Serves 8

115g/4oz large raisins
115g/4oz golden sultanas
115g/4oz currants
4 dessert apples, cored and thinly
   sliced (try to find fairly sour eating
   apples – see page 2)
4 semi-dried figs, halved and sliced
30g/1oz butter, melted

30g/1oz Demerara sugar
55g/2oz ground almonds
extra virgin olive oil, for glazing

For the olive oil pastry:
150g/5½oz plain flour
½ teaspoon salt
1½ tablespoons extra virgin olive oil
about 125ml/4fl oz iced water

First make the pastry. Put the flour and salt in the bowl of a tabletop mixer and attach the dough hook. Add the oil as it mixes, then add the water, a tablespoon at a time, until the mixture forms a dough. You may not need to add all the water; stop when it forms a stiff dough. Continue to mix for about 2 minutes, until the dough is smooth and elastic, then wrap it in cling film and store in the fridge for an hour. (Alternatively, you can make and knead the dough by hand, which should take about 15 minutes.)

Mix together all the filling ingredients and set to one side. The butter will cool and set.

Preheat the oven to 190°C/375°F/Gas Mark 5. Roll out the pastry into a very large, thin round. You will find it very elastic and pliable. Use your hands to thin and stretch it further, then place it on a baking sheet, spoon the filling into the centre and spread it into a round. Bring the pastry edges up and over the filling, pleating them in towards the centre and stretching them if necessary. You will probably have too much; just snip off the surplus. Pinch the pastry folds together in the centre but leave a little hole so the steam can escape as the pie cooks. Brush the surface with oil, then place in the oven and bake for about 30 minutes, until golden. Serve hot or cold.

Mayonnaise

Using pure olive oil is not always a given with mayonnaise. For some salads with a mayonnaise dressing, the powerful flavour can ruin the other ingredients, so I often substitute a proportion of sunflower oil. But mayonnaise made with a low-acid olive oil tastes like a sauce made from the fruit of the olive tree itself. Don't be alarmed by the ghoulish green colour.

Makes about 300ml/ ½ pint

3 egg yolks
1 teaspoon Dijon mustard
300ml/ ½ pint extra virgin olive oil
1 tablespoon lemon juice or white
    wine vinegar
sea salt and ground white pepper

Put the egg yolks in a mixing bowl and add the mustard. Begin to whisk in the oil bit by bit – starting with a teaspoonful at a time and progressing to larger amounts. After each addition, give it a good whisk so it emulsifies. An electric mixer will speed things up. When nearly all the oil has been incorporated, add the lemon juice or vinegar. Whisk again and add the rest of the oil. Taste and add salt, then a pinch of white pepper. Store at room temperature, or in the fridge if it is for more than 12 hours.

Kitchen notes
To flavour the oil with garlic, omit the mustard and add a garlic clove that has been chopped, then mashed to a purée with a little salt.

To flavour with chilli, substitute 1 tablespoon of harissa paste for the mustard. You can combine harissa and garlic, if you like.

To flavour with herbs, use white wine vinegar rather than lemon juice and add a tablespoon each of chopped parsley, chives, basil and tarragon, stirring them in at the end. The addition of 2 grated hardboiled egg yolks at the end will make a sturdy, rich mayonnaise.

The Lost Kitchen

Look closer at that leafy weed on the verge by the side of the road.
Could it go into the pan, then on to a plate? Or take some of those wild,
plum-like fruits that grow on the bush beside the footpath – find out
what they are and make a juicy tart with them. You never know, one
day you may be credited with a discovery, or at least for carrying out a
rescue. There are hundreds of neglected, underused species of food plants,
animal breeds and fish in the world. In spite of those long supermarket
aisles packed with thousands of 'lines', humans are very dull omnivores.
Around 50 per cent of the world's food requirements is taken from three
cereal crops: rice, wheat and maize. It is estimated that 90 per cent of our
vegetable and fruit supply derives from 103 species. That is out of a
possible 7,000 plants either grown or collected. It points to a very
interesting 10 per cent of underexploited foods. Genetic resource experts
say these other species are eaten by the poor, and not just in developing
countries. Findings in the UK's Low Income Nutrition and Diet Survey,
published in 2007, show that 20 per cent of our low-income groups gather
wild berries.

Paradoxically, as we become more sophisticated and resourceful,
the food supply is becoming increasingly monolithic. In 1949 there
were 10,000 wheat species cultivated in China; by the 1970s this
number had dropped to 1,000.

The downside of this slide into monoculture is the risk to the
developing world. Grow just one species of rice and the whole crop
will be lost if disease hits. Famine is the ultimate danger. But there
is the nutritional and economic impact to consider, too. Bioversity
International (BI), the UN-backed organisation set up to study loss
of crop biodiversity and the threats this poses, says that people who eat
more diverse diets live longer and have lower states of chronic diseases.
It is also true that many underexploited species have exceptionally high
vitamin and mineral contents. Of course it is possible to argue that in

the developed Western world we are perfectly well fed. But how well nourished are we? All the while that diet has become more uniform, incidences of obesity and food-related chronic illness have increased. The food industry's response is to use food technology and synthetic additives to turn the few raw materials we do eat into an unending list of 'convenience' foods.

It is not totally daft to suggest eating weeds. During the 1980s, a genetic resource expert, Dr Stefano Padulosi, remembered how as a child growing up near Naples, he would nibble the peppery wild rocket leaves growing among the ruins of Pompei. Padulosi later discovered that historically rocket had been an important crop, so he took the wild seed and developed it for commercial cultivation. That is the rocket that now pops up in every other European sandwich or salad.

There are many lost English foods. We have our own rocket in young dandelion leaves and many others, but there are also those foods that grew contentedly here once but which few people bother with now. Spelt, quinces, figs – there is evidence that lentils were once grown in the southeast of England. There are the lost animal breeds. The last true Alderney cow, the small beast that provided the 'king's' butter in A. A. Milne's poem, was born in 1927. Much of this loss is put down to low yield, but there is evidence that low-yielding crops can contain higher-grade nutrients. In the UK we eat abysmally few types of vegetables, grains and seeds. We must be the only country in the world that has sacrificed its national nut, the walnut, for a love of grey squirrels…

Seeking out foods derived from rarer breeds, trying those strange-coloured carrots or rough-skinned apples, eating fish you have never heard of before, or giving alternative flours a go in breads and baking, is not only healthy, it is also more interesting. It is one thing to die poorly nourished, but quite another to expire with boredom.

OX TONGUE

Braised Tongue

Leftovers
Sandwiches
Hot Tongue with Potato Salad
Hash

We were fed ox tongue as children, and I remember not always being happy to see the tongue itself just before cooking, a grey and not at all pretty-looking shape on the kitchen counter. I don't remember at what point it no longer mattered that it was ugly. Once simmered for hours, skinned and trimmed, the small, square pieces of meat – and it is like a lean beef – become something else. The ritual of preparing ingredients that are difficult to love at first sight removes disgust, as long as it is sensitively done. It's fine for the ones who wait and see only the *fait accompli* looking neat as ironing; so it is a brave cook that tackles challenging cuts such as tongue for the first time. Your efforts will pay off, though. When you serve an ox tongue that has been carefully brined by a butcher – not too long in the salt tub, not too dehydrated – the admiration for it will soon, I promise, override the horrors.

The first meal will be a hot one, consisting of comforting slices of meat with a cheerful green sauce – make lots of buttery mashed potatoes to eat with it. After that there is the happy prospect of leftovers – cold meat to eat with pickles and rye bread for a weekday lunch or on returning home from work.

Buying tongue

Traditional butcher's shops will brine a fresh ox tongue, ready for the pot, but not all do. To find your nearest butcher who buys from local farmers, see The Guild of Q Butchers' website, www.guildofqbutchers.com, or contact their helpline on 01738 450443.

Braised Tongue

Serves 8

1 brined ox tongue, the skin on and
   the root bones removed
2 carrots, peeled but left whole
2 onions, quartered
2 celery sticks, sliced

1 bay leaf
8 black peppercorns
2 juniper berries
1 tablespoon Worcestershire sauce

Put the ox tongue in a large pan, cover with cold water and leave to soak for a few hours. Drain well, then return the tongue to the pan, add the vegetables, bay leaf, peppercorns, juniper berries and Worcestershire sauce and cover completely with fresh water. Bring to the boil, skim away any foam that rises to the surface and simmer for 3–4 hours, until a knife can pierce the meat with ease. Remove the tongue and allow to cool for a few minutes. Skin it, using a small knife to peel the membrane away. Remove any bone or fibrous tissue at the base.

Slice the tongue and serve hot, with green sauce (see page 55).

Sandwiches

The obvious, but natural, way to use up thin slices of braised tongue. Use buttered brown bread and choose your mustard: hot English, with a dash of Tabasco stirred in, Dijon (Maille makes delicious *noix*, or hazelnut, mustard which is good with tongue) or sweet German mustard, which reminds me of hot salt beef bars – you could warm the slices of tongue in a pan and make a hot tongue sandwich.

Hot Tongue with Potato Salad

Boil some salad potatoes until tender (use one of the salad potato varieties recommended on page 335). Slice into rounds, then dress with a mustard dressing (1 tablespoon of Dijon mustard, a pinch of sugar, a pinch of salt, 1 tablespoon of red wine vinegar, 2 tablespoons of water, a crushed garlic clove and 4 tablespoons of olive oil, all shaken together in a jar). Warm some slices of tongue in a pan and serve over the top of the potato salad, with a few sliced cornichons.

Hash

Cut leftover tongue and some boiled potatoes into 1cm/½ inch dice, put in a bowl and season with black pepper. Fry some sliced white onion in a frying pan until softened but not coloured, then add to the bowl. Allow to cool, then add 1 beaten egg. Place the frying pan back over the heat with a little olive or sunflower oil and tip in the hash mixture. Fry gently for a few minutes, until browned underneath – check by lifting the edge of the hash with a knife. Place a plate (one that fits inside the pan) over the hash and invert the pan quickly. Then slide the hash back into the pan and fry for a few minutes longer, until browned. Eat with Worcestershire sauce, ketchup or Tabasco.

OYSTERS

Grilled Oysters with Butter, Watercress, Celery
and Aniseed

Once you have mastered opening them, native oysters are a wonderful food to eat at home. Oysters from Colchester and West Mersea have the most extraordinary resonant flavours. Eat one and your cheeks tingle with pure, clean marine memories for up to 15 minutes. They are the fugu of the Thames Estuary, but nothing like as dangerous. Oysters travel well for several hours and do not need to be kept freezing cold, but they should be icy cold when you eat them, as it improves the taste.

Choosing and opening oysters

An oyster that is tightly shut when you try to open it is healthy. What matters is its origin – always buy from reputable shops or mail-order suppliers (see below).

To open an oyster, place it in the palm of your hand on a folded cloth. The hinged end should be closest to your body and the flat half of the shell uppermost. Insert an oyster knife, or other small knife with a strong, thin, inflexible blade, into the hinge. If you keep the knife level with the flat half of the shell, it should slip in easily until it reaches and breaks the muscle holding the two shells together. Don't rush it – a slipped knife can cause a nasty injury. And don't twist the knife aggressively, or it will fill the interior with shards of shell. When you feel the grip loosen, twist the knife once, then discard the flat shell. Inspect the oyster inside – it should look clear, and have a sweet smell of clean seawater and fresh fish. Use the tip of the knife to cut the ligament that attaches the meat to the shell and flip it over. Serve the oysters in their shells, with lemon juice – it is a bit of a shame to put anything stronger on this delicious fish.

Buying oysters

Native oysters are available from fishmongers from September to April. To buy natives by post – quite safe, as oysters travel well even when not packed on ice – contact Falmouth Bay Oysters in Cornwall, who buy wild oysters from local fishermen: www.falmouthoysters.co.uk; tel: 01326 316600. Richard Haward harvests legendary oysters in the creeks around West Mersea Island, at the mouth of the Thames: www.richardhawardoysters.co.uk; tel: 01206 383284.

Grilled Oysters with Butter, Watercress, Celery and Aniseed

These oysters are a favourite at Bentley's, the old London restaurant now run by Richard Corrigan. This is my own version, using similar ingredients, but if the chance arises, try his.

Oysters flashed under the grill with a sauce can be delicious, but don't buy natives, as their flavour will be wasted. Buy Pacific farmed or Gigas oysters (the ones with tear-shaped shells). For 2 people, open a dozen oysters and arrange on 2 ovenproof plates. Put in a food processor the leaves from 2 bunches of watercress, 1 small stick of celery (pull the strings from it first), the leaves from 4 sprigs of parsley, a tablespoon of softened butter, 2 tablespoons of fresh breadcrumbs and 2 tablespoons of Pernod. Blitz to a fine purée (or you can chop it by hand if necessary; the texture will be rougher but it will still be lovely). Season with salt and pepper and put a heaped teaspoon on to each oyster.

Either preheat the oven to its highest setting or preheat the grill. Put the oysters in the oven or under the grill and cook until the butter melts. The oysters do not need to cook through – they should be partly raw.

PARTRIDGES

Pot-roasted Partridges with Breadcrumbs

Partridge Legs

Partridge and Pears

Potted Partridge and Pistachio

Leftovers

Cold partridge with Wood-roasted Peppers

Partridge Stock

A roasting dish packed with two rows of partridges, during the short season when they are abundant, is a festive joy. Just in advance of Christmas, just when we want to splurge a bit on ingredients, there is this bird that is a meal in itself. Just enough for one. Most of the partridges you see in butcher's shops, farmers' markets and supermarkets (some of which are beginning to make them a stock autumn/winter fresh food) are the red-legged variety. This breed has been in Britain a long time. They are farmed and released into the wild, the quarry of game bird shoots throughout the country. If you are arguing about the ethics of shooting, the pros of partridges are many. A responsible shoot will rear the young birds in confinement for a short period before releasing them into the wild, where they will forage for their own food. The existence of shooting as a field sport subsidises the real cost of the birds – they are worth a good deal more than we pay – but not all shoots stick to the basic idea that it is a bit of fun for participants and has environmental benefits. Large-scale commercial shooting can result in too many birds being reared just so a few guns can boast an enormous bag – a practice that is giving the sport a bad name and could see it banned.

The other partridge on the market is totally wild. Grey-legged partridges are indigenous in Britain but their number has been badly affected by the use of agricultural chemicals and, in particular, pesticides.

Their flavour is more pronounced than that of the red-leg, which can even – though delicately delicious – be accused of being close to chicken. Recently conservation groups and the game authorities have done much to encourage a revival of the breed. This has been so successful in certain areas that they are a bird that can be eaten with a clear conscience.

Buying partridge

The season for partridge runs from 1 September to 1 February, and butchers with a licence to deal in game will continue to sell fresh birds for about two weeks after the season closes. Contact The Thoroughly Wild Meat Company (www.thoroughlywildmeat.co.uk; tel: 01963 824788 or 07770 392041) in Somerset, which sells partridges whole and also the legs (see page 293). The organisation Game to Eat has a directory of game suppliers: www.game-to-eat.co.uk. All types of game birds (woodpigeon, partridge, pheasant, grouse) are available direct from game expert David Hammerson at the Everleigh Farm Shop (www.everleighfarmshop.co.uk; tel: 01264 850344) and also from fellow expert Ben Weatherall at Yorkshire Game (www.yorkshiregame.co.uk; tel: 01748 810212). Game birds are increasingly available in supermarkets.

Pot-roasted Partridges with Breadcrumbs

While it is no trouble tackling the breast meat of a roast partridge, the leg meat is not so easy to get at with a knife and fork. The answer is simple: cut off the legs before cooking and braise until the meat is falling off the bone. Roast the breast crowns separately, then serve them together.

Serves 4

4 partridges
4 sprigs of thyme
5 tablespoons extra virgin olive oil
1 garlic clove, crushed
2 wineglasses of dry West Country cider
300ml/½ pint chicken stock (see page 116)
sea salt and freshly ground black pepper

For the breadcrumbs:
30g/1oz unsalted butter
4 tablespoons sourdough breadcrumbs
a few gratings of lemon zest
1 teaspoon ground allspice
a pinch of ground cloves
2 tablespoons finely chopped curly parsley
½ teaspoon sea salt

Sever both legs from each partridge, cutting away the whole thigh. Trim the backbone away from the carcasses. Use scissors to snip down either side of the backbone, leaving the 'crown' with both breasts and wings attached. You could ask your butcher to do this for you, but do give him notice. Put the legs and breast crowns in a bowl. Add the thyme sprigs and some black pepper, plus 4 tablespoons of the oil. Turn the meat over in the bowl so all gets a good covering, then leave for about 30 minutes.

Put the remaining oil and the garlic into a casserole (large enough to hold all the legs and which has a well-fitting lid) and fry for a minute or two over a low heat without letting the garlic brown. Add the partridge legs from the marinade and turn them in the hot oil, letting them brown slightly. Add the cider, bring to the boil and then pour in the stock. Bring back to the boil and skim away any foam that rises to the surface. Turn down the heat so the contents are just simmering, put the lid on the casserole and cook for about 40 minutes, until the meat on the legs is tender and comes away from the bone easily. Turn off the heat.

Meanwhile, preheat the oven to 230°C/450°F/Gas Mark 8. Just as the partridge legs begin their 40-minute simmer, take the breast and wing crowns from the marinade and put them in a roasting tin, breast-side up. Season with salt and pepper, put them in the oven and roast for 20 minutes. Take from the oven, cover with foil and leave to rest for 15 minutes,

Melt the butter in a pan and add the breadcrumbs, lemon zest, allspice, cloves, parsley and salt. Fry until golden, then set to one side. To serve, put the legs on 4 warmed plates with some of the cooking juices, put a crown on top, then some breadcrumbs beside. Eat with lentils (see page 253), or black cabbage or spring greens.

Partridge Legs

I buy partridge legs from a farmers' market in Somerset in the middle of the shooting season, season them with salt, pepper and cumin and roast for a good half an hour at 200°C/400°F/Gas Mark 6. I serve them with yoghurt that has been blended with green chilli and coriander, as something to chew on with a drink.

Partridge and Pears

Spatchcocked partridges served with pickled pears. To eat at Christmas.

Serves 4

4 partridges
2 tablespoons melted butter
sea salt and freshly ground black
  pepper

For the pickled pears:
300ml/½ pint cider vinegar or white
  wine vinegar

200g/7oz golden granulated sugar
3 pink peppercorns
1 bay leaf
6 pears, quartered lengthways and
  cored
12 long French breakfast radishes,
  halved lengthways

To make the pickled pears, put the vinegar in a pan, add the sugar, peppercorns and bay leaf and bring slowly to the boil. Simmer for 5 minutes, until syrupy, then add the pears and radishes, making sure both are covered with the mixture. Bring back to the boil, turn off the heat and store until needed.

Preheat the oven to 230°C/450°F/Gas Mark 8. To spatchcock the partridges, turn them over so the backbone faces you, then snip (using scissors) 2 lines down either side of the backbone to remove it. Turn the partridges over again, so the breastbone is uppermost, and use the heel of your hand on the actual ridge of the breastbone to press them flat. If given plenty of warning, a butcher will do all this for you.

Use a pastry brush to paint the birds all over with melted butter (undersides, too), then season with salt and pepper. Put them in a roasting tin and roast for 20–25 minutes (no red juices should appear when the thicker part of the breast or thigh is pricked with a skewer). Once cooked, cover with foil and leave to rest in a warm place for 15 minutes. Serve with the pickled pears and a bitter leaf salad (chicory or radicchio) dressed with a sweet mustard dressing.

Potted Partridge and Pistachio

Pretty and festive, a potted recipe to show off at Christmas and so good to have in the fridge. More than once I have been rescued by a supply of something to spread on toast. To make lighter work, ask the butcher to prepare the meat for you.

You will need a large ceramic rectangular or oval terrine dish with a lid, approximately 30cm/12 inches long. Alternatively, use one or two metal loaf tins, with aluminium foil for the lid.

Serves 10–12 generously

1kg/1¾lb pork shoulder meat, cut into 1cm/½ inch chunks
1kg/1¾lb lean pork belly, minced
3 partridges, the breast and leg meat taken off the bone and cut into strips
1 wineglass of London gin
30g/1oz softened butter
2 bay leaves
10 very thin rashers of unsmoked (green) streaky bacon
70g/2½oz pistachio nibs or shelled whole pistachios
sea salt and freshly ground black pepper

Preheat the oven to 200°C/400°F/Gas Mark 6. Put the pork and partridge into a bowl with the gin and leave to marinate for 1 hour. Use the butter to grease the inside of the terrine dish, put the bay leaves in the bottom, then line it neatly with the bacon rashers, laying them across the width of the dish. Add the pistachios and seasoning to the partridge mixture, then pack it into the terrine, making sure the partridge slices run lengthways in the dish. Wrap any stray pieces of bacon around the meat. Cover with a lid or foil, place in a roasting tin containing 3cm/1¼ inches of boiled water and bake for 1½ hours, until the meat is shrinking away from the sides of the dish. Add more water to the dish if it evaporates during cooking. Remove from the oven, place a weight on top and leave to cool, then chill.

To serve, cut into 1cm/½ inch slices. Eat with any of the suggestions on page 327.

There is always something left on the carcass of roast partridge after the meal – unless my husband has been at the table. He eats them with his fingers and gets to every bit.

Cold Partridge with Wood-roasted Peppers

If you can buy the Navarro brand of peppers, which are roasted over charcoal and then peeled, you will save yourself a lot of time. Although one tin seems expensive, it contains a lot of peppers and they go a long way. You can, of course, roast and peel your own. Strip off as much partridge meat as you can and set it to one side. Arrange 2 roasted peppers on a plate with 3 tablespoons of cooked lentils (see page 252) or some white beans (see page 33). Hardboil an egg, then chop the white only. Scatter the partridge meat over the peppers, followed by the egg white. Push the yolk through a sieve and sprinkle over the top. Add a few chopped parsley leaves, a pinch of Maldon salt and finally shake a little olive oil over the top. You could omit the lentils or beans and put the peppers, meat and egg on a piece of bread that has been brushed with oil and rubbed with garlic, then grilled.

Partridge Stock

Make as for chicken stock (page 116) and use for soup or in any recipe needing meat stock.

PEAS

Pea Stock
Pea Soup with Lettuce and Herbs
Pea and Wild Garlic Broth
Living Pea Salad with Mint
Pea Pies

I doubt there is a time when peas are not in my freezer. Very economical, they are a crop that for once grows only for the benefit of everyone and everything around it. Once the harvest is over, peas (which belong to the legume family) leave a present of nitrogen in the soil, ready for the next food plant. Compared to other vegetables, they have an extraordinarily good record on pesticide residues, coming up clean in test after test. And – thankfully – most sold in the UK, albeit frozen, are grown here. It must be said, however, that the concentration of peas grown for the frozen market seems to wipe out the possibility of growing any other legume. It would be a whole lot better if more mangetout, sugarsnap (both whole pod peas) and petits pois could be grown in East Anglia. Instead we rely too heavily on African countries to produce and airfreight these to the UK. And farmers could experiment with more exotic legumes. Asparagus peas (a pea with a peculiar ridged edible pod about 2cm/¾ inch long) may be worth a try, and climate change could see the return of the lentil (once grown in southern Britain), presently cultivated in Europe and Asia (see Lentils, page 249). A little diversity might address the fact that there are too many garden peas in Britain, although I am not suggesting in a million years the return of the enormous, floury, starchy marrowfat pea – it is to be hoped that that one will become a victim of natural selection.

Buying peas

I buy Bird's Eye peas because they are all UK grown and have a good record on pesticide use, and also organic peas, especially organic petits pois (the small ones) from Waitrose, which are excellent value for money and have a genuine fresh flavour despite all that time in the freezer.

Frozen peas can never be as good as fresh – a crop I look forward to but often become frustrated by, because the 'fresh' peas in shops (both greengrocer's and supermarkets) are usually anything but. Peas become starchy very soon after picking, hence the efforts of the frozen pea industry to freeze them within an hour or two of harvest. I have bought good peas from farmers' markets, but not every time. If there is a doubt about the freshness, and the urge is still there for a pea supper, I buy UK-grown mangetout or sugarsnap instead. Pea shoots are another relative, and are the crunchy stalks and leaves, plus flowers, of young snow peas. You can buy Aconbury pea shoots online from Goodness Direct (www.goodnessdirect.co.uk; tel: 0871 871 6611).

Pea Stock

A greenish broth that will turn up the pea flavour in your pea soup and can also be used in other vegetable soups. With fresh peas being relatively costly (compared to frozen), it is an enormous relief to use up pods that would otherwise be chucked in the bin.

To make the stock, put the empty pods in a pan, cover with water, then bring to the boil and simmer for about 20 minutes. Strain through a sieve. This stock freezes well.

Pea Soup with Lettuce and Herbs

This is the soup, or pottage, I imagine being eaten in medieval Britain. Peas grew with ease then, feeding people and pigs. Herbs and edible leaves were randomly used and a little cream at the end of cooking would make the broth feel nice in the mouth. I use fresh British peas when available, or frozen ones.

Serves 4

3 tablespoons cold-pressed
   rapeseed oil
2 onions, chopped
1 garlic clove, crushed with a little salt
1.2 litres/2 pints water, or any stock
   (including pea stock, made from
   the pods if you are using fresh peas
   – see page 301)
450g/1lb podded green peas,
   defrosted if frozen
4 teaspoons salted butter
sea salt and freshly ground black
   pepper

Any or all of the following:
a few celery leaves
hearts of romaine or Cos lettuce,
   roughly chopped
a few lovage leaves
4 sprigs of chervil, chopped
red mustard leaves
young spinach leaves
sorrel leaves (be aware that sorrel
   turns dark when cooked)

Heat the oil in a large pan and add the onions and garlic. Cook over a low heat until they soften. Cover with the water or stock, bring to the boil, then add the peas with the leaves of your choice and bring back to the boil. Allow to simmer for 1 minute, then turn off the heat. Season with salt and pepper. Spoon into bowls and put a knob of butter on the surface of each to melt.

Pea and Wild Garlic Broth

Follow the recipe above but omit the leaves and herbs. Substitute 225g/8oz chopped wild garlic leaves, adding them with the peas. Chop a few extra leaves and add them to the butter that is melted on top of the soup.

Living Pea Salad with Mint

Green pea shoots with a creamy dressing, fresh mint leaves and black pepper – eat with cold ham or avocado.

Serves 2

3 punnets (about 200g/7oz) pea
   shoots

For the dressing:
1 teaspoon dry English mustard
1 teaspoon golden caster sugar

a pinch of sea salt
1 tablespoon white wine vinegar
4 tablespoons extra virgin olive oil
2 tablespoons crème fraîche
6 mint leaves, torn into pieces
a pinch of freshly ground black
   pepper

Wash the pea shoots and leave to dry on a towel. Put them into a shallow dish. Mix all the dressing ingredients together and pour them over the pea shoots. Done.

Pea Pies

Crisp little parcels, filled with spicy mashed peas. You can use filo pastry or, if you prefer, the olive oil pastry on page 280.

Makes 16

32 sheets of filo pastry (about 30cm/
   12 inches square)
100g/3½oz butter, melted

For the filling:
1 tablespoon butter or olive oil
1 tablespoon good-quality medium-
   strength curry powder

1 teaspoon turmeric (if it is not in the
   curry powder)
a large pinch of sea salt
2 onions, finely chopped
2 garlic cloves, crushed with a little
   salt
1kg/2¼lb frozen petits pois, defrosted
leaves from 2 coriander sprigs,
   chopped
leaves from 2 mint sprigs, chopped

Preheat the oven to 230°C/450°F/Gas Mark 8. Heat the fat in a pan, add the spices, salt, onions and garlic and cook gently for a minute or two, until the onions soften but don't take on any colour. Add the peas and herbs and cook for 3 minutes, then use a handheld potato masher to crush to a rough purée.

To assemble, brush one sheet of pastry with melted butter, then lay another sheet on top. Brush with butter again, then put 2 tablespoons of the pea mixture in the centre. Bring up the sides of the pastry around the little mound of filling, pinching the edges together in the centre. Brush the outside with melted butter. Repeat with the remaining pastry and filling. Place on a baking sheet lined with baking parchment and bake for 10–15 minutes, until crisp and golden. Eat immediately – the pea mixture will lose its greenness fairly quickly.

PHEASANT

Bacon-wrapped Pheasant
Stir-fried Pheasant with Ginger and Black Beans

Leftovers
Pheasant Stock
Cold Pheasant with Chickpeas, Pine Nuts, Aubergine
and Mint

Pheasant feels so English, so Edwardian, yet it isn't at all. It is an Asian bird that originated in the Caucasus. You only have to look at its totally incongruous plumage to know it's not really meant to be here. But it has been, for several hundred years, and I look forward to October when the season begins, because the first roast pheasant with bread sauce is a great feast – not least because the pheasants are still fat from the summer's foraging. In the middle of the glut, when you can buy pheasants for very little, I give up chicken and use their testily dry meat for whatever Brit-Asian fusion food I feel like. So they go into green curries, pilaffs and most of all into Chinese-inspired stir-fries.

Pheasants are not properly wild birds. Many that end up in butcher's shops will have been reared in farms, then released into woodland when old enough and strong enough to look after themselves. Rearing techniques vary, but they are rarely in an organic system, so they can be treated with drugs to fight infection. They are sometimes 'protected' from their own and their fellows in the pen with beak guards – these are small plastic clips that prevent them damaging others during their regular fights and are removed after a period. These clips are not necessary when the early rearing stages are non-intensive, but there are some large commercial shoots in the UK that use beak clips routinely. It would be good to know when you buy a pheasant if this is the case. But you have to ask (some butchers will be able to tell you, especially if their game birds are delivered by a local shoot). I tend towards choosing pheasant because much of their lifetime is spent in the wild, and many escape the shot pellets.

Buying pheasant

Butchers have licences to sell game stock pheasants during the season
(1 October–1 February) and for about two weeks after it ends. To find a
local butcher, contact www.bigbarn.co.uk or see the Shop Local archive link
on www.roseprince.co.uk.

Pheasants and all other game birds are available from game expert David
Hammerson at the Everleigh Farm Shop (www.everleighfarmshop.co.uk;
tel: 01264 850344) and also from fellow expert Ben Weatherall at Yorkshire
Game (www.yorkshiregame.co.uk; tel: 01748 810212). Game birds are
increasingly available in the main supermarkets.

Bacon-wrapped Pheasant

If you share your table with a pheasant-loving person, who cannot return
from a trip to a butcher's or the countryside without charging through the
door clutching yet more of them, fatigue sets in around December. It does
not help that the older the birds get, and the deeper into winter, the more
the little traces of yellow fat under the skin disappear and you are left with
a bird with no inbuilt basting tool. Pheasants do not have much of a skin to
speak of, so create your own and solve both problems. Buy 225g/8oz very
thinly sliced smoked streaky bacon. Lay a few small sprigs of woody herbs
(sage, thyme, rosemary – the latter in tiny amounts) on to the skin, season
the bird with pepper, then cover with the bacon slices until completely
wrapped. Secure with string and roast for 45–55 minutes in an oven
preheated to 230°C/450°F/Gas Mark 8. The pheasant is ready when the
juices in the leg run clear when pricked with a skewer. Inside, the meat
should be as juicy as a pheasant can be. To serve, pull off the bacon wrapper
and divide it among the plates, then carve the pheasant.

Make a reservoir of bread sauce to eat with it: 300ml/½ pint hot milk
infused for half an hour with 1 chopped white onion, 4 cloves, a few
gratings of nutmeg, a bay leaf and 6 crushed pink peppercorns, strained,
then reheated with enough dryish breadcrumbs to make a sloppy sauce.

Stir-fried Pheasant with Ginger and Black Beans

Pheasant cooked with ingredients from a country that values this beautiful bird.

Serves 4

2 tablespoons sesame oil
700g/1lb 9oz pheasant meat, filleted
   from the breast and legs of
   2 pheasants, then cut into bite-
   sized pieces (remove the sinews)
4cm/1½ inch piece of fresh ginger, cut
   into matchsticks

6 spring onions, sliced into rounds
2 red chillies, deseeded and chopped
4 garlic cloves, peeled and cut in half
4 tablespoons sake or dry sherry
2 tablespoons soy sauce
1 teaspoon light brown sugar
4 tablespoons Chinese black beans,
   cooked in water until just soft
coriander leaves

Heat the oil in a large frying pan or wok and add the pheasant pieces. Cook, stirring, over a medium to high heat until they begin to turn opaque, then add the ginger, spring onions, chillies and garlic. Stir-fry until the pheasant is cooked through, then add the sake or sherry, soy sauce, sugar and black beans. Cook until the juices begin to sizzle, scatter with coriander leaves and stir. Serve over egg noodles or long grain rice.

Pheasant Stock

Make as for chicken stock (see page 116) and use in any recipe that needs meat stock, or as a replacement for water in soups. Pheasant stock can be a little grainy – strain it through a fine sieve before use.

Cold Pheasant with Chickpeas, Pine Nuts, Aubergine and Mint

A quick supper to make in one pan. Cut cold leftover pheasant into strips, then fry in a pan with a chopped garlic clove, 2 chopped shallots, 1 small aubergine, diced small, and a can of drained chickpeas. Add a teaspoon of ground coriander, ½ teaspoon of ground cumin and a spoonful of tomato paste. Add a little of the liquid from the chickpea can if the mixture is too dry. Season with a little salt (it should not need much) and scatter over a few mint leaves. Shake over a little olive oil and eat with hot pitta bread.

See also Pheasant Halves Stuffed with Cobnuts, Bread and Butter on page 137.

PISTACHIO NUTS

Pistachio Biscuits

Pistachio and Lamb Rice

Should you ever pass a Middle Eastern food shop in August, step in to check if there are any fresh pistachio nuts. Sweet and delicate, they are a rare and special nut to add to a lamb pilaff, flavour a biscuit or use in a trifle. With so few English-grown nuts to choose from, pistachios, like almonds and pine nuts, have become store-cupboard must-haves. They are not costly, in environmental terms, to freight compared to other imports, and belong on the English table, which has always had a thieving nature. Dried pistachios come a very close second to fresh ones, and now that shelled unsalted pistachio nuts are easier to find, they are also becoming one of the most used nuts in my kitchen. Perhaps used too much, but I remember doing the same with pine nuts when they arrived in our shops and impinged on our consciousness with the discovery of pesto and rustic Italian cooking.

Nuts like pistachio remind me how bad we are at snacking. In the Middle East a handful of nuts is essential for staving off the hungry hour – or hours – between teatime and supper. Here at home, witness the dread tube of Pringles. Nuts are low-status snacks, and have had to make way for canapés – mini meals that are now sold ready to heat or arrange on a plate. Offering pistachio nuts with a drink is thought idle when you could be reheating a mini Yorkshire pudding with Lilliputian slices of beef inside and a squeeze of industrial horseradish cream. But nuts are a more loving snack because, being highly nutritious, they do the job properly.

Like all nuts, pistachios can cross from savoury to sweet dishes easily.

Buying pistachios

Shelled unsalted pistachios are available from Waitrose, branches of Fresh & Wild and Whole Foods Market (www.wholefoodsmarket.co.uk). I also buy fresh and nibbed pistachios from the Reza patisserie and grocery at 346 Kensington High Street, London W8 6NW (tel: 020 7603 0924). Mr Ali's shop is a treasure trove of the highest-quality nuts and dried fruit.

Pistachio Biscuits

Delicate, buttery biscuits made from natural pistachios – if you can make them with fresh kernels they will turn out a pretty khaki green.

Their mild taste adapts to spicy dishes but also to the buttery flavours of sweet biscuits to eat with ice cream.

Makes 20–25

85g/3oz shelled unsalted pistachio nuts, or fresh nibbed pistachios (available from Middle Eastern shops in season)

140g/5oz unsalted butter, softened

40g/1½oz light brown muscovado sugar

140g/5oz plain superfine or Italian '00' flour, plus extra for dusting

a few drops of vanilla extract, or the seeds scraped out from ½ vanilla pod

Put the pistachios in a food processor and whiz until fine. Set to one side. Put the butter and sugar in a mixer or food processor and whisk or blitz until light and fluffy. You could also with some extra effort do this by hand. Fold in the nuts, add the flour and vanilla and mix to a dough. Wrap the dough in a plastic bag and put in the fridge to rest for about 1 hour.

Preheat the oven to 150°C/300°F/Gas Mark 2. Roll out the dough thinly (no more than 5mm/¼ inch) on a work surface dusted with flour. This is a very buttery dough that will stick to the work surface, so work quickly. Use a cutter, any shape, to cut out the biscuits and then put them on a baking sheet lined with baking parchment. Roll any trimmings into another ball of dough and cut out more, repeating until all the dough has been used up. Bake the biscuits for about 12 minutes, until pale gold. Lift off the baking sheet and leave to cool on a wire rack.

 Kitchen note
These biscuits can be made with other ground nuts, such as walnuts, pecans, peanuts and almonds.

Pistachio and Lamb Rice

This is my standard recipe for leftover lamb. Cooking the onions for a good long time is vital to it.

Serves 4

200g/7oz basmati rice
a pinch of sea salt
2 tablespoons lamb dripping from the roast (or butter)
2 onions, chopped
½ teaspoon ground allspice

2 tablespoons shelled unsalted pistachio nuts, roughly chopped
2 tablespoons sultanas, preferably golden sultanas (available from Reza – see page 309)
about 450g/1lb leftover roast lamb, sliced

Put the rice in a saucepan, cover with cold water and leave to soak for 10 minutes. Pour off the water, then cover with fresh water to about 1cm/½ inch above the level of the rice. Add the salt and bring to the boil. Boil, uncovered, for 5 minutes, then cover with a lid, turn down the heat and cook for a further 5 minutes. Take the pan off the heat, leave the lid on for a further 5 minutes and it should be perfectly cooked.

Heat the dripping in a large frying pan and add the onions. Cook over a low-medium heat for 10–15 minutes, until the onions begin to take on a little golden colour. Add the allspice, pistachios and sultanas, followed by the lamb, and cook until thoroughly heated through. Stir in the rice, giving it a thorough coating of the cooking juices and mixing it well. Serve with whole-milk yoghurt.

POMEGRANATES

Fresh Pomegranate Jelly
Mutton Leg Chops with Ginger and Pomegranate Salsa

Speaking up for a fruit that has undergone what I now come to recognise as a health-claim takeover, can I urge you away from the dreaded pomegranate drinks and back to the fruit itself? Pomegranates may not be a British-grown fruit (although I suspect they might be one day if our winters continue to warm up), but they have great keeping qualities, lasting for ages after picking. This means that pomegranates, like bananas, are never air-freighted. Fruits such as these, and citrus fruits, can be justified as imports because in the UK, after the summer is over, there are few fresh, home-grown fruits available.

It is possible to buy genuine (not in a carton) freshly pressed pomegranate juice in cities where there are Middle Eastern shops. In one I know, Mr Ali (see Pistachio Nuts, page 309) peels pomegranates and sells cupfuls of their seeds to passers-by at his shop in Kensington High Street, London. That's what I call fresh pomegranate juice. If you want 100 per cent of pomegranate goodness without added powdered vitamins (there to replace what is lost in processing) – eat the real thing, or crush it and drink the juice.

Buying pomegranates

The season for pomegranates begins in summer but their hard shell makes them a good, long-lasting fruit, so for an import I can feel happy about buying them, compared to, say, a punnet of raspberries. Most pomegranates come to the UK from the southern Mediterranean, but there is also a supply of a very bright-red species, shipped by boat from the USA. Both types are available in supermarkets and greengrocer's shops; I tend to go for the Mediterranean type because it is nearer.

Fresh Pomegranate Jelly

This jelly can be made a day or two before it is needed. It is a wonderful winter festival fruit, and holds much symbolism for Middle Eastern countries at that time.

Pomegranates have lovely sweet seeds but bitter pith. When squeezing them, it is better to use a levered citrus press (which looks like a giant garlic press). You can also use an electric citrus press but you will need to cut the pomegranates in half. Do not overwork them or the flavour of the pith will enter the juice.

Serves 6

8–10 large, ripe pomegranates, cut
   into quarters
caster sugar (optional)
4 gelatine leaves
extra pomegranate seeds, to
   decorate

Use a levered citrus press to extract as much juice as possible from the pomegranates (you will need approximately 600ml/1 pint), then pour it through a small sieve into a bowl. Do not be put off if the juice is cloudy; it will have a far more intense flavour than fully filtered juice. Taste the juice – if it is very sour, stir in sugar to taste.

Soak the gelatine leaves in cold water for about 10 minutes. Put half the pomegranate juice into a small pan and heat gently. Squeeze the cold water from the gelatine leaves, add them to the pan and stir until they are dissolved. The juice must become slightly warmer than hand hot for the gelatine to dissolve. Remove from the heat, pour into the remaining juice and stir once or twice. Pour the mixture into 6 glasses and leave to cool, then chill for several hours until set. Serve decorated with a few spare pomegranate seeds.

Mutton Leg Chops with Ginger and Pomegranate Salsa

A dish that feels very old English, from a time when both spices and mutton were revered and the word salsa often used. Now it feels contemporary, in tune with a revived piratical attitude to food that is curious about everything yet strives to eat what is local or low impact environmentally. This is a dish that not only sets an example as to which meat to choose – eating mutton is essential if we are to preserve our hill country (see page 226) – but also which ingredients it is acceptable to import. Long-lasting imports like pomegranates and ginger make sense, as do lightweight storage items such as spices, because they do not need to travel via airfreight and they have good storage qualities. Either barbecue the mutton for this recipe or cook it on a ridged cast-iron pan. Be a little careful where you buy mutton – not all will be tender when grilled, though leg steaks are fairly reliable. I buy salt-marsh mutton steaks direct from The Thoroughly Wild Meat Company (www.thoroughlywildmeat.co.uk; tel: 01963 824788) or Scottish Blackface mutton from www.blackface.co.uk; tel: 01387 730326.

Serves 4

4 leg steaks of mutton, cut 5cm/
    2 inches thick
olive oil for brushing
sea salt and freshly ground black
    pepper

For the salsa:
1 sweet red onion, finely chopped
a large handful of parsley, chopped
seeds from 1 pomegranate
4cm/1½ inch piece of fresh ginger,
    grated
1 teaspoon coriander seeds, toasted
    in a dry frying pan and then
    ground
5 tablespoons virgin olive oil
1 tablespoon sherry vinegar

Combine all the salsa ingredients and set aside for an hour or two before eating so the flavours develop. Season the leg steaks, brush with olive oil and grill over a high heat for about 4 minutes on either side. Ideally they should be cooked over coals: light the barbecue, making a deep bed of charcoal – when the flames have died down and the coals are pale grey, it is the perfect moment to put the meat on the grill. Once cooked, allow it to rest for 5 minutes, then slice across the grain and serve with the salsa and some fresh watercress or other salad leaves.

PORK

Roast Middle Loin of Pork

Roast Spare Rib of Pork Stuffed with Prunes

Leftovers

Warm Pork Sandwiches with Apple Sauce

Cold Pork with Anchovy and Caper Sauce

Cheap cuts

Potted Pork with Basil

 Things to eat with potted pork

  Toast

  Butter and Radishes

  Leek Jam

  Pickled Pears

  Lettuce with Dressing

  Cucumber Pickle

Pork Chump Chops Braised with Lentils, Cider
 and Cream

Raised Pork and Duck Pie

Braised Hand of Pork with Wine

From the tips of their noses to the points of their trotters, and down to the end of their tails, pigs are the most generous providers. Roasted, potted, packed into skins as sausages, chopped into chops, filleted into fillets, torched into crackling – this is only the beginning. I have covered cured pork elsewhere in this book (see page 15) and dealt with trotters and sausages separately (see pages 410 and 386). This section is about fresh pork and a few of the ways in which it can be used. It also suggests what to do with leftovers and how to make the most of paying more for higher-quality pork.

Paying more is related to the welfare of pigs. Pork can be produced cheaply but only in a system that confines the animals in tight spaces and exhausts them, restricting their natural behaviour. Like hens kept in a broiler house, an indoor-reared pig will experience none of the natural foraging or satisfy its curiosity roaming in fields and woodland. The intensive pork farming industry is geared only to producing the largest possible pigs in the shortest possible time. Choosing to buy free-range pork, or pork reared in welfare-friendly organic systems, will inevitably cost more money. The only way to economise is to use as many cuts as you can, especially the cheaper cuts, and then use up any leftovers.

Roast pork was the least favourite Sunday lunch for me as a child. The loin or leg joint was always huge, its flesh milky white and dry, no matter how carefully cooked. There was no choice of breed then. For farmers, the modern crossbreeds were sacred in their profitability. Welfare came second to fast growth. Indoor rearing of pigs was all the rage and only later did I realise how evident this was in the flavour of the meat. But now that an interest in traditional breeds has been revived, and free-range farming on a natural diet is seen as the way forward for premium pork, I can look forward to those roasts again and begin some kitchen adventures.

The higher cost of traditional, naturally reared pork means the roast loin becomes something of a luxury, though nowhere near the high cost of a joint of prime beef. I tend to look more at the cheap cuts, how they can be used in ways to nourish but not take the fat off my purse. Potted pork is an answer – packing cuts of meat into a terrine dish with herbs and a little marinade, cooking slowly, then pressing and cooling it. The potted pork – pâté to the French – will keep in the fridge for two weeks, a bountiful supply of exceptional meat at low cost that does lunches and suppers or occasional snacks for visitors.

Buying pork

Pigs are reared almost all over the country in abundance (though less in Scotland), so it should be easy to find a supplier from a farm close to your home. Buying locally reared, locally slaughtered pork not only reduces food miles and boosts the local economy, it is kinder to the pigs themselves, who suffer if they travel long distances. To find a local supplier such as a farm shop or butcher, see the food maps on www.bigbarn.co.uk, or seek out farmers' markets in your area by checking www.farmersmarkets.net or www.lfm.org.uk (for London markets). Recommended regional producers can also be found in the Shop Local archive link on www.roseprince.co.uk. To learn more about traditional breeds and to find a supplier or butcher near you, see the Rare Breeds Survival Trust website for a list of accredited butcher's shops: www.rbst.org.uk.

Roast Middle Loin of Pork

This is the prime lean cut – the most valuable on the pig. It is still reasonably priced enough, though, to choose this as a good cut to serve at a party. The whole loin, either with the bone in or boned and rolled, looks spectacular.

Ask the butcher to bone, roll and tie it and score the rind. I often ask the butcher to pare off the rind and then re-attach it with string, which makes it much easier to carve. I also always ask for the rib bones and roast the pork sitting on top of them, with large sprigs of sage, rosemary and thyme between the two.

For good crackling, boil a kettle and pour the water over the pork. This will open out the score marks and dry it a little. I then rub it with olive oil, which helps to soften the crust of the crackling without making it soggy. I have come round to this after some disappointments leaving it dry – which can often result in crackling that is hard and chewy.

Sprinkle the loin with salt and roast in an oven preheated to 200°C/400°F/Gas Mark 6 for about 20 minutes. Reduce the temperature to 160°C/325°F/Gas Mark 3 and cook for about 2½ hours. To test for doneness, insert a skewer deep into the meat and leave it there for a few moments. Test the temperature of the section of the skewer that was in the centre of the joint by tapping it quickly with your finger – if it is hot, the meat is thoroughly cooked. Remove from the oven and let it rest for 20 minutes before serving.

Roast Spare Rib of Pork Stuffed with Prunes

Ask the butcher to prepare this cheap cut for you, boning out the neck end and removing the rind (ask to keep it – it can be slow roasted to make pork scratchings). There is no need for the butcher to roll the meat – you will be doing this bit.

Lay the meat out on the worktop, skin-side down. Scatter about 12 prunes down the centre of the cut with a sprinkling of dried sage and some freshly ground black pepper. Roll up the pork and tie tightly in several places with kitchen string. Roast in an oven preheated to 200°C/400°F/Gas Mark 6 for about 10 minutes, then reduce the temperature to 160°C/325°F/Gas Mark 3 and cook for approximately 1¼ hours (for a 1.25kg/2¾lb joint of meat).

To check if it is done, insert a skewer deep into the meat and leave it there for a few moments. Test the temperature of the section of the skewer that was in the centre of the joint, tapping it quickly with your finger – if it is hot, the meat is thoroughly cooked. Remove the meat from the oven and let it rest for 20 minutes before serving.

Roast pork leftovers

Warm Pork Sandwiches with Apple Sauce

More leftovers, this time in my daughter Lara's favourite way. Use tart eating apples or cooking apples for the sauce.

55g/2oz butter	For the apple sauce:
4 thick slices of cold roast pork	6 apples, peeled, cored and
4 fresh bread rolls, split in half	quartered
rocket leaves	juice of ½ lemon
freshly ground black pepper	

To make the sauce, put the apples in a pan with 4 tablespoons of water, place over a medium heat and cook until soft. Stir in the lemon juice and set aside to cool.

Melt the butter in the frying pan and fry the pork slices over a medium heat so they reheat gently. Put a warm slice in each bread roll, spoon in some sauce and add a handful of rocket. Season with black pepper and serve.

Cold Pork with Anchovy and Caper Sauce

Carve the pork as thinly as possible to make this salad a success.

Serves 4

350g/12oz cold roast pork, sliced as
   thinly as possible

For the sauce:
2 egg yolks
1 teaspoon Dijon mustard
300ml/½ pint extra virgin olive oil

2 tablespoons lemon juice
4–6 anchovies, depending on
   preference
2 tablespoons capers, rinsed and
   squeezed dry, then chopped
leaves from 8 sprigs of parsley, finely
   chopped
3 hardboiled eggs, finely chopped
ground white pepper

Arrange the pork slices on a large plate. To make the sauce, put the egg yolks in a mixing bowl and add the mustard, then begin to whisk in the oil bit by bit – starting with a teaspoonful at a time and progressing to larger amounts. Each time oil is added, give it a good whisk so it emulsifies. An electric mixer will speed things up. When nearly all the oil has been incorporated, add the lemon juice. Whisk again and add the rest of the oil. Season with a pinch of white pepper. Pat the anchovies on kitchen paper to remove excess oil, then chop them finely and add to the sauce with the capers and parsley. Fold in the chopped hardboiled eggs. If the sauce is very thick, let it down with a little water – you need to be able to pour it, but slowly. Dress the pork with the sauce, zigzagging it over the surface. Serve with watercress or peppery leaves such as rocket, or sorrel if you can find it.

Potted Pork with Basil

The most humble of the 'potted' recipes on the New English Table. This is food I live off. Potted pork in the fridge means money saved for treats and feasts – it means the odd dish of langoustines or a wild mushroom or two. It is my essential protein when balancing the scale between fast and feast. The pig's liver in the recipe is optional. It is unusual for butchers to have it on the counter so you may need to order it. They may ask you to buy a whole liver (about 2.5kg/5lb in weight). If you have freezer space, this is well worth it not only because pig's liver is cheap but because it adds richness to the taste and texture of the potted pork. It is also worth asking the butcher to prepare (mince and chop) the pork for you, as it will then take little time to prepare after the meat is marinated.

    You will need a very large ceramic rectangular or oval terrine dish with a lid – approximately 30cm/12 inches long. Alternatively, use one or two metal loaf tins, using aluminium foil as a lid.

Serves 10–12 generously

- 1.5kg/3¼lb fresh pork (lean belly or shoulder), half of it cut into 1cm/½ inch chunks, half minced
- 125g/4½oz pork liver, minced or chopped very small in a food processor (optional)
- 100ml/3½fl oz sherry (not too sweet), or vermouth or white wine
- 30g/1oz softened butter
- 10 very thin rashers of unsmoked (green) streaky bacon
- 20 basil leaves
- sea salt and freshly ground black pepper

Put the pork cubes, mince and liver into a bowl with the liquor and leave to marinate for 1 hour.

Preheat the oven to 200°C/400°F/Gas Mark 6. Grease a terrine dish with the butter and line it neatly with the bacon rashers, laying them across the width of the dish. Now put half the marinated meat in the terrine, followed by a good layer of basil leaves, then the rest of the pork, remembering to season with a little salt and pepper as you go. Wrap any stray pieces of bacon around the meat.

Cover with a lid or foil, place in a roasting tin containing 3cm/1¼ inches of boiled water and bake for 1½ hours; the meat should be shrinking away from the sides of the dish when done. Add more water to the tin if it evaporates during cooking. Remove from the oven, place a weight on top and leave to cool, then refrigerate. The potted pork will keep, wrapped, in the fridge for at least a week.

 Kitchen note
Omit the basil and add about 6 semi-dried Smyrna figs, trimmed of their stalks and pre-soaked in white wine until soft, placing them in a line down the centre of the pâté so that every slice shows a little bit of fig. Scatter thyme leaves in among the figs.

Alternatively, replace the sherry with Pernod and place 2 star anise in the bottom of the dish before layering.

Things to eat with potted pork

Toast

Self-explanatory, but toast looks good torn, rather than cut, in half. Sourdough and seeded or wholewheat breads are especially good with preserved things.

Butter and Radishes

See page 358.

Leek Jam

1 litre/1¾ pints white wine vinegar
1kg/2¼lb golden granulated sugar
1 bay leaf
12 coriander seeds

6 white peppercorns
1kg/2¼lb young leeks, cut into
1cm/½ inch dice

Bring the vinegar and sugar to the boil, adding the bay and spices. Allow to bubble until the liquid reduces a little, becoming a syrup. Add the leeks, bring to the boil and turn off the heat. Put into jars and seal.

Pickled Pears

See page 259. Good for all pork-based pâtés, and will go with duck, too.

Lettuce with Dressing

Any lettuce, even the flabbiest oh-so-English kind, is good beside potted things *provided it is covered in a decent dressing*. This one works:

Dressing for green salad:

2 tablespoons Dijon mustard
1 teaspoon sugar
½ teaspoon sea salt
1 garlic clove, peeled and cut in half

3 tablespoons white wine vinegar flavoured with tarragon, or red wine vinegar
9 tablespoons extra virgin olive oil
1 tablespoon cold water
freshly ground black pepper

Put all the ingredients in a bowl and whisk until emulsified. Leave for a while so the garlic infuses the dressing. Store any excess in a sealed jar in the fridge.

Cucumber Pickle

1 cucumber, halved lengthways, deseeded and very finely sliced
115g/4oz golden granulated sugar
8 shallots, chopped
1 teaspoon sea salt

1 teaspoon ground white pepper
1 tablespoon yellow mustard seeds
2 green chillies, deseeded and chopped
300ml/½ pint white wine vinegar

Put all the ingredients in a saucepan, bring to the boil and cook for about 5 minutes, until the cucumber slices have softened but not fallen apart. Spoon into jars and store in the fridge.

Kitchen note
The above companions for potted pork are also good with potted rabbit (see page 356), or put them on the table when you are having one of those cold meat and baked potato lunches.

Pork Chump Chops Braised with Lentils, Cider and Cream

A quick braise of cheap chops to throw together on returning home.

Serves 4

2 tablespoons extra virgin olive oil
4 large or 8 small pork chops, the fat
    trimmed off
1 onion, chopped
2 eating apples, cored and grated
1 small sprig of rosemary
200g/7oz brown Italian lentils

300ml/½ pint dry cider
300ml/½ pint chicken stock (or more)
    (see page 116)
1 teaspoon Dijon mustard
2–4 tablespoons double cream, to
    taste
leaves from 1 sprig of tarragon
sea salt and freshly ground black
    pepper

Heat the oil in a large pan and brown the pork chops on both sides. Add the onion, apples and rosemary and cook until the onion is soft. Add the lentils, then the cider and stock, bring to the boil and simmer for about 45 minutes, until the pork chops are tender and the lentils cooked. Add more liquid during cooking if the braise becomes too dry. Taste and add salt if necessary. Add freshly ground black pepper, then the mustard and cream. Serve with the tarragon leaves stirred in.

Raised Pork and Duck Pie

The thought of making a raised pie may fill you with dread but it is a way to fill an afternoon of cooking that leaves a heady sense of achievement. I usually make the stock for the jelly the previous day, partly to lighten the load of the recipe, so I can enjoy the construction part of making the pie, and partly to check that it is going to set, which it should. If it doesn't, soak 2 gelatine leaves in cold water for 10 minutes, squeeze them out and add to the stock when it is warm and you are about to pour it into the pie. Make sure the gelatine is well mixed and dissolved before you pour.

Serves 8–12

For the jelly:
900g/2lb pork bones
2 pig's trotters
1 onion, peeled
2 carrots
1 celery stick
1 bay leaf
1 litre/1¾ pints water
lemon juice, to taste
sea salt and freshly ground black
    pepper

For the filling:
1kg/2¼lb boned duck leg meat, left in
    large pieces (or substitute chicken
    leg meat, game, rabbit or hare)
800g/1¾lb boned pork shoulder, half
    minced, half cut in 1cm/½ inch
    cubes

250g/9oz raw smoked gammon, cut
    into small dice
4 sage leaves, chopped
a large pinch of ground coriander
a large pinch of grated nutmeg
12 fennel seeds
1 wineglass of white wine
250g/9oz thinly sliced smoked streaky
    bacon or pancetta
sea salt and freshly ground black
    pepper

For the pastry:
900g/2lb plain flour, plus extra for
    dusting
2 egg yolks
1 teaspoon fine sea salt
2 tablespoons icing sugar
400g/14oz unsalted butter, melted
300ml/½ pint iced water
1 egg, beaten, to glaze

To make the jelly, put the pork bones, trotters, vegetables, bay leaf and water in a pan and bring to the boil. Turn down to a simmer and cook for 3 hours. Strain through a sieve, return the liquid to the pan and boil hard until reduced by half. Season with a squeeze of lemon, some black pepper and salt. Leave to cool, then refrigerate if not using immediately.

Meanwhile, put all the filling ingredients apart from the bacon, salt and pepper in a bowl and leave to marinate for 1 hour.

To make the pastry, put the flour in a mixing bowl with the egg yolks, salt and icing sugar and add the melted butter. Mix well with a wooden spoon until you have a crumb texture. Add the water and continue to mix (you could do this in an electric mixer at low speed) until a soft dough forms. Wrap in cling film and chill for 1 hour.

Preheat the oven to 150°C/300°F/Gas Mark 2. Roll out two-thirds of the pastry on a floured board to about 5mm/¼ inch thick. Use to line a large, round cake tin, approximately 25cm/10 inches in diameter, making sure there are no cracks or holes and letting the pastry overlap the sides. Line the pie with the bacon slices. Season the filling with salt and pepper, then pile it into the lined tin, making a nice mound shape. Roll out the last piece of pastry to fit the top of the tin, brush the edges with beaten egg and lay it on top of the meat. Pinch the edges together and trim if necessary. Brush the pie with egg wash.

Pierce the centre of the pie with a knife, making a small hole. Cut a strip of leftover pastry about 7.5cm/3 inches long and 1.5cm/⅔ inch wide. Roll it into a little cylindrical chimney, using more egg wash as glue, then position it over the hole in the lid, pressing down gently so it sticks. The hole in it needs to be large enough for the liquid jelly to be poured in after the pie is baked. Decorate the pie with leftover pastry, making flower shapes and leaves, etc. Stick each piece on using beaten egg. Brush the whole surface with egg again, then place in the oven straight away and bake for about 2 hours. If the surface becomes too brown, lay a sheet of foil on top.

Allow the pie to become completely cold before pouring in the jelly. If the jelly has set, warm it carefully until just runny – don't pour boiling-hot jelly into the pie. Put a funnel in the pastry 'chimney', then carefully pour in the jelly about a tablespoon at a time. Be careful that it does not overflow. Put the pie in the fridge for a couple of hours to set. Serve sliced, with any of the pickles and other accompaniments for Potted Pork (see page 325).

Braised Hand of Pork with Wine

The 'hand' is a cut taken from the shoulder of the pig. The meat has a wide grain and is best for slow braising. It's an easy job; ask the butcher to part-bone and roll the hand, put it in a casserole with 2 wineglasses of white wine, 2 peeled, halved onions, 2 halved carrots, a chopped celery stick, a few sprigs of parsley, a bay leaf, a star anise and 6 black peppercorns. Cover with meat stock or water, bring to the boil, then turn down to a simmer, cover with a lid and cook for about 2 hours, until the pork is tender. Lift out the pork and keep warm. Skim the fat off the cooking liquid, then strain it into a clean pan. Boil the stock until it reduces, becoming richer to taste. Add salt if necessary, and black pepper.

To serve, cut the string off the meat, remove the rind, then cut the pork into generous chunks. Bring the stock back to the boil and add the meat. Eat with plenty of mashed potato, or boiled new potatoes, and a good handful of chopped parsley. You could serve it with butterbeans (see page 40) or lentils (see page 253).

POTATOES

Whipped Potatoes with Lancashire Cheese
Potato and Fresh Cheese in an Olive Oil Pastry Pie

Lamb's wool for the tummy, a few good potato dishes are always needed to please and warm. The quest, though, is to find good potatoes that taste of rather more than starch. Relief sets in when I see the first red-skinned Desiree potatoes. Their yellow flesh has a flavour so citrus it makes sense that potatoes are a rich source of vitamin C.

I have written a lot in the past about monoculture, and especially in terms of the potato. In a bid to please the big buyers of potatoes for processing (into frozen catering products and potato crisps), British farmers have narrowed down the choice to so few that we are left with little to choose from but Maris Piper and King Edwards. For salads, the Charlotte is everywhere.

The loss of potato varieties is a loss of diversity – a factor that leads to environmental problems. Growing only one or two types encourages heavy use of chemicals, too. In a monoculture, diseases can take hold and wipe out a huge crop, so farmers blanket spray or treat as 'insurance'. In a polyculture, lots of varieties are grown, each coming into season one after the other. If one crop develops problems, another may not.

But the world of potatoes is becoming more interesting again, with farms growing traditional or new breeds. There is even a crisp manufacturer, Burt's, that makes seasonal potato crisps depending on what is cropping. It is all to the good, and some supermarkets are following suit. So the message is, be bold with potatoes, venture out and experiment. And remember to buy the butter when you are out shopping, too.

Buying potatoes

Waitrose and Sainsbury have both made impressive efforts to sell a wider variety, many of which are organically grown. Organic potatoes are also a good farmers' market buy, but remember to take a trolley or your arms will suffer. Keep an eye out, too, for roadside sales – local farmers will often put some sacks out with an honesty box for the cash. This is the way to potato bargains. For special, traditional-breed potatoes, you can buy all sorts direct from Carroll's Heritage Potatoes in Northumberland (www.heritage-potatoes.co.uk; tel: 01890 883060 or 8803833). They also sell to shops, so call for stockists.

Which potato to use

A bag might label the potatoes inside as 'floury' or 'salad' potatoes but, with the gradually increasing number of renaissance breeds available, here is a guide that will help identify the appearance, flavour and uses of both the familiar main crop and the rarer types. It was compiled with the help of Carroll's, the farm responsible for reviving the lost, weird and wonderful historic breeds.

Unusual potatoes to eat in a salad

Ratte A long, finger-shaped potato with white flesh and yellow skin. Be careful not to overcook it; it is best to stop boiling when it still feels slightly underdone.

Pink Fir Apple Another long shape, this time pink skinned but with knobbly eyes. Like the Ratte, it is susceptible to overcooking despite its waxy texture.

Roseval A beautiful, blushing-pink potato with yellow flesh, which is adored by the French for its fruity flavour; delicious and colourful with mayonnaise.

Salad Blue Early Dark blue skin and flesh, pretty in a salad with green leaves, peas or broad beans.

Unusual potatoes to eat boiled and hot

Sharpe's Express A white-skinned, pear-shaped potato with lemony, pure white flesh.
Jersey Royal A kidney-shaped potato tasting of lemon and minerals, classically eaten with butter and mint.
Red Duke of York Bright red skin and yellow, full-flavoured flesh.
Arran Victory One of the many blue-skinned, blue-fleshed potatoes.
Yukon Gold A yellow American variety, tasting strongly of butter.
Red King Edward A red-skinned, less usual version of a King Edward. Good boiled, then served bashed, not mashed, with butter, beside boiled ham and parsley sauce.
Epicure A delicious potato with a traditional-looking bumpy surface.
Romano A red-skinned Italian potato normally boiled in its skin and made into gnocchi. Ideal for the potato pie on page 339.

Unusual potatoes to roast, mash or fry

Dunar Rover A very rare potato with extra-floury flesh.
British Queen A round potato with white skin and an unusually high number of eyes; peeling is recommended.
Red King Edward A red-skinned version of the ubiquitous supermarket potato.
Mr Little's Yetholm Gypsy Patches of blue, red and white on the skin, with white, floury flesh.
Shetland Black Mottled black flesh and skin; makes a striking plate of chips.

Common or garden potatoes

All-purpose potatoes *(but no good in salad)* King Edward, Maris Piper, Desiree.
Potatoes to eat in salad Nicola, Charlotte, Maris Peer.
Potatoes to eat boiled, mashed, roast and hot Saxon, Nadine, Estima.
Potatoes to bake Cara, Marfona, Estima.
Potatoes to roast Wilja (the best, in my opinion), Desiree, King Edward.

Whipped Potatoes with Lancashire Cheese

It is only right to credit the Aubrac region of France for this wonderful potato recipe. Its real name is *l'aligot* (pronounced lally-got). It is mashed potato, with added garlic and cream, briskly whipped over the heat while adding handfuls of loose-textured cheese. A spoonful of it lifts out of the pan in steaming, glorious strings. It is truly the best way to eat potatoes as a dish in their own right on a cold day; pure, cuddly cashmere. It is also good with rare roast beef. Follow with a big green salad.

In France this dish is made in a copper pan but any heavy-bottomed pan will do (it is important that the potato does not burn during the whipping phase).

Traditionally, *l'aligot* is made with the Aubrac's own *tomme* cheese, Laguiole, which is hard to buy in the UK, but *tommes* or Cantal cheese from France's other high regions will do. On experimentation, Mrs Kirkham's Lancashire cheese, which is also loose textured and slightly wet, is the closest British alternative.

Serves at least 6

800g/1¾lb floury potatoes, peeled and cut into chunks
2 tablespoons softened unsalted butter
1 small garlic clove, grated
2 tablespoons crème fraîche
600g/1lb 5oz Lancashire cheese, chopped into small squares
sea salt

Boil the potatoes in salted water until tender, then drain and put through a mouli-légumes, or grate them. Do not use a food processor because it will make them go gluey; a handheld masher is better than that. Put the potatoes back in the pan and place over a very low heat. Add the butter, garlic and crème fraîche and beat with a wooden spoon. Add the cheese a handful at a time, stirring constantly in a figure-of-eight pattern – local cooks insist on this. Once all the cheese has been incorporated, taste for salt and serve immediately.

Potato and Fresh Cheese in an Olive Oil Pastry Pie

Paper-thin olive oil pastry, filled with mashed potato and cheeses. Don't be alarmed by the method for the pastry. It is easy to handle with a little patience and the results are good enough for applause.

Serves 8

4 medium-sized red-skinned
   potatoes, such as Romano or
   Desiree
1 egg
100g/3½oz loose-textured cheese,
   such as Lancashire, Cheshire or
   Wensleydale, grated

115g/4oz ricotta or cottage cheese,
   drained for an hour on a cloth
150ml/¼ pint double cream
30g/1oz butter
1 quantity of Olive Oil Pastry (see
   page 280)
extra virgin olive oil for brushing

Cook the potatoes whole in boiling water until tender. Drain and leave to cool, then rub off the skins. Pass the flesh through a mouli-légumes (or a potato ricer), then beat in the egg, cheeses, cream and butter.

Preheat the oven to 190°C/375°F/Gas Mark 5. Roll out the pastry into a large, thin round. You will find it very elastic and pliable. Use your hands to stretch it further until it is very thin, and approximately 75cm/30 inches in diameter. Place it over a baking sheet lined with baking parchment, spoon the filling into the centre and spread it into a round approximately 30cm/12 inches in diameter. Bring the pastry edges up and over the filling towards the centre; stretch them if necessary. Pinch the pastry folds into the centre but leave a little hole so steam can escape as the pie cooks. Brush the surface with the oil and bake for approximately 30 minutes, until golden. Serve hot or cold.

PRAWNS AND SHRIMPS

Prawn Salad with Raw Apple, Rhubarb and
    Walnut Oil
Pint of Shell-on Prawns with Scrumpy Butter
Shrimp (or Prawn) Shell Broth with Ale and
    Straw Mushrooms
Potted Shrimps with Egg Pasta
Prawn and Shrimp Stock
Mathias's Prawn Curry with Coconut 'Tea'

Since I discovered that it is fine to eat plenty of North Atlantic prawns, as their number is not in danger, it has been something of a binge. Once defrosted carefully, so that the salty glaze that is there to protect them in the freezer drains away, the pink prawn can be added to the pan with garlic, olive oil and other flavours; or stirred into a curry at the last minute; or used in a salad with leaves and herbs; or marinated with lemon and oil for a recherché starter (see Mushroom Salad with Lemon, Parsley and Prawns, page 265) – yet they still taste as if they were added fresh. The price is reasonably low, and a few seem to go a long way.

    Less everyday are the rich-tasting brown shrimps that are native to British coastal areas, and whose tiny frames are mostly picked and potted with butter and spices. It is possible to buy these shrimps peeled and plain, but expect to pay quite a high price for them.

    In spite of being farmed and harvested in the tropics, warm-water tiger and king prawns seem very much more visible than Atlantic prawns when food shopping, and especially in restaurants. In Asian restaurants, it would be a shock not to see them on the menu. But these are the problem prawns. Farming them has dire effects on the coastal landscape, polluting water with sulphates and other chemicals and medicines used in aquaculture. Coastal mangrove forest is cleared to make way for the ponds or is damaged by effluent, removing yet more essential oxygen-puffing greenery from the surface of the planet. And then there is the people element. The journalist

Felicity Lawrence made the shocking discovery that there is nothing lucrative in tiger prawn farming for farmers in developing countries. It is a very high-risk business that has left many of them destitute.

However, I have found a source of farmed prawns that I can feel happy about buying and they are worth highlighting because they are widely available in the UK. They are reared organically in northern Madagascar by a visionary Malagasy, Mathias Ismail. When I went to see his farm in 2007, I was shown verified records demonstrating that soil, water and vegetation are healthy in the area. The water is as clean when it leaves the ponds as it is when it comes in from the river. The prawns are loosely stocked (no more than 240g/8½oz prawns to 1.3 tonnes of water) and are given an organic-certified feed. An obvious bonus is that they taste good and are 'clean' – you do not need to remove the black gut that runs down the back of conventional prawns and which may be contaminated.

The 'people' element of this story is truly heartening. Ismail employs 900 local people on a rate much higher than the minimum wage. He offers training to those who want skilled jobs, skills they could one day have the opportunity to use elsewhere. His company provides water and plantations of non-mangrove species firewood to the surrounding villages and has built a school and medical centre. It is a happy place – not put on for the visiting journalist. Locals who had nothing are buying their own bicycles and can now pay for their children's schooling. He also leaves alone those who prefer their traditional way of life and do not want to be modernised. All this was verified by Andrew Mallinson, marine specialist (not fish buyer) at Marks & Spencer, who I have mentioned before in this book (see Mackerel, page 255). He has policed the standards and monitored this new project with Ismail from the beginning, five years ago. I am going on about this a bit because it is the first time that anyone has achieved 'clean' tiger prawn farming and shown that aquaculture can have genuine sociological benefits. For more information about Ismail's prawns, see www.madagascar-gambas.com.

Buying prawns and shrimps

I buy shell-on North Atlantic prawns from fishmongers, keeping an eye out for excessive shell, tail and feeler damage – they are usually trimmed of their feet, which is a pity. At least buying them with the shells on determines that they come straight to the UK and have not taken a detour to Asia for processing. Peeled ones are widely available and vary in quality – the larger ones seem to be the best. Young's prawns are recommended. They are fished off the coast of Greenland, frozen as soon as they are caught, then defrosted, cooked, peeled and refrozen in Greenland before being transported to the UK by boat.

Potted brown shrimps are widely available, in supermarkets and specialist food shops, but it is more economical to buy them via mail order. James Baxter & Sons pots brown shrimps caught in Morecambe Bay, cooking and peeling them, then smothering them in spiced butter. There is a minimum order of 10 pots; phone on 01524 410910. Furness Fish, Poultry and Game will also send potted shrimps and can provide peeled, cooked shrimps, too: www.morecambebayshrimps.com; tel: 015395 59544.

Bridgewater Bay prawns are available only in summer, from a tiny shop run by the prawn fishermen who fish on the mud flats: Stolford Fishermen's Shop, Bridgewater Bay, Somerset TA5 1TW; tel: 01278 652297. Drop in if you are in the area, but call in advance to check that they are open.

Mathias Ismail's organic tiger prawns are available raw and frozen from Marks & Spencer stores throughout the UK (not always in their smaller shops, though). They are transported to the UK by boat. For Marks & Spencer product enquiries, phone 0845 302 1234.

Prawn Salad with Raw Apple, Rhubarb and Walnut Oil

A trip to Somerset to visit the prawn fishermen on Bridgewater Bay provided inspiration for the following two recipes. Not sure what to eat the cooked prawns with, I dropped into a farm shop where Somerset's crop of apples and summer fruit was piled high. The raw fruit and prawns dressed with walnut oil made an unusual salad, a happy accident, which I recommend.

Serves 4 as a starter or light lunch

2 British apples, cored and very thinly sliced, then tossed with a little lemon juice

2 sticks of green rhubarb, cut into very thin slices

1 spring onion, sliced

4 tablespoons walnut oil

1 teaspoon cider vinegar

350g/12oz shelled, cooked prawns or shrimps

sea salt and freshly ground black pepper

Combine the apples with the rhubarb and spring onion. Shake together the walnut oil, vinegar, a pinch of sea salt and some pepper in a jar with a lid and pour over the salad ingredients. Mix well, divide between 4 plates, then scatter an equal amount of prawns on to each one.

Pint of Shell-on Prawns with Scrumpy Butter

Part two of the Somerset prawn experiment (see page 343) took a strong apple liquor as the base for a butter sauce. Highly successful, and further confirmation that raw materials that share a landscape are happy on a plate together, too.

Use strong dry cider or white wine in place of the scrumpy, if you wish.

Serves 4

4 pints of shell-on pink prawns, or
   brown shrimps (brown shrimps are
   more fiddly so serve a smaller
   amount, for a starter)
1 shallot, chopped

2 blades of mace
5 tablespoons scrumpy
175g/6oz unsalted English butter,
   softened and cut into chunks
sea salt and freshly ground black
   pepper

Divide the prawns between 4 bowls. Put the shallot, mace and scrumpy in a small pan, bring to the boil and simmer until the liquid has reduced by half. Strain, reserving the liquid. Put the liquid back in the pan with a piece of the mace and place over a low heat. Whisk in the butter, piece by piece, until you have a smooth, yellow sauce. Add salt to taste and a little black pepper. Divide between 4 small dishes and serve as a dipping sauce for the prawns as you peel them. Put plenty of napkins or finger bowls on the table. Reserve the prawn shells for soup (see page 347).

Shrimp (or Prawn) Shell Broth with Ale and Straw Mushrooms

The easiest use for fresh leftover shells that still hold the flavour of the shrimps or prawns. For 2 people, put a handful of shells in a pan, cover with 300ml/½ pint water and bring to the boil. Simmer for no more than 20 minutes, then add some little straw or fairy ring mushrooms, or very thinly sliced button mushrooms. Pour in about 100ml/3½fl oz real ale, simmer for 5 minutes, then taste for salt and serve. You could be more extravagant and make this with Japanese sake instead of beer, if you wish, and scatter on chopped chillies for piquancy.

Potted Shrimps with Egg Pasta

I had never thought of it before but of course potted shrimps from Morecambe Bay are an instant pasta sauce. For 4 people, cook 400g/14oz egg pasta (thin linguine is best) in boiling salted water until tender, then drain. Divide between 4 bowls and put an individual serving of potted shrimps on each; add a little chopped red chilli and some parsley.

Prawn and Shrimp Stock

Make a stock, and you will extract further value from the leftover shells of all prawns and shrimps. Put the heads, legs and shells from approximately 500g/1lb 2oz prawns or shrimps into a large pan with two tablespoons of olive oil or butter and fry until they are pale gold. You can add a few chopped vegetables (carrot, celery, onion) and a wineglass of wine if available. Add 1 litre/1¾ pints water and bring to the boil, skimming away any foam that rises. Turn down to a simmer and cook for 20 minutes. Strain the stock and use in rice dishes and soups. (See photograph overleaf.)

Mathias's Prawn Curry with Coconut 'Tea'

We ate this light, fragrant curry in Madagascar. The use of coconut tea is the secret – it has none of the fattiness of many coconut-based curries.

Serves 4

100g/3½oz desiccated coconut
750ml/1¼ pints boiling water
3 tomatoes
2 tablespoons sunflower oil
1 heaped tablespoon medium-strength Madras curry powder
2 spring onions, chopped
½ cucumber, peeled, halved lengthways, deseeded and cut into chunks

24 tiger 'bikini' prawns (that is, head and tail left on, back shell removed)
2 red chillies, deseeded and chopped
a few fennel seeds, crushed, or fresh fennel flowers if available (or use the soft leaves from a fennel bulb, chopped)
sea salt

Put the desiccated coconut in a bowl, pour over the water and leave to steep for 20 minutes. Nick each tomato with a knife and put in a bowl. Pour over boiling water to cover, leave for 1 minute, then drain and remove the skins, which should come away easily. Halve the tomatoes, discard the seeds, then slice. Set to one side.

Heat the oil in a large pan, add the curry powder and cook over a low heat for 1 minute. Add the spring onions and the tomatoes. Strain the coconut water, discarding the pulp. Add the coconut 'tea' to the pan. Bring to the boil and add the cucumber and prawns. Simmer until the prawns change to pink and feel firm when squeezed. Add salt to taste, scatter with the chopped chillies and fennel and serve with steamed rice.

QUINCE

Roast Quince

A perfect example of a lost fruit, one that was once grown in our orchards but gave way to easy-to-eat apples and pears. It might resemble those fruits but in fact is nothing like them. To eat a quince raw would be a good moment to phone a dentist. They are rocks until cooked. Imported *membrillo*, the quince paste made to eat with cheeses and dry-cured meats, is quite well known but, as quince trees become fashionable to grow again in the UK, a British quince supply might burgeon. The quince you can buy are usually imported from Spain, Portugal or the southern Mediterranean. They are larger than the British ones and suffer often for looking good but lacking the heavenly fragrance of the real thing.

Buying quince

Your best bet is to look in farmers' markets during the picking season in September and October; you may see them in greengrocer's shops but they are likely to be imports from Spain or the Middle East. British quinces are barely grown commercially, so do not pass through the markets that supply the greengrocers, but you may be lucky and have a local supplier selling them to high-street shops.

Roast Quince

Once roasted, quince can be eaten with both sweet and savoury things. They are good with game birds and roast pork, but also with vanilla ice cream.

Preheat the oven to 200°C/400°F/Gas Mark 6. Wash 4 quince, rubbing away any dusty flock on their skins. Quarter each quince, holding it firmly and using a knife with a strong blade. Boil the quinces in water for about 3–5 minutes, until just soft. Drain them, then cut out the hard core from each quarter. Brush with melted butter, then place in an ovenproof dish and roast until golden. Add sugar as they come out of the oven if you are eating them sweet, or leave the sugar out if you are serving them with meat, or eat hot and sour with cheese.

To serve the quince with ice cream, I make a sauce with 115g/4oz butter, 115g/4oz brown sugar, ½ lemon grass stalk, chopped, and 1 wineglass of sweet wine or other unused Christmas-present liquor. Boil the ingredients together until you have a slightly thickened sauce to pour over the quince and ice cream.

RABBIT

Potted Rabbit with Pork, Rosemary, Pink Pepper and Lemon

A meat that is so dismissed it is a crime. Rabbit was superseded by cheap, intensively farmed meat, has had its reputation trashed by myxomatosis and has generally been ignored. But the corpse is twitching, if you'll forgive the inauspicious reference. I have bought several prepared (that is, skinned and paunched – or gutted) rabbits from butchers and farmers' markets, all as fresh as can be. This is essential with rabbit, whose meat can taint in no time unless it is eaten quickly (within about three days of being killed). I have, however, also bought decent rabbit that has been blast frozen straight after killing, which retains its fresh taste.

The countryside is no longer ridden with rabbits – myxomatosis saw to that in the 1950s and 60s – although farmers may disagree. It was wrong to attack rabbits with germ warfare, just as it has been wrong to deal with weeds slash-and-burn-style with herbicides. The balance between Nature and human nature was shifted to panic mode of all-out warfare. The over-population problem was blamed on a public aversion to eating an animal people had had no choice but to consume endlessly throughout the War years. But I blame the cooks. Rabbit needs careful handling and seasoning. It is no good chucking rabbit fricassee on the table each day if it is dry, tastes and smells as if it has been delayed on its way to the pot and, worse, is branded chicken. I am thinking of my schooldays, when a glaringly obvious rabbit bone, or a rib cage, would turn up in the stew and our complaints were ignored.

But a fresh young rabbit – and you are advised to interact with the butcher, stallholder or mail-order service on the subject of age – is a bunny you can roast gently with butter and herbs and a paring of lemon rind. After cooking, let it rest in a warm place while you place the roasting tin over the heat and pour in wine, scrape to get the bits off the bottom of the tin, then finish with cream and mustard. It's an easy dish. A little more of a challenge is a potted version (see page 356), a ready supply of slices of cold rabbit and pork to eat with salad or toast.

Few rabbits are farmed in the UK. The farmed rabbit that you see in butcher's shops will most likely have been imported from Europe, and just as likely reared intensively in cramped conditions. I have only found 'farmhouse'-style rabbits (those that are hand reared slowly) for sale in artisan farmers' markets when on holiday in France. Farmed rabbit is very easy to eat – 'delicate', some would call it – but it could also be described as bland. It is a pity no enterprising farmer has explored the possibility of reviving the Roman-style enclosures that were once a useful source of inexpensive meat for country people.

Buying rabbit

Rabbit are in season all year round. Ask first at the butcher's; they will certainly get rabbit for you if they have a game licence. Various specialist game merchants will send fresh rabbit to you direct. Try Everleigh Farm Shop (www.everleighfarmshop.co.uk; tel: 01264 850344), Yorkshire Game (www.yorkshiregame.co.uk; tel: 01748 810212) or The Thoroughly Wild Meat Company (www.thoroughlywildmeat.co.uk; tel: 01963 824788 or 07770 392041).

Potted Rabbit with Pork, Rosemary, Pink Pepper and Lemon

Who could have imagined rabbit to be so glamorous? The aromas of pink pepper and lemon, the neat layers that look so pretty when you cut the first slice – this is a dish that does more than respect the modest rabbit.

Serves 8

1kg/2¼lb fresh pork (shoulder or lean belly), minced
the filleted meat from 1 fresh, wild rabbit, cut into strips
1 wineglass of white wine
grated zest of 1 lemon
about 1 teaspoon crushed pink peppercorns

3 garlic cloves, crushed with a little salt
leaves from 1 sprig of rosemary, plus 1 extra small rosemary sprig
leaves from 1 sprig of thyme
30g/1oz softened butter
12 very thin slices of green (unsmoked) streaky bacon
sea salt and freshly ground black pepper

Preheat the oven to 200°C/400°F/Gas Mark 6. Put the pork and rabbit into a bowl with the wine, lemon zest, pink peppercorns, garlic and herb leaves (except the small rosemary sprig) and leave to marinate for 1 hour. Use the butter to grease a terrine dish or loaf tin about 25cm/10 inches long by 10cm/4 inches wide. Put the single rosemary sprig in the bottom, then line it neatly with the streaky bacon, laying it across the width of the dish. Season the marinated meat mixture and put it into the terrine dish. Wrap any stray pieces of bacon around the meat. Cover with a lid or foil, place in a roasting tin and pour boiling water into the tin to a depth of 2cm/¾ inch. Place in the oven and bake for 1½ hours; the terrine is done when the meat shrinks away from the sides of the dish. Add more water to the tin if it evaporates during cooking. Remove from the oven, place a weight on top – 3 cans of beans or tomatoes will do – and leave to cool, then store in the fridge.

To serve, cut into 1cm/½ inch slices and accompany with lettuce – the rabbit's favourite food.

Radishes

Butter and Radishes
Radish and Horseradish Sauce

It always seemed a pity to cut off and throw away radish leaves, until one day tasting the green leaf of an especially fresh bunch changed all that. True, radish leaves can be a little prickly, but that disappears when they are dressed with oil. The fresher they are, the more of a peppery taste there will be. Using them as a bed for warm salads sees them wilt as gracefully as rocket. Have a go next time. Checking the leaves is a certain indication of freshness. The better the leaves, the better the root.

The radishes best known to us are, of course, the red English ones, the famous old variety being Scarlet Globe. This is a juicy (perhaps too juicy) sphere of a radish, with a thickish skin. Less liquid inside and more tender, yet with a sharp, peppery taste to finish, are French breakfast radishes, which are paler pink with a white tip. They are grown in the UK, along with the little red globes, and usually both will be on offer in shops. Other species include a white version of the salad radish, and winter radishes – great big tough, black things that are occasionally grown in the UK. When I think of radishes I often group them with beetroots, which have similar uses in salads when raw and very fresh. They could be substituted for pink radishes (grated, their young leaves chopped) in the Radish and Horseradish Sauce on page 358.

Butter and Radishes

Long-bodied French radishes, spread with a little of the very best-quality unsalted butter and dipped in Maldon sea salt, are the best friend to a plate of Potted Pork (see page 325) and toast. Put all the component parts – radishes, butter, salt – in three separate dishes and let everyone diy.

Radish and Horseradish Sauce

Get the radish family together for a salsa. It sounds terrible, but is irresistible when eaten with grilled mackerel, sardines, pork, beef or chicken.

Serves 4

1 bunch of radishes (about 20), with their leaves
5cm/2 inch piece of fresh horseradish
2 spring onions, chopped

juice of 1 lemon
1 teaspoon English or French mustard, whichever preferred
6 tablespoons extra virgin olive oil
sea salt and freshly ground black pepper

Separate the leaves from the radishes, then chop both leaves and radishes into small dice. Put them in a bowl. Grate the horseradish into the bowl and add the remaining ingredients. Stir well and leave for 20 minutes or so, until the flavours have amalgamated.

RICE – Short Grain

Tomato Rice

The process of cooking rice while continuously adding meat stock, letting the rice absorb it before adding more, has become so embedded in daily cookery it almost feels like our own. In truth, rice has been eaten in the UK for over 1,000 years, so we can make some claim to it as 'ours', even as an import. I almost hate to use the word risotto now that the dish is on every other restaurant menu. Rich yet healthy, infused with ingredients such as mushrooms, beef marrow, shellfish, broad beans, asparagus... Few recipes have such richness and elegance yet cost so little to make. Maybe it is vulgar always to look at the price tag on a dish, but perhaps it is snobbery not to. It's a matter of some pride, as far as this cook who lives with a budget-wary man is concerned, that a basic risotto comes in at 24 pence per helping, based on using 75g/2¾oz rice per person. Keeping a little check on the spend always makes way for some extravagances – sometimes ones to add to the rice dish itself.

The stumpy grains of rice that are the hard core of risotto-style dishes fall into two main types. Arborio becomes soft and soupy after the cooking process, releasing its starch nicely into the dish like soap left in water; Carnaroli stays slightly chewy and heavier, even when it has taken in as much liquid as it can. For this reason I began using it more for a while, as insurance against overcooking. I went back to Arborio, though. For an effect as sublime as it delivers, it deserves us cooks to be reliable and stand over the pot, adding and stirring, waiting for the moment when it has to go into the bowl. Cancel all jobs until the dish is made.

I used to make rice pudding with short grain rice, until I went to India and had it made with basmati, whose extra fragrance adds something special – see Brokens Pudding with Caramelised Pineapple (page 366).

Buying short grain rice

Two brands are widely available, both imported from northern Italy – Riso Scotti and Riso Gallo are recommended. Vialone Nano is a specialist breed that delivers a lovely creamy risotto, even more soupy than Arborio, and does not have Carnaroli's ability to stay *al dente*. You can buy the Gli Aironi or Principato di Lucidio brands of this and others direct from importers, Savoria, bagged up in cloth sacks (www.savoria.co.uk; tel: 0870 242 1823). Carluccio cafés are also a good source of rice, or try the top Spanish brand, Calasparra, which is used to make paella. For outlets, contact Brindisa (www.brindisa.com; tel: 020 8772 1600) – I have seen it in branches of Sainsbury and Budgen.

Tomato Rice

Made with chopped, deseeded fresh tomatoes and seasoned with basil and garlic, this is a light rice dish, pale pink in colour, that 'does tomatoes' in a subtle way. If you find that the tomato flavour will not come through due to them being too watery, add a few tablespoons of passata or a little tomato purée (but go carefully), or one or two chopped sundried tomatoes.

Serves 4

450g/1lb tomatoes, as ripe as possible
3 tablespoons extra virgin olive oil
1 garlic clove, chopped
1 white onion, chopped
300g/10½oz Arborio rice
1 wineglass of white or rosé wine

approximately 1 litre/1¾ pints beef, veal or chicken stock (see pages 64, 116) – you may need more
2 tablespoons softened butter
6–8 tablespoons freshly grated Parmesan, pecorino or Twineham Grange cheese
leaves from 1 sprig of basil, torn
sea salt and freshly ground black pepper

Put the tomatoes in a deep bowl, nicking each one with the tip of a knife as you go. Pour over boiling water from the kettle, making sure all the tomatoes are totally submerged. Leave for 1 minute, then drain and peel off the skins. Cut the tomatoes into quarters, remove and discard the seeds and chop the flesh.

Heat the oil in a large shallow pan and add the garlic and onion. Cook until soft but do not let them brown. Add the rice, stir to coat with the oil, then add the wine. Bring to a simmer over a medium heat and cook gently until the liquid is absorbed by the rice. Add the tomatoes, then begin to add the stock (it can be added cold or hot), ladle by ladle, stirring slowly but constantly and allowing the rice to come back to the boil and absorb the liquid in between each addition. Continue until the rice has absorbed enough liquid to become tender but not too soft – about 18–20 minutes from the moment you begin to add the stock. Stir in the butter, with 1 tablespoon of the cheese, making sure they are well mixed. Taste and season with salt and pepper. Serve the risotto immediately, with the basil and remaining cheese scattered over the top, and bread on the table.

RICE – Long Grain

Spiced Rice with Cauliflower, Coconut, Cloves
  and Ginger
Brokens Pudding with Caramelised Pineapple

Buying long grain rice is activism by shopping trolley. Buy American long grain and you support an intensive, high-tech farming system; buy long grain from a Far Eastern country and it is possible that it was grown by farmers labouring on a pathetic minimum wage. It's a world fraught with politics, both environmental and sociological. In countries where rice is the staple food, the inferior-quality rice is eaten and the better rice exported as a cash crop.

A visit to the northern province of India to see the basmati harvest gave me some surprises. Until the trip to Aryana, I believed that all Indians – and the people of Pakistan, who also grow this particularly fragrant, polished white rice – ate it by the sackful. They don't. At least not much outside the area where it is grown. Real basmati, which is best described as the Tamworth pig of rice, a breed that grows slowly and has a low yield for the labour it involves, is far too valuable for the growers to keep. Most is exported to the expats who migrated to the Middle East and Europe – and America, where higher incomes make it affordable.

The second surprise about basmati, considering the quantity that is grown, is that it is fairly traded. A system exists in India, regulated by the government, that ensures individual farmers get to sell at auction, so their harvest is not bagged up in one mountainous pile and traded on the worldwide commodity exchange. It is also grown in an utterly traditional way, using little fuel, natural irrigation and no harmful chemicals. It is a slow-growing 'rare' breed, a factor that has pushed up its price. Some remarkable businesses are involved, who put the interests of the Indian people up there with their own.

Protecting the breed has been paramount. There is an enormous difference between the hybrids and the real thing. Mostly it is a matter of how the rice behaves in the pan – pure basmati remains sturdy and lengthens to twice its size when cooked – but it is also evident in the taste. The scent of basmati, too, is so good it is a pity it is not harnessed and used in scented candles, like vanilla or smouldering logs.

Buying long grain rice

Tilda imports pure basmati rice to the UK, where it is available everywhere. It is scrupulously checked for inauthentic or broken grains before arriving at the docks in Rainham, where it is milled. Tilda is a privately owned company and the family funds community projects in Aryana and gives free training and advice to farmers who produce in the area. Buy large bags for good value.

Spiced Rice with Cauliflower, Coconut, Cloves and Ginger

There are several biryani methods; this one involves cooking the rice first. The finished dish is glorious. Eat it with chutneys or serve with curries (see pages 122, 124, 161, 229, 349) or roasted poultry or lamb.

Serves 4

250g/9oz pure basmati rice
125ml/4fl oz sunflower oil
4 garlic cloves, crushed
4cm/1½ inch piece of fresh ginger, grated
4 onions, chopped
6 cardamom pods
3 cloves
1 teaspoon ground turmeric
4 tomatoes, chopped
55g/2oz cream cheese or paneer
flesh of ½ coconut, grated

8–10 green chillies, cut lengthways into slivers
12 green beans
2 potatoes, unpeeled, cut into thin sticks
½ cauliflower, divided into florets
sea salt

To serve:
a handful of mint leaves
a handful of coriander, chopped
2 teaspoons ground cinnamon
1 lime, cut into quarters

First prepare the rice: soak it in cold water for 20 minutes, then wash it by tipping off the cloudy water, rinsing the rice and draining again. Put it in a pan with a large pinch of salt. Add enough water to come about 1cm/½ inch above the level of the rice, bring to the boil and cook, uncovered, for 5 minutes. Cover the pan, turn down the heat and simmer for 5 minutes. Turn off the heat and leave the rice to steam for a further 5 minutes. Take off the lid and fork through the rice. Spread it out on a large plate and leave to cool.

Heat half the oil in a wide frying pan, add the garlic, ginger and onions and fry until golden brown. Add the cardamoms, cloves, turmeric and ½ teaspoon of salt, followed by the chopped tomatoes. Add the cream cheese and coconut and cook for 10 minutes.

Meanwhile, heat the remaining oil in a separate pan, add the chillies, green beans, potatoes and cauliflower and fry until the vegetables begin to soften round the edges. Add the cooled rice to the onion and tomato mixture, then stir in the fried vegetables.

Pack the mixture into a casserole and keep warm in a low oven for about half an hour to let the flavours blend. Serve with the mint leaves, chopped coriander and cinnamon scattered over the top, putting a wedge of lime on to each plate.

Brokens Pudding with Caramelised Pineapple

Ask for brokens in an Asian supermarket and they'll know what you are talking about. These are the reject basmati grains that snap during milling, and are siphoned off and sold cheaply. They make great rice pudding, but you can also use regular basmati rice.

Depending on how runny you like your rice pudding, you may want to add slightly less milk in the final stages of the recipe.

Serves 4–6

115g/4oz pure basmati rice 'brokens'
1 litre/1¾ pints whole milk
115g/4oz golden caster sugar
a pinch of ground cardamom
10 pistachio nuts
10 blanched almonds, chopped

For the caramelised pineapple:
40g/1½oz unsalted butter
½ pineapple, the skin cut off, cored and sliced
1 heaped tablespoon soft light brown sugar

Soak the rice in plenty of cold water for 20 minutes, then wash it by tipping off the cloudy water, rinsing the rice and draining again.

Heat half the milk in a pan with the rice until it reaches boiling point. Reduce the heat and simmer for 5–6 minutes, until the rice is just tender.

Meanwhile, prepare the pineapple. Melt the butter in a frying pan, add the pineapple slices and fry for about a minute, sprinkling with half the brown sugar before you turn them. Turn and sprinkle with sugar again, so both sides are tinged with brown caramel. Place on a dish ready to serve.

Add the remaining milk, sugar, cardamom, pistachios and almonds to the rice mixture. Bring back to the boil, stirring gently but continuously. Reduce the heat, simmer for 2–3 minutes, then serve with the pineapple.

ROOTS

Roasted Mixed Root Vegetables

Raw Roots

Sweet Potato Stew with Crab, Coriander,
  Lime and Butter

Carrot Butter Sauce

Carrot Soup

Carrots, beetroot, parsnip, swede, celeriac and turnips. How good it is to
see them in September, when the young specimens are at their best. How
delighted I am to kiss them goodbye when the asparagus shoots in late
spring. But last year was different. The local city farmers' market featured
extraordinary roots: pink and white carrots, knobbly beets in various
shades, and small, snow-white parsnips. Whenever I could get to the
market, the basket was filled; £10 bought a week's worth and all I did was
roast them and eat with roasts or alone with soured cream – a root junkie
right until the last of the winter's supply had softened and wrinkled and the
stall could barely sell any more. Farms that produce the unfamiliar deserve
so much respect. They try out different varieties, carving out large areas
where they could stick in a plantation of dull but predictably saleable Maris
Piper, and work at converting consumers accustomed to a dogma of
monoculture and visual perfection.

Buying roots

Seek out organic market gardeners at farmers' markets, where there should
be greater diversity. See www.farmersmarkets.net, or www.lfm.org.uk for
London, to find your nearest market. The maps on www.bigbarn.co.uk
feature organic growers, farmers' markets and farm shops.

Roasted Mixed Root Vegetables

It is not only the richness of the colours – the orange, yellow, purple and pink stripes – that makes this hot pan of vegetables remarkable, it is also the sweet toffee smells, the myriad flavours and, last but not least, the ease with which I can throw it together.

I often make this for big Sunday lunches because it provides a wide variety of vegetables without having to hover over individual pans of boiling water on top of the stove. Once all is in the oven, you can forget it for at least 40 minutes while tending to other vital things, like mixing Bloody Marys. And tasting them. Having said this, if you have a small oven that can hold only the roast on one shelf and one other roasting tin, you can make this in advance and reheat quickly while the meat is resting. Vegetables cooked this way are delicious with sausages, Pearl Barley with Turmeric, Lemon and Black Cardamom (see page 27), or Farro with Potatoes and Basil Oil (see page 445).

Serves 8

4 large carrots, peeled and cut into diagonal chunks about 3cm/ 1¼ inches thick, or 8 whole smaller (not baby) carrots, scraped

2 parsnips, peeled and cut into diagonal chunks

8 medium beetroot (any colour – red, stripy pink 'chioggia' or golden), halved (do not trim the pointed end)

8 small turnips, cut into quarters

1 large salsify, peeled and cut into diagonal chunks

125ml/4fl oz olive oil

4 sprigs of thyme, or 1 teaspoon dried thyme

sea salt and freshly ground black pepper

Preheat the oven to 200°C/400°F/Gas Mark 6. You will probably need 2 large roasting tins. Put the prepared vegetables into the tins and add half the olive oil to each. Add the thyme, season with salt and pepper and mix with your hands. Cover with foil and bake for 40 minutes. Remove the foil and roast until the vegetables are lightly browned and tender when pierced with a knife – about 15 minutes. They will be quite sugary at this stage and can easily burn, so keep an eye on them.

Raw Roots

Four vibrant salads made from grated vegetables: parsnip and apple; beetroot; celeriac and broad bean; and swede. Eat them with charcuterie, boiled bacon or any of the potted meats and fish on pages 108, 296, 325, 356 and 452.

I like to eat these rich little salads, which the French call *rémoulade*, with other vegetables – they match the Potato and Fresh Cheese in an Olive Oil Pastry Pie on page 339 well. Good food for feeding the masses. An electric grating attachment to the mixer helps enormously. Save washing-up time by making the beetroot salad last.

Serves 10 as part of a meal with cured meat or the potato pie on page 339

600ml/1 pint single cream

For the parsnip and apple:
2 medium parsnips, peeled and grated
3 crisp, fibrous apples (such as Cox's), cored and grated
juice of 1 lemon
leaves from 4 sprigs of flat-leaf parsley, roughly chopped
10 cornichons (baby gherkins), sliced into small rounds
sea salt and freshly ground black pepper

For the celeriac and broad bean:
1 large celeriac, peeled and grated
400g/14oz broad beans, blanched in boiling water for 1 minute, then pinched from their skins (or use frozen beans, which do not need blanching)

2 tablespoons capers, washed and chopped
leaves from 4 sprigs of tarragon, roughly chopped
sea salt and freshly ground black pepper

For the swede:
1 large swede, peeled and grated
2 carrots, scraped and grated
juice of 1 lemon
2 tablespoons unsalted shelled pistachio nuts, toasted in a dry frying pan, then chopped
1 teaspoon cumin seeds, toasted with the pistachios
sea salt and freshly ground black pepper

For the beetroot:
3 fresh, crisp beetroot, peeled and grated
leaves from 4 sprigs of dill
10 pink peppercorns, crushed
sea salt

Put all the ingredients for each *rémoulade* except the salt and pepper into separate mixing bowls. Pour 150ml/¼ pint of cream over each and mix well. If the salad is too stiff, add a little water. Taste each and add salt if necessary. Add black pepper where applicable. Refrigerate until ready to eat.

Sweet Potato Stew with Crab, Coriander, Lime and Butter

A stew that crosses the line between luxury and good basics.

Serves 4

4 tablespoons extra virgin olive oil	1 litre/1¾ pints fish stock (see page 202) or vegetable stock
4 shallots, chopped	200g/7oz brown and white crab meat
4 garlic cloves, crushed with a little salt	4 tomatoes, deseeded and chopped
2 chillies, deseeded and chopped (optional)	115g/4oz butter
2 sweet potatoes, peeled and cut into 1cm dice	juice of 2 limes
	leaves from 4 or 5 sprigs of coriander
	sea salt and freshly ground black pepper
	Tabasco sauce, to serve

Heat the oil in a large pan, add the shallots, garlic and chillies, if using, and cook over a low heat until soft. Add the sweet potatoes, stir-fry for a minute or two, then cover with the fish stock or water and bring to the boil. Simmer for a few minutes; the potatoes should be tender. Stir in the brown meat from the crab, then spoon the stew into 4 warmed bowls. Scatter over the tomatoes and the white crab meat.

Melt the butter in a separate small pan, stir in the lime juice and season to taste with salt and pepper. Heat to boiling point and pour the mixture over the crab. Scatter over the coriander leaves and eat immediately, with lots of bread. Shake over some Tabasco if you like.

Carrot Butter Sauce

The Irish chef Richard Corrigan showed me how to make this sauce.
He put it beside turbot but you could serve it with steaks cut from brill –
a flat fish with a flavour (when very fresh) that comes near to the valuable
turbot – or pollock (a cod alternative). I have since tried it with roast duck
legs, eating it with egg noodles. Buttery carrots and duck like each other,
and it is an unusual way to dress pasta.

Serves 4

15 green cardamom pods
400g/14oz unsalted butter
1kg/2¼lb carrots, finely grated

vegetable stock, to cover
a little white wine vinegar (preferably
    Forum Chardonnay vinegar)
sea salt and freshly ground black
    pepper

Crush the cardamom pods and extract the seeds. Melt the butter in a pan
and add the grated carrots and cardamom seeds. Cook over a low heat for
3–4 minutes, then cover with vegetable stock and cook for 15 minutes.
Take the pan from the heat and allow it to sit for at least 15 minutes so
the flavours can develop and amalgamate.

Set a metal sieve over a second pan and tip the contents of the first pan into
it, pushing through as much liquid as you can with the back of a wooden
spoon. Taste the sauce and add a drop or two of white wine vinegar to
sharpen it, then season with a little salt and pepper. Serve with grilled fish
or try other things with it, such as grilled goat's cheese or braised
butterbeans (see page 40).

Carrot Soup

Humble carrot soup is traditionally eaten to break a fast but it is not a dull soup. With a few spices and some citrus to sharpen and aromatise it – then it ranks among the best.

Serves 4–6

2 tablespoons butter
2 onions, roughly chopped
6 medium-sized carrots, cut into small chunks
12 coriander seeds, crushed, or 1 level teaspoon ground coriander
½ teaspoon ground allspice
1.2 litres/2 pints chicken or vegetable stock (see page 116) or water

juice and grated zest of 1 lemon
sea salt and freshly ground black pepper

To serve:
150ml/¼ pint whole-milk yoghurt or Greek-style yoghurt, warmed slightly in a pan (do not let it boil)
leaves from 4 sprigs of flat-leaf parsley, chopped
4 tablespoons melted unsalted butter

Melt the butter in a large pan over a medium heat, add the onions, carrots and spices and cook for about 5 minutes, stirring occasionally. Pour in the stock, bring to the boil and simmer for 15 minutes or until the carrots are soft. Cool a little and then blitz in a liquidiser or food processor.

To serve, reheat gently and stir in the lemon juice and zest. Season with salt and black pepper to taste. Ladle into bowls, pour in about 2 tablespoons of the warmed yoghurt per portion and scatter over some parsley. Add some melted butter to each bowl.

ROSES

Lamb with Rose and Almonds

Blancmange with Crystallised Rose Petals

The flavour of my namesake is one I like. I haven't grown to love lavender, except when it is my friend the chocolate maker Chantal Coady's lavender chocolate in her shop, Rococo. Roses do a subtle thing, adding scent and colour. If you have ever travelled to Greece and been offered a spoon of jam as a teatime snack, it is likely to be one infused with rose petals. They also turn up in *ras al hanout*, a complicated spice mix that is added to food at the last minute. No flower is more festive than a rose, and decorating a pudding with the crystallised petals of the smellier types is a ritual that attracts helpers. It is better to pick roses from a garden that you hope has not been sprayed. Florist's roses may well have been.

Lamb with Rose and Almonds

Use the neck fillet, an inexpensive cut, to make this quick but unusual supper dish.

Serve 3–4

2 lamb neck fillets
olive oil for frying
sea salt and freshly ground black
    pepper

For the salsa:
petals from 2 pink roses (or use dried
    edible rose petals bought from
    Middle Eastern shops, soaked in
    water)
2 tablespoons whole blanched
    almonds
1 teaspoon ground coriander
2 garlic cloves, peeled
4 tablespoons olive oil

Put all the salsa ingredients in a food processor and blend to a rough paste. Set to one side. Season the neck fillets and gently fry in olive oil for about 8 minutes on either side; the lamb should be served quite pink. Cook the rose and almond mixture in a separate small frying pan for 2–3 minutes, until it softens.

Slice the neck fillets into chunks 2cm/¾ inch thick and serve with the sauce.

Blancmange with Crystallised Rose Petals

The best rose petals to use are from the Provins rose, or *Rosa gallica officinalis*, but other red or dark-pink damask rose petals will be fine.

Serves 4

250g/9oz ground almonds
600ml/1 pint whole milk
85g/3oz caster sugar
6 egg yolks
2 gelatine leaves

200ml/7fl oz whipping cream, lightly whipped

For the crystallised rose petals:
about 24 rose petals
2 egg whites, lightly beaten
caster sugar

You will need a wire rack and some tweezers when crystallising the rose petals. Pick up a petal with the tweezers, dip it in the egg white and then in the sugar, coating it well. Place on a wire rack and repeat with the remaining petals. Leave to dry in a warm place for several hours – an airing cupboard is perfect.

Put the ground almonds in a bowl. Heat the milk to boiling point, pour it over the almonds and leave to infuse for several hours.

Strain the milk through a fine sieve, pushing every last drop of it from the almonds with a spoon. Throw away the almonds. Measure the milk, making it up to 600ml/1 pint with fresh milk if necessary.

Whisk the sugar and egg yolks together in a separate bowl until pale and thick. Bring the almond milk to the boil and gradually stir it into the egg mixture. Return the mixture to the pan and cook, stirring, over a very low heat until it thickens enough to coat the back of the spoon lightly; do not let it boil. Meanwhile, soak the gelatine leaves in cold water for about 10 minutes.

As soon as the mixture has thickened, pass it through a sieve into a bowl. Squeeze the excess water out of the gelatine and drop the leaves into the mixture. Stir until dissolved. Sit the bowl in a second one filled with iced water and stir until the mixture begins to thicken. Fold in the cream, using a whisk, then divide the mixture between 4 glasses and leave in the fridge until set.

Scatter the crystallised rose petals over the surface just before serving.

RUNNER BEANS

Runner Beans with Shallot, Mustard, Oil and Vinegar

Beans, Beans and Beans

During summer, runner beans seem to have such a long season that they deserve a category of their own. I tried to grow them this year, in my dark city garden. I have harvested eight so far and expect the total to be less than 15. Perhaps better to give my money to successful growers of these leggy plants, who paid rather more care – although the freak July hailstorm last summer, which turned half the leaves to Honiton lace, was an act no one could have predicted. Runner beans have a season, not that you would know this looking at supermarket shelves, where the runners are packed in plastic and have none of the coarse sturdiness of home-grown ones. These beans, sold outside the British season, are usually grown in African countries: Kenya, Gambia, sometimes Egypt. Oh dear, it's the Kenyan bean issue. Problematic to its toes. Of course, the answer to the problem is to let countries like Kenya grow their own food, not ours, which they could do if only the European member states and US government stopped dumping our subsidised excess on them in the name of food aid.

In theory, African countries growing for us is not a bad idea. Based on the principle that the more variety we eat, the healthier we will be, there are many crops we need and cannot grow. And Africa deserves an agricultural renaissance whether the wilderness tourists like it or not. This is all dependent on various environmental concerns being noted, namely water and soil erosion, but do not forget about traditional production methods. Developing countries have great traditions in farming and have been known to grow far more plant species than now. Biodiversity International, the organisation that promotes an increase in the number of species grown in the world, puts forward a convincing argument that using more traditional techniques to grow a greater number of food plants is the way to sustain the food supply for all countries. Embracing ideas like this might find a food plant with great assets that need not be air-freighted like the bad bean.

Buying runner beans

British beans are available in season from July to November. Local greengrocer's shops are the best source because in many cases they buy beans at the nearest wholesale market from the previous day's cropping – a feat few supermarkets can match, since all their produce must go to distribution depots, picking up food miles on the way. Choose beans that are not oversized, do not have huge beans bulging through the pods and release juice when bruised with your fingernail. They are less likely to be stringy when cooked.

Runner Beans with Shallot, Mustard, Oil and Vinegar

A useful dish to eat at room temperature. Like the purple sprouting broccoli with lentils on page 73, it will sit happily waiting while you prepare other food. At the height of their season, the green beans will be crisp and fresh-flavoured, and the piquant mustard dressing will not overpower them.

Make a dressing with 1 tablespoon of Dijon mustard, 2 chopped shallots, 5 tablespoons of extra virgin olive oil, 1 tablespoon of water and 1 tablespoon of cider vinegar. Mix with cooked runner beans while they're still warm, leaving for a few minutes to let the flavours develop.

You can eat these beans alone or with almost anything – cold ham or roast chicken (see page 115). But I like them with semi-soft boiled eggs. Put the eggs into a pan of cold water, bring to the boil and cook for 5 minutes, then plunge into cold water. Peel and quarter the eggs, then put them on top of the beans.

Beans, Beans and Beans

Make a large warm salad of beans, mixing blanched French beans or bobby beans with blanched, sliced runners and a few flageolets – which can be bought canned, then drained and rinsed. Dress with olive oil and scatter over some sea salt and thinly sliced shallot.

SARDINES

Grilled Sardines with Bread, Walnut and Chilli Sauce
Canned Pilchards with New Potatoes

Sardines are one of Cornwall's success stories, a fishery recently revived by concentrating on keeping the fish in the freshest state. Still fished using small-scale short-trip boats, they are netted and kept in slush ice – a mixture of seawater and ice that chills them literally to the bone, stopping the decay that would previously have begun before reaching the auction at the market.

Sardines are, of course, pilchards. Both names cover the same species; the difference is purely geography and size. By the time the shoals reach Cornish waters, they have grown larger than those found further south but if they are well cared for after the catch, there is nothing in the claim that small sardines are better fish. Inexpensive, a fish and a dish for every day, they are widely available in supermarkets and from good fish merchants. They do give off strong (and delicious) smells when cooked, but my preference for cooking them outdoors is more connected to the fact that they taste phenomenal when grilled over charcoal embers. I occasionally cook them in the fireplace, over charcoal, since they have a season that runs from August through to April, and barbecuing outdoors during winter feels a little desperate.

Buying sardines

Cornish sardines are available in Marks & Spencer, Waitrose, Tesco and Sainsbury during the season, and direct from Nick Howell at the Pilchard Works: www.pilchardworks.co.uk; tel: 01736 332112. Nick Howell also produces exceptional canned pilchards, which are sold as Cornish sardines and are grilled before canning in extra virgin olive oil.

Grilled Sardines with Bread, Walnut and Chilli Sauce

Sardines are nicest eaten with a generous squeeze of lemon juice and a robust sauce like this one, which doubles as a mop for the juices. There is no need to gut the sardines; once cooked, the meat fillets easily.

If you are grilling the sardines outdoors, British hardwood charcoal is the most eco-friendly. Contact the Dorset Charcoal Company for stockists (southwest England and London only): www.dorsetcharcoal.co.uk; tel: 01258 818176. Or buy Welsh charcoal via mail order from Graig Farm Organics: www.graigfarm.co.uk; tel: 01597 851655.

Serves 4

8–12 fresh whole sardines
olive oil for brushing

For the sauce:
6 tablespoons extra virgin olive oil
2 garlic cloves, chopped
2 shallots, chopped

85g/3oz walnuts, finely chopped, then toasted in a dry frying pan until golden
2–3 slices of sourdough bread, processed into crumbs
2 red chillies, deseeded and chopped
a handful of curly parsley, finely chopped

To make the sauce, heat the olive oil in a pan, add the garlic and shallots and cook until soft and slightly coloured. Add the walnuts, breadcrumbs and chillies and fry for a minute or two. Stir in the parsley then spoon into a bowl.

Make a deep bed of hardwood charcoal in the barbecue and light it, letting it burn until the coals are powdery white and the flames have died down. Brush each sardine with oil and lay them over the hot coals. Cook for 2–3 minutes, then carefully turn and grill the other side. Serve the fish with the sauce on the side.

Kitchen note
Sardines can be cooked indoors, too. Prepare as above, then put in a roasting tin and cook in an oven preheated to 220°C/425°F/Gas Mark 7, or fry them for about 4 minutes on each side, depending on size.

Canned Pilchards with New Potatoes

The easiest salad, in desperate need, however, of Nick Howell's canned pilchards (see Buying Sardines, above) and good, waxy new-season Cornish potatoes.

For 4 people, brush or scrape the skin off 12–16 new potatoes and boil until just tender; they should not be falling apart. If the potatoes appear not quite done when pierced with a sharp knife, take them off the heat anyway. They tend to continue cooking even after they have been drained. Leave to cool, then slice and serve with 1 can of drained pilchard fillets, some lemon juice, parsley, chives and olive oil. Some good-quality olives are an asset, as is a halved semi-soft boiled egg. To cook an egg in this way, put it in a pan of cold water, bring to the boil, simmer for 5 minutes, then run it under a cold tap.

SAUSAGES

Sausage Meatballs and Farro Broth with Mustard
Wurst with Butterbeans, Tarragon, Leeks and Cream

The best way to eat sausages is cooked in a pan with a little double cream and no other fat. A nice thing occurs as the cream cooks slowly with the bangers, forming toffee-ish strings that stick to them. The cream burns a little, becoming a sticky lace. The same happens if you bake them in the oven, and can be done with all plain pork sausages, but it helps to use well-made sausages stuffed with good ingredients, or the stickiness outside will be hiding inner disappointment.

Well-made sausages have a high meat content and that meat is from naturally fed, slow-grown pigs. The rest is a cereal, usually specially manufactured 'rusk', but it is always good to see sausages that are still made the traditional way with bread. The meat content is ideally 80 per cent, including an essential proportion of fat, but contrast this with budget sausages, which can contain 30 per cent pork and 20 per cent mechanically recovered meat (MRM) – a process that sucks the remaining meat, fat and connective tissue from the bones of a pig, extruding it as a slimy paste. The rest of the sausage could be 15 per cent water, 30 per cent cereal rusk and 5 per cent assorted additives, including flavourings, colour, sugar, flavour enhancer and preservatives.

The best sausages are no longer cheap as chips, but they are good value for money because there is less water and fat lost during cooking and a higher proportion of leaner meat. Tasting a budget sausage is like eating a slice of white bread spread with a greasy, pork-flavoured paste. Need I go on?

Putting a good sausage in a pan with some other filling yet nutritious ingredients is a way to stretch the budget. Beans are the obvious match, but grains are good too, and eating them with potato is compulsive.

Buying sausages

When possible, buy sausages that have been produced with locally sourced free-range meat. Ask your local butcher or farmers' market supplier how they make them. I make the following recommendations with the proviso that there be no complaints about my personal taste. Sausage appreciation is an emotional zone, but the following suppliers make sausages of integrity. Sillfield Farm sells a variety of beautifully seasoned sausages made from the farm's own wild boar and pork: www.sillfield.co.uk; tel: 015395 67609.

Well Hung Meat makes its sausages naturally with 95 per cent meat and they taste delicious, too: www.wellhungmeat.com; tel: 0845 230 3131.

The butcher John Robinson & Sons makes a long-standing favourite of mine. Visit the shop at High Street, Stockbridge, Hampshire SO20 6HE; tel: 01264 810609 – no home delivery.

Donald Russell makes simple pork sausages and also the best Continental wurst (smoked pork sausages) I have found: www.donaldrussell.com; tel: 01467 629666.

Sausage Meatballs and Farro Broth with Mustard

A recipe that sprang out of an unexpected-friend-for-supper situation, and which is now much loved. Splitting open a sausage provides an instant meatball to simmer with stock and grains.

Serves 4

3 tablespoons extra virgin olive oil
1 tablespoon yellow mustard seeds
8 sausages
4 bacon rashers, cut into small pieces
2 onions, chopped
4 garlic cloves, crushed with a little salt
200g/7oz farro (whole wheat – see page 445)

1 litre/1¾ pints meat or chicken stock (see pages 64, 116 and 238)
150ml/¼ pint passata (puréed tomatoes)
1 tablespoon cider vinegar
1 tablespoon Dijon mustard
sea salt and freshly ground black pepper

Heat the oil in a large casserole, add the mustard seeds and cook until they pop. Scoop the sausage meat from the skins and shape into meat patties the size of golf balls. Brown them in the casserole with the bacon, then add the onions and garlic. Stir-fry for half a minute, then stir in the farro. Add the stock and passata, bring to the boil and simmer for about 20 minutes, until the farro is tender. Taste and add salt if necessary, then pepper. Gently stir in the cider vinegar and mustard. Serve in bowls, with sourdough bread.

Wurst with Butterbeans, Tarragon, Leeks and Cream

The slight smokiness on the skin of the sausage invades this creamy stew. Put mustard on the table.

See page 387 for where to find good wurst.

Serves 4

2 tablespoons extra virgin olive oil
1 medium-sized leek, sliced
2 cans of butterbeans (drained weight 470g) – or use cannellini beans

4 smoked wurst
900ml/1½ pints chicken stock (see page 116)
90ml/3fl oz single cream
leaves from 2 sprigs of tarragon

Heat the oil in a casserole, add the leek and cook over a low heat until it softens slightly. Drain the butterbeans and add them to the pan with the wurst. Add the stock and cream and bring to the boil. Turn off the heat and leave for 3 minutes for the meat and beans to heat through properly, then add the tarragon. Ladle into shallow bowls and serve.

SCALLOPS

Scallops Baked in Their Shells with Mace

I buy mostly hand-dived scallops, not ones that are dredged up from the sea by machinery, and so think of them as an exceptional meal. I buy them rarely but when I do I want the best. Too many scallops sit sadly in pools of water in the shop, looking matt and grey. It is best to buy them live, on the shell, and ask the fishmonger to open them and remove the meat, there and then.

To open and remove the scallop yourself, slide a short, sharp knife inside the shell (it will probably slam shut) and cut the muscle at its base in the rounded half of the shell. The shell should then release and can be opened. Trim off the organs – the frilly bit around the scallop – but save the white cylinder of meat, the coral and the white strips of meat that are attached in a circle towards the edge of the shell.

Buying scallops

You can buy hand-dived scallops from Steve Hall and Matt Baldwin of Handpicked Shellfish in the West Country, who catch them near Weymouth. They also sell a wide variety of other fish, including many unfamiliar ones. To order, and to check availability, tel: 07968 176485 or 07785 571023.

Hand-dived scallops and other extra-fresh shellfish and fish are also available from Angela Harrison, who runs Pengelly's Fishmongers with her daughter, Jackie, in Looe, South Cornwall; tel: 01579 340777 or 01503 262246.

Not all dredger fishermen are irresponsible. In Rye, Sussex, there is a small co-operative of 30 local boats who fish around Camber Sands. They have too much to lose if they overfish the valuable scallops. Contact Market Fisheries, tel: 01797 225175.

Scallops Baked in Their Shells with Mace

These look wonderful, wrapped up like a present as they come out of the oven, but smell even better when they are opened and a stream of mace-scented steam touches the tip of your nose.

Serves 4

8 large, fresh scallops
4 scallop shells (both parts)
2cm/³/₄ inch piece of fresh ginger,
    crushed and then chopped
55g/2oz butter
¹/₂ lemon
4 small pieces of mace blade, or
    4 pinches of ground mace

Preheat the oven to 240°C/475°F/Gas Mark 9. Put 2 scallops in each shell and divide the ginger between them. Put a quarter of the butter in each, plus a squeeze of lemon. Add a mace blade to each, or a pinch of ground mace, then put the flat shell on top. Place each shell on a large square of baking parchment, bring it up round the shell and twist tightly at the top to seal the contents. Bake for 10–15 minutes.

To serve, put a scallop shell on each plate and let everyone unwrap their own and get the first whiff of the heady ginger-butter-mace effect.

SQUASH AND PUMPKIN

Baked Gem Squash
Pumpkin Soup

The squash family is an exciting bunch. Ravishing to look at, heavy to carry home, no two look alike or taste the same. I buy a squash if I see one and leave it sitting pretty in the kitchen; its good keeping qualities make it an emergency vegetable with class. Small chunks can be added to onions, butter and rice, then cooked with stock or water for a dish as warming as a blanket; squash soup is up there with watercress as a favourite and it can replace meat in any of the curries on pages 122, 124, 161, 229 and 349. Simply cut into crescent moons, brushed with oil and roasted, it is something substantial on its own.

Buying squash and pumpkin

West Indian markets are the best source for small pumpkins, but these are imports – always sea freighted, though, which is more eco-friendly than any other way. You will have to wait until late summer to see the British glut invade the shops and markets.

Baked Gem Squash

Gem squash are the small, dark-green cannonballs available in most supermarkets from September until they run out. They have an amazingly long shelf life. The flesh is pale yellow, turning a deeper butter colour when cooked. To cook them, cut in half and bake in a moderate oven for 30–40 minutes, until soft. Remove from the oven, scoop out the seeds and add a small blob of butter, some chopped herbs, a few grains of salt and some freshly ground black pepper. Eat them alone, or place a large dish of them on the table next to the Dry-roast Chicken on page 115. I like the fact that the chicken would have enjoyed eating the seeds, had it had the chance.

Pumpkin Soup

The first time I tasted pumpkin soup I found it very sweet. In the USA the pumpkin's sugary nature is celebrated in sweet pies; in Italy, northern cooks mix it with even sweeter amaretti biscuits and use to fill ravioli or tortellini. They are wonderful in small doses, dusted with Parmesan and drenched in butter. A great festive dish. But I like to cut the sweetness down a bit, and garlic is the way to do it – plus sourdough bread – in a smooth, golden-yellow soup.

Serve 6–8

6 garlic cloves, crushed with a little salt
6 tablespoons extra virgin olive oil
4 slices of sourdough bread
1 medium Caribbean pumpkin (or a 2kg/4½lb slice from a large pumpkin), peeled, deseeded and cut into chunks

600ml/1 pint whole milk
900ml/1½ pints chicken or other stock (see page 116), or water
sea salt and ground white pepper

To serve:
toasted pumpkinseed oil
crushed toasted green pumpkin seeds

Preheat the oven to 220°C/425°F/Gas Mark 7. Mix the garlic with the oil and leave to infuse for a while – about 15 minutes should do it. Dip a brush into the oil and paint each side of the bread slices. Put the slices on a baking tray and bake until golden brown.

Meanwhile, put the remaining garlicky oil, complete with garlic bits, in a large pan. Add the pumpkin and stir-fry over a low heat until it starts to soften. Add the toasted bread, then pour in the milk and stock or water. Bring to the boil and cook over a medium heat for about 20 minutes, until the pumpkin is tender. Remove from the heat, allow to cool a little, then liquidise until smooth. Reheat, season to taste and serve with a little pumpkinseed oil dotted on top and crushed toasted pumpkin seeds scattered over.

SWEETBREADS

Lamb Sweetbreads Wrapped in Ham with Peas and Lovage

We are in offal territory, but offal that is the least challenging to eat. When prepared and cooked carefully, sweetbreads, a gland taken from lamb or veal, yield white meat as easy to love as a chicken breast. Their flavour is gentle and mildly meaty. Since so much offal never reaches the butcher's, sweetbreads can be hard to find, but ask all the same – it should be easy for the butcher to order some for you.

Buying sweetbreads

See Lamb and Mutton chapter, page 226, for suppliers. Some may be able to supply sweetbreads.

Lamb Sweetbreads Wrapped in Ham with Peas and Lovage

Sweetbreads parcelled up in thinly sliced, air-dried ham, either prosciutto or a British variety. With pea and lovage purée, they are an elegant little meal or a big starter, depending on the event. See page 213 for suppliers of dried cured ham.

Serves 4

12 sweetbreads
6 slices of cured ham (use Italian prosciutto or even thinly cut streaky bacon), cut in half
a little oil for frying
a knob of butter
sea salt

For the pea and lovage purée:
600ml/1 pint chicken stock (see page 116) or water
225g/8oz shelled peas – preferably fresh spring peas, though frozen will do
a knob of butter
about 10 lovage leaves, chopped
sea salt and freshly ground black pepper

To prepare the sweetbreads, put them under a slowly running cold tap for 20 minutes to remove the blood. Put them in a pan, cover with fresh cold water, add a teaspoon of salt, then bring to the boil and simmer for 5 minutes. Remove from the pan and refresh in iced water. Peel off the tough outer membrane. Lay 2 squares of cling film on top of each other, place a sweetbread in the centre, then bring up the corners and twist into as tight a ball as you can. Wrap the remaining sweetbreads in the same way. Chill for 2 hours.

Remove the sweetbreads from the cling film and wrap each one in half a slice of ham. Heat a little oil in a frying pan until smoking hot, then add the sweetbreads and butter. Cook quickly until golden and crisp, then remove from the pan and keep warm.

To make the pea purée, bring the chicken stock to the boil, add the peas and boil for 1 minute, then drain. Blitz the peas in a food processor, then stir in the butter and lovage leaves. Season with salt and pepper. Serve the sweetbreads with the pea purée.

TEA

Tea-soaked Fruitcake
Lemon Lapsang Souchong Jelly

All the while the debate over imported food versus local sourcing carries on, 200 million cups of tea will be drunk in one day in the UK. One thing is certain, no green campaigner is likely to cherish the idea of giving up his or her ration. Life without tea? Unthinkable. It is estimated that per capita consumption is 2.5kg/5½lb dry weight each year and that overall 200 million kg of tea are consumed annually in the UK. It is a national addiction, and with good reason. Drinking a glass of cold water on a wet day may be good for you but a hot cup of tea is less chilling, even cheering. It also, say scientists, contains flavonoids – nutrients not present in water that protect against disease. Typically the latest research making this claim was paid for by a tea trade organisation, but it was stressed at the time that the work was 'independent'.

Tea is obviously an import to the UK, yet there are some imports that can be justified. I have included a few in this book not only because they are deeply embedded in our diet historically but also because as imports they impact less catastrophically than air-freighted asparagus from Peru. Tea is one of those. But even though it weighs little, has a long shelf life and can be imported via boat – the transport with the lightest carbon footprint – it is still something to buy with caution. Tea growing does have an impact on the environment. For the vast majority of tea produced in the world, just one plant variety is grown. Growing a plant in a 'monoculture' will affect the balance of the ecosystem that protects plants from disease – hence the routine spraying of non-organic tea crops. In 2005, 96 samples of tea were tested for pesticides by the UK Government's Pesticides Residue Committee (PRC). Out of these, 18 samples contained residues of more than one pesticide. Although, as it always seems to, the PRC commented that the levels were 'acceptable', I wouldn't say that any level is acceptable in a drink that simply says 'tea' on the label. How about 'tea with added Endosulfan' – how comforting is that?

Added to these problems are those concerning the workforce. There are tea gardens that still uphold a working regime that could be matched to slavery.

The upshot of all this is that it is best to buy organic, and to buy Fairtrade (www.fairtrade.org.uk). There is also another organisation, the Ethical Tea Partnership (ETP), whose members buy tea only from gardens that stick to a strict code of practice (see its website for a list of members: www.ethicalteapartnership.org). It would be better, however, if the ETP and the Fairtrade Foundation were one and the same organisation. Tea is a commodity that needs to change.

George Orwell wrote a lot about tea. He even penned a recipe for the perfect cup (it works). His tea grumbles were not about chemicals or fairness to the workers but about the favourite addition to tea in the UK after milk: white sugar. In *The Road to Wigan Pier*, he complained that too much household income was spent on sugar, going into the endless cups consumed by the unemployed in Britain. Nutritionally negative sugar spoiled tea, which he wrote should taste bitter, like ale. If the money had been spent on nutrient-rich brown flour to make bread... I know what he was driving at, but try to come between an Englishman and his sweet cup of tea.

Recently I have tried cooking with tea, using it as a marinade for fruit and making a lemon tea jelly in an old-fashioned ceramic mould. You can taste the bitter aromatics in both recipes but, with apologies to Orwell, some sugar was also necessary.

Buying tea

The Fairtrade Foundation website, mentioned above, has a long list of certified suppliers of tea. I suggest experimenting to find a tea that you enjoy, and especially recommend the new 'green' and 'white' teas now available, made from non-fermented leaves, which are caffeine free and have a high antioxidant content. Of the smaller suppliers, Yorkshire-based company Steenbergs Organic has beautiful teas, and can send them by post: www.steenbergs.co.uk; tel: 01765 640 088. The Rare Tea Company (www.rareteacompany.com) sells unusual, even 'limited-edition' teas, including delicious jasmine-scented green teas and an amazing 'flowering' tea. The leaves are tied in a posy, which unravels in the hot water like a blossom. Pricy, but they make lovely presents.

Tea-soaked Fruitcake

A boiled cake made with dried fruit, steeped in tea until nearly bursting. The bitterness of the tea tempers the sweetness of the fruit.

225g/8oz mixed dried fruit, such as raisins, sultanas, currants, chopped prunes, natural 'brown' apricots, dried Bing cherries
1 litre/1¾ pints boiling-hot Earl Grey or jasmine green tea, medium strength

115g/4oz unsalted butter
115g/4oz soft brown sugar
280g/10oz golden syrup
2 eggs
85g/3oz plain flour
½ teaspoon bicarbonate of soda
140g/5oz ground almonds

Put all the dried fruit in a bowl and pour over the tea. Leave to steep for about 45 minutes, until the fruit is soft and swollen.

Preheat the oven to 150°C/300°F/Gas Mark 2. Strain the fruit, then put it in a large pan with the butter, sugar and golden syrup. Place over the heat, bring to the boil and boil gently for exactly 5 minutes. Set aside to cool until just hand hot. Beat in the eggs, one by one. Sift in the flour with the bicarbonate of soda and ground almonds and fold in well.

Line a 23cm/9 inch long loaf tin with baking parchment. Turn the mixture into it and bake for 45–55 minutes, until a skewer inserted in the centre comes out clean. Remove from the oven, turn the cake out on to a wire rack and leave to cool.

Lemon Lapsang Souchong Jelly

A pretty pudding for grown-ups, to set in a mould or small glasses. The mint leaves can be replaced with strawberries, redcurrants or blackberries. Never add pineapple to jelly – it ruins the set.

Makes 8–10 individual jellies

10 gelatine leaves
1 litre/1¾ pints strong Lapsang
   Souchong tea, kept quite hot
4 teaspoons golden caster sugar, or
   to taste
juice of 1 lemon, strained
8–10 fresh geranium or mint leaves

Add the gelatine to a bowl of cold water, one leaf at a time. Soak for about 10 minutes, until soft. Meanwhile, combine the tea with the sugar and lemon juice and pour a third of it into a bowl. Squeeze out the excess liquid from the gelatine and discard the water. Add the gelatine to the smaller amount of tea and stir with your fingers to dissolve. Have ready a metal sieve and another clean bowl. Pour the remaining lemon tea into the gelatine mixture and stir again. Pour the whole mixture through the sieve into the clean bowl then pour it back into the former bowl, but without the sieve this time. This process cools the jelly a little, so it will set faster.

Pour enough jelly into 8–10 individual moulds, or 1 large one, to leave a 2cm/¾ inch space at the top. Put in the fridge for 45 minutes–1 hour, until just set, then pour over the remaining jelly mixture. Submerge the leaves in the unset jelly. Refrigerate again until set.

To unmould the jelly, dip each mould into hot water for a few seconds, until you can see the jelly is coming away from the edges of the mould. Turn out on to serving dishes and serve straight away.

TOMATOES

A Cooked Tomato Store
Tomato and Spelt Soup
Chilled Tomato, Lime, Basil and Lemon Grass Soup
Skinned Tomato and Dandelion Salad

I quake when I buy a fresh tomato with a destination other than a salad. Wet summers make the British crop – one that I am anxious to buy into and so support the farmers – a watery bunch. They feel firm when picked up but can reduce to nothing when cooked. Unlike an Italian plum tomato, they release so much liquid during cooking that my regularly made batch of tomatoes stewed with oil, garlic and basil, which I use throughout the week, may need to simmer for hours just to reduce. Having to add passata, and especially concentrated tomato purée, feels like failure when the objective is to buy as much fresh food locally as possible. The trick is to plan ahead. Buy a quantity of tomatoes and leave them to ripen, even to dry a little. They should then have more substance. Alternatively, remove the seeds and the water around them before adding the tomatoes to the pot.

Buying tomatoes

Farmers' markets and box schemes are undoubtedly the best source. Organic growers produce an endless variety, so that the tomato harvest will last for longer. To find a farmers' market, look at your local council website or at www.farmersmarkets.net for a nationwide list. London markets can be located at www.lfm.org.uk. There are other independently run produce markets, like Borough Market in southeast London, and you will sometimes find locally grown tomatoes in ordinary street markets across the country. Look out also for country markets, run by the WI. Your nearest can be located on www.country-markets.co.uk.

A Cooked Tomato Store

A treasure of a recipe that has got me out of more trouble more times than I can count. How often do you run out of time, both for cooking and shopping, yet yearn for something home cooked? Or need to provide children with a quick plate of pasta but want to give them something you made yourself? A store of stewed tomatoes, cooked with olive oil, whole garlic cloves (which can be removed later) and basil leaves, becomes an instant pasta sauce, or the base of a sauce for grilled meats, or a supply to tap into and make a quick soup by adding a little stock (from your other store) and some spelt grains.

It is economical, too. I buy boxes of overripe tomatoes at the vegetable market on Saturdays. I try to buy British but fall for plum tomatoes when I see them. If I make a large enough supply in my big pan, it will keep me going for at least three weeks. I store the cooked tomatoes in double plastic bags and put about two-thirds of them into the freezer, one third in the fridge. The olive oil content means they keep a good, long time.

To make the sauce, halve 2kg/4½lb ripe tomatoes and put them in a pan with 3 peeled garlic cloves and 6 tablespoons of olive oil. Add a few basil leaves, bring to the boil, then turn down to a simmer and cook for 30 minutes. Add 3 tablespoons of passata and another 2 tablespoons of olive oil. Bring back to the boil and simmer for 30 minutes. Taste and season with salt and pepper, adding a little sugar if the sauce is not sweet – this is often the case with tomatoes that have ripened in a box and not in the sun. Put the sauce through a food mill (mouli-légumes) or whiz in a food processor until smooth. Store in bags, jars or containers, in the fridge or freezer, until needed.

Tomato and Spelt Soup

I eat this soup so often that I keep the cooked tomato base in the fridge with any available stock and make up as much as I need.

chicken or other stock (see page 116), or water

whole spelt (allow about 55g/2oz per person)

sea salt and freshly ground black pepper

For the tomato base:
6 tablespoons extra virgin olive oil
1 onion, finely chopped
1 garlic clove, finely chopped
leaves from 2 sprigs of oregano, or 1 teaspoon dried oregano

2kg/4½ lb ripe tomatoes (preferably ones that are going soft), roughly chopped

To serve:
grated hard ewe's milk cheese, such as Somerset Rambler, Italian pecorino or Twineham Grange (an English Parmesan-style cheese) or Italian Parmesan

extra virgin olive oil (chilli olive oil is good, too)

To make the tomato base, heat the oil in a large pan and add all the remaining ingredients. Cook for about an hour, until the sauce tastes sweet, then season with salt and pepper. Cool and put through a food mill (mouli-légumes) or blend in a liquidiser.

To make the soup, heat equal quantities of tomato base and stock (about 150ml/¼ pint of each to make one generous serving). Add the spelt, simmer for 20–25 minutes, then season to taste and ladle into bowls. Serve with grated cheese and a splash of olive oil.

Chilled Tomato, Lime, Basil and Lemon Grass Soup

A cooling soup, and a little different from a gazpacho.

Serves 4–6

2kg/4½lb ripe tomatoes, deseeded
    and the hard area of stalk removed
juice of 4 limes
1 tablespoon palm sugar (available in
    Asian shops) or soft brown sugar
2 lemon grass sticks, thinly sliced,
    then chopped
4cm/1½ inch piece of fresh ginger,
    grated

600ml/1 pint tomato juice
sea salt

To serve:
finely chopped Thai holy basil leaves,
    or ordinary basil if you can't get it
chopped deseeded green chilli
    (optional)
a little flavoured olive oil (basil, chilli
    or sesame would be good)

Put all the ingredients in a liquidiser in several batches and blend until smooth. Taste and add sea salt if necessary, then chill thoroughly. Serve in soup bowls or cups, scattered with a little basil and green chilli, if using, and with a little flavoured oil zigzagged over the surface to bring out the flavour.

Skinned Tomato and Dandelion Salad

Crucial to the success of a good tomato salad is the removal of the tomato skins. This allows the dressing, which should be pepped up with a good dose of Dijon mustard, to penetrate the tomatoes.

Serves 8

8–12 ripe tomatoes
4 handfuls of dandelion leaves

For the dressing:
1 tablespoon Dijon mustard – more if
　you like a dressing that makes your
　eyes water

1 teaspoon sugar
½ teaspoon sea salt
1 garlic clove, peeled and cut in half
3 tablespoons red wine vinegar
135ml/4½fl oz extra virgin olive oil
freshly ground black pepper

Nick the skin of each tomato with a knife. Submerge the tomatoes in boiling water for a minute, then drain and push the skins off. Cut into quarters and remove the seeds.

Shake the dressing ingredients together in a jar. Put the tomatoes, dandelion leaves and dressing in a bowl, toss and serve.

Kitchen note
This salad is lovely with any other leaves, but especially young red chard or red amaranth in spring, or sorrel for a sharp, lemony salad.

TROTTERS AND KNUCKLES

Spelt Groats, Knuckle of Pork and Herbs

Pig's Trotter, Woodpigeon and Wheat Soup with
   Cobnut and Watercress Sauce

No one sums up pig's trotters better than the chef Fergus Henderson, who fills his menu at St John restaurant in Clerkenwell, London, with extreme pieces of meat. They are his special subject, the magic budget ingredient he uses to 'bring an unctuousness to everything'. And they do, but not without a certain amount of work. The simplest way to use a pig's foot is to drop a split one into a stew with the other meat and braise until the meat begins to fall off the bone. If you then carefully remove it and pick out the little pieces of meat from the skin, avoiding the bone but keeping some of the delicious, gelatinous connective bits, the stew will not only benefit from the taste of the braised trotter but will also have added morsels of exceptional meat.

Buying trotters and knuckles

You may have to order trotters or knuckles – the cut just above the trotter that has more meat on it – from your butcher, because they do not always have pork delivered with the trotters. Many butchers will say there is 'no call for it'. So call for it and kickstart a trend.

    To find a local butcher, check the maps on www.bigbarn.co.uk or contact The Guild of Q Butchers (www.guildofqbutchers.com; tel: 01738 450443). Ask the butcher for naturally reared, slow-grown pork; the trotters are still a bargain.

Spelt Groats, Knuckle of Pork and Herbs

The knuckle can be cut as a large piece and include the more generously muscled part of the leg, or just be the lower part, like the shank on lamb, which the Italians call *stincotto*. It yields more meat than the trotter and is a more valuable cut for it, but it still has much of the trotter genius.

Serves 4

1 pork knuckle
4 tablespoons extra virgin olive oil
2 onions, finely chopped
1 fennel bulb, sliced
2 garlic cloves, chopped
1 teaspoon coriander seeds, ground
1 teaspoon fennel seeds
½ teaspoon ground allspice

a handful of celery leaves
200g/7oz spelt groats
1.2 litres/2 pints meat stock (see
    pages 64 and 116), or water
leaves from 4 sprigs of parsley
leaves from 4 sprigs of bronze fennel
    (or leaves from the top of the fennel
    bulb)
leaves from 2 sprigs of lovage
sea salt

Soak the pork knuckle in water overnight, then drain, put it in a pan and cover with fresh water. Bring to the boil and simmer for 2 hours or until the meat begins to fall away from the bone. Drain, remove the meat from the bone and set to one side.

Heat the oil in a separate pan, add the vegetables, garlic, spices and celery leaves and cook until they begin to soften. Add the groats with the cooked pork, then the stock or water. Bring to the boil and simmer for 15–20 minutes, until the spelt is cooked, adding the herbs during the last 10 minutes. Taste and add salt if necessary. Ladle into bowls and serve.

Pig's Trotter, Woodpigeon and Wheat Soup with Cobnut and Watercress Sauce

I go to Dorset often, and this soup sums up the field and the produce there.

Serves 4–6

2 tablespoons dripping
6 shallots, chopped
2 sprigs of thyme
1 bay leaf
3 woodpigeon
2 pig's trotters, split in half (the butcher will do this for you)
3 wineglasses of red wine
2 litres/3½ pints water or stock

200g/7oz whole wheat groats or spelt
sea salt and freshly ground black pepper

For the cobnut and watercress sauce:
115g/4oz Kentish or other cobnuts (use hazelnuts out of season)
leaves from 1 bunch of watercress
5 tablespoons olive oil
1 garlic clove, peeled (optional)

Heat the dripping in a very large pan and brown the shallots with the thyme and bay. Add the pigeons and roll them around in the hot fat, then add the pig's trotters and the wine. Allow the wine to come to the boil, cook for half a minute, then add the water or stock. Bring to the boil, skimming off any foam as it rises. Turn down to a very slow simmer and cook for at least 2 hours, until the meat from the pigeons and trotters is falling off the bone. Turn off the heat and leave to cool.

Skim the fat off the surface – there will be substantial amounts of pork fat, which you can reserve for roasting potatoes. Lift out the birds and trotters and pick the meat off both, discarding the carcasses, bones, skin, gristle and fat. Strain the cooking liquid into a pan (if it has cooled to a jelly, heat it slightly, then strain).

Add the wheat to the cooking liquid, bring to the boil, then turn down to a simmer and cook for about 20 minutes, until the wheat is tender but still has some bite. Return the meat pieces to the pan and heat to boiling point. Taste and add salt and pepper if necessary.

To make the sauce, toast the cobnuts in a dry frying pan, then put them in a mortar and pestle or food processor with the watercress, oil, garlic, if using, and a pinch of salt. Blend to a rough-textured sauce.

Serve the pottage in bowls, very hot, with a spoonful of cobnut and watercress sauce over each.

Rhythms of Dinner and a Time to Eat Soup

There is a moment, just after the Christmas lights are taken down, when the whole population goes into mass, voluntary hibernation. Try to get someone to come over for a meal and they will tell you they are not drinking, or have given up potatoes, sugar and bread. The days are very short, and your bed seems charged with a magnetic force drawing you towards its soft covers. Holding back comes naturally – a rare moment of reverting to ancient custom. A time to eat soup.

What is it about the British and soup? Soup loses out to sandwiches and pies as daily sustenance. Soup does not mean a clear pond of shimmering broth, spiked with vegetables, white beans and herbs and seasoned with green olive oil and pepper. Soup means soup kitchen. I have always believed that consommé, a delicious soup but one without calories, is not 'food' to the ever status-conscious British but a statement: 'I do not need to eat soup.'

A thousand years ago, the peasant labourer and his family would eat a thick, nutritious pottage every day. So would his feudal landlord and everyone between the two, from immediate family to the coopers, agents, herdsmen and merchants. The base of this soup was vegetable protein – a leguminous vegetable like peas, or a cereal. The soup you ate embodied where you were. Every fresh item that went into the pot would have been grown locally. There is something very democratic about soup. History books reveal that during this hiatus a thousand years ago, a moment when all the English ate well, only the sick and the elderly were thin. Keep in mind that at the time England was essentially a province of France – or Normandy. Society was feudal, and all land belonged to the king (or to God, some would say). There was no ownership. The king would grant land to his knights, who in turn would grant rights to those beneath them. In some ways it was communistic. Telling people how to eat, an anathema today with the general loathing for the nanny state, was quite normal. If the lord of the manor was not bossing, the Church certainly was.

There were approximately 150 feast days, with periods of abstinence and fasting round them. Diktats were issued over what could and could not be eaten and when. I doubt the peasant farmer with his bowl of pottage and a rabbit stolen in the dead of night registered a fast as such, but the greater point is that the wealthy, who had the potential to exhaust the food supply, were not permitted to do so at certain times. It was not long before soup began to solidify into puddings and pies and our soup era came to a close. The better and more efficient farming became, the faster the diversity of species began to diminish in favour of a few bulky grains. That little window closed, finally, with the dissolution of the Catholic Church. Goodbye feast days; so long, soup. The Mediterranean countries kept their soups: their chickpea broths, bolstered with dry bread, herbs and olive oil; the smooth cress and lettuce veloutés, the magnificent gazpachos and minestrones. We admire the southern European diet now, for its vibrancy and also for its nutritional benefits.

I am not too keen on the idea of a feudal landlord, zero land ownership, or the clergy breathing down my neck, telling me what is on the menu. But I do acknowledge a certain built-in rhythm, a seasonal body clock that will tell you, if you listen to it, the right and wrong moment to eat something. There is also, I am glad to say, that innate human pendulum between strength and weakness that should mean that a period of richness is followed by a time of clean, simple foods that impact lightly on both your body and the environment around you.

There are foods for those rich moments, like wild salmon and strawberries, and foods for everyday, like green lentils, barley, bacon and vegetables. Herbs, spices and good cooking ensure, however, that every meal, including soup, is a feast.

TURKEY

Roast Turkey with Dried Cherry, Apple and Cornbread
   Stuffing and Duck and Chestnut Forcemeat
Turkey Legs Stuffed with Nettles and Garlic

Leftovers
Using Turkey Stock
Using Cold Turkey

Well, it is not often that you have to get to grips with a turkey, but when the time comes it is worth knowing what to do and what not to do, especially as some of the better-quality birds come with big price tags. A turkey will repay you in kind, being the base for literally gallons of fantastic stock with which to go into the New Year, when light broths feel so right.

Dismantle some of the dogma that comes with traditional turkey advice, though. First, forget stuffing any part of it apart from the small cavity at the neck end. Stuffing the main cavity of the turkey means it will take a long time to cook and the meat will dry out in the process. Never stuff a turkey again – think of it as a liberation. No more piles of bread and sage, no more uneaten cold stuffing to be thrown away.

Next, unless cold turkey meat is something you actually enjoy eating for a week, buy the smallest bird you can get away with. You will still have that giant carcass for the broth store. Smaller turkeys take less time to cook, obviously, but that frees the cook yet again.

The most important change, though, is to buy a turkey you can celebrate with that has not suffered. There is a bad side to turkey farming that matches the worse chicken broiler houses. The enormous bodies of fast-grown birds cannot be supported by their weak, under-exercised legs. It does not take much to imagine the scenes in some overcrowded indoor farms. Free-range and organic turkeys are readily available, however, and so are the slow-growing traditional breeds such as Norfolk Bronze and Norfolk Black.

Buying turkey

Try to find a local producer of traditional free-range bronze, black or white turkeys through www.bigbarn.co.uk or go to www.ukturkeys.co.uk for a list of turkey producers in your area. If you find a producer, ask about how the birds have been reared: natural feed? Access to outdoors?

There are plenty of producers who sell turkeys online. Try Franklins of Thorncote (www.franklinsfarm.co.uk; tel: 01767 627644), Kelly Bronze (www.kellyturkeys.com; tel: 01245 223581), Sheepdrove Organic Farm (www.sheepdrove.com; tel: 01488 674747), Copas Turkeys (www.copas.co.uk; tel: 01628 474678) or Daylesford Organic (www.daylesfordorganic.com; tel: 01608 731718).

Turkey weights and cooking times

I have always used the guide recommended by the Kelly family, who were the farmers responsible for reviving the bronze turkey breed and putting some flavour back into the Christmas bird. They sell their turkeys online (see above).

Cooking times are based on stuffing the neck only, roasting at 175°C/350°F/Gas Mark 4 and not wrapping the bird in foil. When buying a whole turkey, allow approximately 450g/1lb per person.

3kg/6½lb	1¾ hours
5kg/11lb	2¼ hours
7kg/15¼lb	2¾ hours
9kg/19¾lb	3½ hours
11kg/24¼lb	4½ hours

Roast Turkey with Dried Cherry, Apple and Cornbread Stuffing and Duck and Chestnut Forcemeat

I have been making duck forcemeat for the neck cavity stuffing for 2 years now – it is wonderful with turkey. I do not stuff the big cavity but cook the main 'stuffing' separately, because I find the moisture in the bird is sacrificed for the stuffing.

1 turkey – weight to suit the number of guests (see above)
55g/2oz butter, melted
2 wineglasses of white wine
1 litre/1¾ pints chicken stock (see page 116; it can be made from the turkey giblets, excluding the heart and liver)
sea salt and freshly ground black pepper

For the cornbread:
225ml/8fl oz warm water
1 tablespoon fresh yeast or 1 teaspoon dried yeast
4 tablespoons caster sugar
115g/4oz yellow cornmeal
1 teaspoon salt
75g/2¾oz plain flour
75g/2¾oz wholewheat flour
1 tablespoon butter for greasing

For the main stuffing:
4 tablespoons pine nuts
2 tablespoons hazelnuts
3 tablespoons butter or dripping
8 sprigs of thyme
10 sage leaves, chopped
4 eating apples, cored and finely chopped
150g/5½oz dried Bing cherries, roughly chopped
4 onions, finely chopped
4 celery sticks, finely chopped
2 tablespoons sunflower oil
3 eggs, beaten

For the duck and chestnut forcemeat:
2 whole duck breasts (about 700g/1lb 9oz)
the heart and liver of the turkey
450g/1lb peeled vacuum-packed chestnuts, chopped
2 sprigs of thyme
2 tablespoons whisky
1 egg

First make the cornbread. Preheat the oven to 175°C/350°F/Gas Mark 4. Combine the water with the yeast and sugar and leave in a warm place for about 20 minutes, until the mixture foams. Put the cornmeal, salt and both flours in a bowl and stir in the yeast mixture. Add more water – enough to make a very thick but pourable batter. Generously butter a small baking tin and pour in the batter. Bake for approximately 25 minutes or until the edges of the cornbread are golden, then remove from the oven and leave to cool.

For the main stuffing, toast the nuts in a dry frying pan until golden, then scoop them out and set to one side. Melt the butter or dripping in the same pan, add the herbs, apples, dried cherries, onions and celery and cook gently for 5–7 minutes. Take about 6 slices of the cornbread, cut them into small dice and fry in the sunflower oil in a separate pan until golden. Combine with the nuts and the apple mixture and leave to cool. Stir in the eggs, mix well and season with salt and pepper.

Preheat the oven to 175°C/350°F/Gas Mark 4. To make the duck and chestnut forcemeat, put the duck breasts (including the fat and skin), plus the turkey heart and liver, through a mincing machine, or chop them in a food processor. Do not over-process. Cut 2 more slices of the cornbread and make it into breadcrumbs. Put the chestnuts into a bowl, add the meat, breadcrumbs, thyme, whisky, egg and some salt and pepper and mix well. Stuff the mixture into the neck cavity of the bird, tuck the large flap of skin around it and secure with a small skewer or a bamboo kebab stick. Brush the turkey with the melted butter and season with salt and pepper.

Place the turkey in a roasting tin and place in the oven. Roast according to the guidelines on page 417 (note that fan ovens cook faster; if you cannot turn the fan off, reduce the temperature to 160°C/325°F/Gas Mark 3). The bird is done if the juices run clear when you pierce the thickest part of the leg with a skewer. Remember to baste it from time to time while it is in the oven.

An hour before the expected end of cooking, put the stuffing in an ovenproof dish, put it in the oven and bake until golden on the surface.

When the turkey is done, lift it out of the roasting tin, transfer to a serving platter, then cover with foil and leave to rest for 20–30 minutes. Pour the fat out of the roasting tin, place the tin over the heat and add the wine and stock. Bring to the boil, scraping at the bottom of the tin with a wooden spoon to deglaze the delicious bits that stick to the bottom. Simmer for 5 minutes, season with salt and pepper, then pour it into a gravy jug.

Serve the turkey with the usual good things: potatoes roasted in duck or goose fat (see page 187); chipolatas, bacon rolls, Brussels sprouts and bread sauce (see page 306).

Turkey Legs Stuffed with Nettles and Garlic

Because turkeys love nettles (one of the many reasons farmers love rearing turkeys).

This is a good supper dish to eat with buttered tagliatelle or mashed potatoes. Since nettles are best in spring, you will need to use either frozen turkey legs or meat from a supplier who rears them all year round. Pick only the young tops of the nettles – I wear rubber gloves and cut the nettle tops with scissors.

Serves 6–8

4 handfuls of young nettle tops
4 garlic cloves, crushed to a paste with a little salt
8 tablespoons sourdough breadcrumbs
4 tablespoons butter

a few gratings of lemon zest
a large pinch or two of grated nutmeg
2 turkey legs
sea salt and freshly ground black pepper

Preheat the oven to 190°C/375°F/Gas Mark 5. Bring a saucepan of water to the boil, add the nettles, then bring back to the boil. Drain well. Chop the nettles (which will now have lost their sting) and leave to cool. Mix them with the garlic, breadcrumbs, butter, lemon zest and nutmeg. Season with salt and pepper.

Use your fingers to open a cavity between the skin of each turkey leg and the flesh. Push the stuffing into the cavity, working from the thigh to the drumstick, so all the meat will be flavoured with the stuffing. Truss the legs with string to stop the stuffing leaching out during cooking. Season the legs with salt and pepper, then put them in a roasting tin and roast for 1–1½ hours, until the meat juices run clear when the thickest part of each leg is pierced with a skewer. Leave to rest for about 15 minutes.

Serve with a gravy made from the cooking juices, following the method in the roast turkey recipe above but halving the quantity of wine and stock.

Turkey leftovers

Using Turkey Stock

Use turkey stock, made from the leftover carcass of the roast bird, in any recipe that calls for meat or poultry stock. It has a richer, gamier flavour than chicken stock and becomes beautifully gelatinous. It will also spread the cost of a more expensive free-range turkey across several meals. Make as for chicken stock (see page 116).

Using Cold Turkey

Cold turkey meat can be used in any of the chicken leftover recipes on pages 118–120, and will reheat perfectly in the recipe for Pistachio and Lamb Rice on page 312.

VEAL

Baked Short Pasta with Veal Meatballs and
   Green Ricotta
Stuffed Breast of Veal

So put off veal were consumers by the revelation that calves were crated in tiny spaces all their lives and fed only milk, preventing any normal behaviour that a young animal should show, that even now welfare-friendly English veal is available, no one is persuaded to eat it. Banging a drum for good veal is a lonely busking job. Drink milk, eat welfare-friendly veal, you say. The response has been minimal. But since starting to campaign for a place in the food chain for dairy bulls, which clearly cannot become part of the milk-producing herd, there are more and more British producers. This is a matter for more influential chefs to work on; the more welfare-friendly veal is served in pubs and restaurants, the more acceptable it will become. The term welfare-friendly is a bit unfortunate, but it seems to have stuck. It means that the young animals are reared loose in pens until about six months of age, fed a diet of milk, plus straw for roughage so they can ruminate, and grouped with other calves so they can socialise. There are better ways to make use of the dairy boys, and some farms are experimenting with rearing the males of traditional dairy breeds such as Guernsey to full size, with some success. But milk-fed, welfare-friendly veal is a creditable answer for now. Calves are not crated in the UK – it is against the law – but crating is still permitted in Holland.

The flavour of milk-fed veal is buttery and the meat tender and easy to cook, even from the forequarters. Most cuts can go into the pan for a quick fry on either side, but the trickier cuts need a recipe that magics a difficult – yet inexpensive – piece of meat into a banquet.

But there is good news: in early 2008 an initiative was launched to encourage dairy farmers to produce veal. Additionally, Tesco has asked all farms that supply them with milk to stop killing dairy bull calves just after they are born, and rear them for veal or beef.

Buying welfare-friendly veal

Waitrose sells good English welfare-friendly veal at a price that is friendly too but also try three other producers: Daylesford Organic milk-fed veal was developed along with their herd of rare-breed Gloucester cattle, from which they are making a genuine Double Gloucester cheese. Check www.daylesfordorganic.com; tel: 01608 731718. Or there's veal from Kimber's Farm in Charlton Musgrove, Somerset: www.kimbersfarmshop.co.uk; tel: 01963 33177. Or try the Bocaddon Farm veal near Looe in Cornwall; tel: 01503 220991.

Baked Short Pasta with Veal Meatballs and Green Ricotta

A big baked pasta dish that looks magnificent, serves the masses and costs little to make. More exciting than the usual pasta dish – it looks like a macaroni cheese until you dig into it, finding a meatball here, a green ricotta dumpling there...

Serves 10

For the meatballs:
1kg/2¼lb minced veal (or lean beef)
115g/4oz chicken livers, chopped very small (optional)
a few gratings of lemon zest
1 tablespoon dried oregano
115g/4oz fresh breadcrumbs
2 eggs, beaten
1 tablespoon freshly grated Parmesan cheese
2 tablespoons olive oil
sea salt and freshly ground black pepper

For the green ricotta dumplings:
500g/1lb 2oz fresh spinach
350g/12oz fresh ricotta cheese, drained
1 tablespoon freshly grated Parmesan cheese, or Gruyère
1 tablespoon plain flour
2 eggs, beaten
2 tablespoons melted butter
½ teaspoon grated nutmeg

For the pasta and sauce:
1.5 litres/2¾ pints milk
1 bay leaf
a few gratings of nutmeg
55g/2oz butter
55g/2oz plain flour
6 tablespoons freshly grated Parmesan cheese
3 tablespoons double cream
750g/1lb 10oz short, tubular pasta, such as rigatoni, fusilli or penne
about 300g/10½oz cherry tomatoes, sliced into thirds

First combine all the ingredients for the meatballs except the oil and roll them into spheres the size of golf balls. Heat the oil in a large casserole and gently fry the meatballs until golden all over. Remove from the heat and set aside. They do not need to be cooked through, as they will be cooked again with the pasta.

For the dumplings, wash the spinach, then put it in a pan with just the water clinging to its leaves and cook until wilted. Drain well and squeeze out all the water. Chop the spinach and combine with the ricotta, Parmesan or Gruyerè, flour, eggs, melted butter and nutmeg. Season with a little salt and pepper. Shape into pingpong-sized balls, then flatten them slightly into a lozenge shape. Place on a board and leave to one side, covered with cling film.

For the sauce, heat the milk with the bay leaf and nutmeg until almost boiling. Remove from the heat and leave to steep for 10 minutes. Melt the butter in a large pan, add the flour and cook gently, stirring, until the mixture has a gritty texture. Strain the milk and gradually add it to the butter and flour roux, stirring all the time to ensure that there are no lumps. Bring back to the boil, again stirring all the time. The sauce will thicken as it heats. Allow it to boil for a minute, then add 2 tablespoons of the Parmesan. Stir in the cream and season with a little salt.

Meanwhile, cook the pasta in a large quantity of boiling water until *al dente* (an opaque fleck should be visible inside when the pasta is bitten or cut). Drain the pasta and stir it into the sauce.

To assemble the dish, preheat the oven to 220°C/425°F/Gas Mark 7. Spoon about a third of the pasta mixture into a big, deep gratin dish or roasting tray, then add the meatballs, spacing them evenly. Spoon over another third of the pasta mixture. Place the dumplings on the surface, evenly spaced, then spoon the remaining pasta around them. Scatter the cherry tomatoes on top, then the remaining cheese. Bake for about 20 minutes, until browned on top and bubbling underneath. Serve immediately.

Stuffed Breast of Veal

Served warm, this is a beautiful way to cook veal in summer; the meat is buttery, the stuffing light.

Serves 6–8

1.3kg/3lb veal breast, boned (but ask to keep the bones)
2 hardboiled eggs
55g/2oz unsmoked cooked ham, cut into strips
2 tablespoons extra virgin olive oil
1 garlic clove, peeled
1 each onion, celery stick and carrot, peeled
2 sprigs of thyme
1 bay leaf
3 wineglasses of white wine
1 litre/1¾ pints chicken or veal stock

sea salt and freshly ground black pepper

For the stuffing:
1 tablespoon butter
4 shallots, finely chopped
750g/1lb 10oz minced veal
2 heaped tablespoons fresh sourdough breadcrumbs
2 garlic cloves, chopped
leaves from 4 small sprigs of parsley, chopped
leaves from 2 sprigs of tarragon, chopped
a few gratings of nutmeg

First make the stuffing. Melt the butter in a small pan, add the shallots and cook gently until soft. Mix with rest of stuffing ingredients and season.

Spread the veal breast out on the worktop, skin-side down. Season with salt and pepper, then spread the stuffing all over it. Slice the egg whites and chop the yolks. Scatter them over the surface and then follow with the ham. Roll the veal breast up, the meat grain running the length of the roll, and tie tightly with string. Brown it on all sides in the olive oil. Take it out and brown the leftover veal bones in the pan. Put the veal roll in a large pan with the veal bones underneath, then add the garlic, onion, celery, carrot and herbs. Cover with the white wine and stock and bring to the boil, skimming away any foam that rises to the surface. Turn down to a very slow simmer and cook, covered, for 2–2½ hours, until the meat is tender. Lift out on to a plate and leave in a warm place to rest for 30 minutes. Strain the cooking stock into a clean pan (reserve the vegetables) and boil until well flavoured. Taste and season if necessary. Serve the veal thinly sliced, either hot, with the stock and boiled vegetables, or cold, with salad and pickles.

WATERCRESS

Watercress Soup

Watercress and Radish Sauce for Pasta

The rocket of Britain and greatly underrated, watercress is in fact a much handier leaf than Italian *rucola*, because even after cooking it is there with all its peppery flavours and green, green colour. Much is grown in the south of England, though I have found a supplier of land cress (grown out of water) near Liverpool that gives the species a whole new dimension. The original type, grown in special ponds, has been farmed in this country for 200 years. Before that it grew like a weed in chalk streams and was gathered wild.

Recently I have noticed that there are fewer and fewer bunches sitting in water on view in shops. The industry explains that cutting and tying bunches has high labour costs, and consequently watercress has succumbed to bagged salad culture in many supermarkets. I find that the bagged version needs to be eaten quickly – so am always happy to see bunched watercress, even if the cost is a little higher. The good thing is that the stalks can be used in the soup on page 430, providing you chop them first, or they will be harder to liquidise to a smooth cream.

Buying watercress

Most of the year watercress is widely available, but bunches are found mainly in greengrocer's shops or at vegetable stalls in markets, bought through local wholesalers. Land cress is grown out of water and has a smaller leaf. To buy it, contact Wirral Watercress (tel: 07779 019348) for stockists or visit them at Woodside Nurseries, Childer Thornton, Wirral.

Watercress Soup

I will probably be guilty of putting a watercress soup in every publication
I am involved in, but it is always good to have one close to hand. Its beauty
lies in the strong flavour waves watercress can radiate, even in a quantity
of stock with cream and the potato which gives the soup a little thickness.
That's a lot of blandness to invade, and the watercress pulls it off. Of course,
the more you use, the better it will be. All the bunch can be added but the
stalks may resist the blender, leaving strings in the soup. If you have a food
mill (mouli-légumes), push the soup through it and you will know green,
peppery velvet.

Serves 4

55g/2oz butter
1 white onion, roughly chopped
2 medium-sized potatoes, peeled
    and cut into dice

1 litre/1¾ pints chicken stock (see
    page 116)
4 bunches of watercress, roughly
    chopped
6 tablespoons double cream
sea salt and freshly ground black
    pepper

Melt the butter in a saucepan, add the onion and cook until soft but not
coloured. Add the potatoes and stock, bring to the boil and simmer for
15 minutes, until the potatoes are tender. Add the watercress and simmer
for 2 minutes. Liquidise or blitz in a food processor until smooth. Reheat
gently, stir in the cream, then taste and season. Serve very hot – the soup
will lose colour if not eaten immediately.

Watercress and Radish Sauce for Pasta

A leafy sauce to spoon over pasta and eat with scrapings of hard ewe's milk cheese.

Serves 6–8

3 bunches of watercress, the thicker
    stalks cut off
a few gratings of horseradish
8 French breakfast radishes, thinly
    sliced
1 garlic clove, crushed to a paste with
    a little salt (optional)

2 tablespoons blanched hazelnuts,
    toasted in a dry frying pan and
    then ground
4 tablespoons freshly grated
    Twineham Grange or Parmesan
    cheese
6 tablespoons extra virgin olive oil
sea salt and freshly ground black
    pepper

Chop the watercress, add both types of radish, then mix with the remaining ingredients. Season with salt, if necessary, and add pepper.

WHEAT

Bread Soups

Wild Yeast Bread

Thin Breads

Three-minute Spelt Bread

'Saffron' Buns

Airy Buns

Berkswell Cheese Scones

Farro with Potatoes and Basil Oil

Spelt and Lentil Salad with Lots of Parsley

At the heart of cooking are grains, the single most important food, yet one that is fraught with difficulties. Grains contain almost all we need to be properly fed, but much of the wheat grain we eat daily has been processed, leaving white carbohydrate and few of the essential vitamins, oils and fibre that make grain a good food. This whole subject is so well covered in baker Andrew Whitley's book, *Bread Matters, the state of modern bread and a definitive guide to baking your own* (Fourth Estate, 2006), that I can only urge concerned devotees of bread and pastry to read it. In the case of bread, Whitley explains how at every level, from the choice of grain seed to the milling and baking process, events conspire to make bread a nutritionally empty food.

The evidence is overwhelming. For me, the most depressing side of this is that, predominantly, one product of grain is all most people will ever know – refined white wheat flour – when there are not only dozens of grains and cereals to discover but also the fact that they can be eaten at various stages of processing: from whole pot wheat, which still has the bran, to partially hulled, to cracked wheat and groats. And then there are the various grades of flour. I eat much less white flour than I once did. I do not automatically make white toast for breakfast, much as I like it, but dutifully eat oats and whole grains, having been convinced that they are best for nourishment and refuelling. But baking is the most intoxicating art in cookery. It is chemistry, but when the bread rises, the pastry puffs or a sloppy cake mixture becomes a rich crumb, baking is pure magic. For this kind of work, white flour is a necessary requirement. So, to use it and not contradict my complaint that too much of it is eaten, I try to buy better-quality white flour and bake with it occasionally, in a festive mood, while wholemeal and whole grains are part of my everyday cookery. For all but the lightest pastry and cakes, I use stoneground white, the only flour to retain the oils and nutrients that are lost in commercial roller milling. This flour has a slightly grey appearance and much more flavour. I notice when making bread with it that I need to add less salt than when I bake with conventional white flour.

The story of good wheat begins with breed. Modern wheats are hybrids developed since the advent of agricultural chemicals – in particular, nitrogen fertiliser, plus the myriad herbicides and fungicides that are used in wheat farming. The two go hand in hand. The modern wheats need the chemicals to crop successfully. But what of the forgotten wheats, the pre-War breeds that grew naturally? They grew without help from chemicals – where are they?

If used, they are in organic production, and most probably originate from European stock. Switzerland has an essential bank of pre-War seeds, for example, but I have also seen pre-War breeds of wheat grown in India. The yield of such wheat is sneered at by the conventional farming industry, because the higher the level of protein, the more farmers earn per tonne. Farmers growing these ancient wheats argue that their protein is of a better quality – and it is a claim that is gaining credibility. Higher levels of certain vitamins are being found in samples of traditional wheat breeds and the organic grail may well be in sight, the moment when beliefs that natural farming produces food with better nutrient quality are proven. For me, a riveting aspect of this debate is how it underpins the commonsense philosophy of eating less but higher-grade wheat as part of a more diverse diet that includes other grains and pulses (oats, barley, lentils, etc).

Buying flour

For speciality, British-grown flours such as spelt, rye and pre-War breeds of organically grown wheat flour, I order from Gilchester Organics in Northumberland, who even have their own mill on their farm – Gilchesters Organic Farm, Hawkwell, Northumberland NE18 0QL; www.gilchesters.com; tel: 01661 886119. I also buy white and brown flour, stone milled by Michael Stoate at Cann Mills in Dorset; phone 01747 852475 for stockists. Waitrose's own farm at Leckford in Hampshire also produces very good single-estate flour, which is sold in their stores.

Bread Soups

When good bread ages, it does so with grace. It slowly dries out and all the while it has various uses. Without a breadcrumb coating, I could not have introduced my children to a dozen new varieties of fish. Older bread is also the base of some of my favourite puddings: summer pudding, apple charlotte and a nice gooey one consisting of milk-dipped bread fingers served with a toffee sauce made by boiling together equal quantities of demerara sugar, golden syrup and butter. But, more than anything, my stale bread store goes into soup. It is the sop, the part of an otherwise light lunchtime broth that keeps me going through the rest of the afternoon. A base of lightly fried chopped garlic and onion needs only some vegetables, maybe some chopped bacon or pork, shredded spring greens or black cabbage, chickpeas or beans; clams, mussels or tomatoes – everything is allowed, but not all together, of course. Once the vegetables have been softened in the pan, add the broth and cook until all is tender. At this point add anything that needs only a short cooking time – fish or mussels, for example. Adjust the seasoning, add handfuls of herbs and ladle the broth over a slice of bread, placed in the bottom of a soup bowl.

Wild Yeast Bread

A sourdough by another name, but as dark and ripe as the famous Poilâne loaf. This recipe, which can be adapted to the use of many different flours and formed into a number of shapes, was born out of the need to be efficient and a dislike of commercial yeast. I happily used commercial yeast for a long time, believing it to be brewer's yeast – a by-product of beer making. It is, in fact, grown on molasses derived from a non-organic crop (although it is permitted in organic baking) and the process creates contaminated by-products. So in our fridge we have 'Dave': a container filled with a fermented mixture of flour (wheat and chickpea, or gram, flour), pressed fruit juice and a few organic sultanas. Naming it like a pet is cheesy, exasperating the children, yet at the same time engaging them in a process. They will never forget their pet yeast and the way it is regularly fed.

Making wild yeast is a long process, and it is perhaps better to start with a piece of dough made the conventional way. Putting this in a container and adding flour and water to it regularly (about 3 tablespoons of each every 2–5 days) will get your fermentation off to a good start. Every time you make bread, use part but not all of the wild yeast, then replenish it with more flour and water 'food'. After a while, the contents of the container will be mostly wild – little of the original dough will remain. 'Dave' has been alive and kicking for several months now and not only does he lend a wonderful ripe, fruity taste to the bread but any dough I make with this wild yeast succeeds. Pizza dough can be rolled out thinly and has a perfect texture when cooked; breads are chewy and have a long-lasting quality; yeast-leavened pancakes like blini are many times more delicious than any I have made using commercial yeast.

Another advantage to using a leaven that gives flavour as well as oomph is that you need less salt. Just remember to keep your wild yeast captive in the fridge or it will over ferment and be useless – and feed it weekly whether you use it or not.

700g/1lb 9oz stoneground or organic strong white flour

½ teaspoon fine sea salt or 1 teaspoon soft sea salt crystals

115g/4oz piece of dough from the previous day's baking; or the same

quantity of wild yeast, as described above

350ml/12fl oz water, at blood temperature

1 tablespoon extra virgin olive oil

oil for brushing

Put the flour in a large bowl, stir in the salt and add the piece of dough or the wild yeast. Add the water and oil and begin to mix and knead the dough – to speed things up, I use a tabletop mixer with a dough hook attachment. Knead the dough by hand for 15 minutes or for 5 minutes on the slow setting of a food mixer, until it is smooth and elastic. If the dough feels too sticky after a few minutes' kneading, add a little more flour; if it is too dry, work in a little water. When you have finished kneading it, cover the bowl with a cloth and leave in a warm, draught-free spot for 1½–2 hours, until increased in size (or leave for longer at cool room temperature, or overnight in the fridge).

Knock the air out of the dough, then prepare two 450g/1lb loaf tins by brushing them with oil. Divide the dough in half, place each piece on a floured work surface and shape into a smooth ball. Put one piece of dough in each tin, dust with flour and cut a slash across the top to help the bread expand during cooking. (Alternatively, shape the dough into 2 rounds and put them on separate baking sheets; dust with flour as for the tins and cut a cross in the centre.) Leave the dough to 'prove', or rise, again, uncovered, for 20–30 minutes.

Preheat the oven to 230°C/450°F/Gas Mark 8. Bake the loaves for 30–40 minutes. They are ready when they come easily out of the tin and sound hollow when tapped on the base with a finger.

Kitchen note

You can use any wheat flour in this recipe, such as wholemeal, brown 80 per cent wholemeal, malted Granary or multiseed mixes. You can also make your own seed bread, adding pumpkin seeds, linseed, sesame seeds or poppy seeds; or add a proportion of oats or rye flour; or flavour with honey or herbs; or add yoghurt, milk, ale, dried fruit or molasses... Don't add everything together, though, or you will not be able to identify anything. Be watchful of the quantities, try to stick to the basic flour-liquid ratio given in the recipe, but add more or less liquid if necessary to get a dough of the correct consistency.

Thin Breads

To make these flat discs of bread, substitute soft white flour for a third of the strong white flour in the recipe above. After proving the dough for the first time, so it grows in volume, cut it into 8 equal pieces and roll or pull each one into a round about 5mm–1cm/¼–½ inch thick. Lay them on a floured baking sheet (I am a fan of those round slotted pizza baking trays, as they cook the underside properly) and bake at a slightly lower temperature than in the recipe above. The flatbreads are ready when they are light brown, puffed and lift easily off the baking sheet. They should sound hollow when tapped with a finger.

Flavour them, if you wish, with sesame seeds, nigella seeds or fresh coriander (these must be worked into the dough) or add a pinch of dried herbs such as thyme or rosemary to the dough and brush with olive oil. You can also fill them with roast vegetables, such as parsnips and beetroot (see page 369), and fresh goat's cheese, then fold into a half-moon shape and bake.

I sometimes make these breads with about 80 per cent white flour and 20 per cent wholemeal, then roll them out into small rounds and cook on top of the oven, like a chapatti. You will need a dry, heavy-bottomed frying pan to do this. Cook each one for a minute or two over a fairly high heat, then flip over and cook for another minute until puffed and light. Eat with the curries on pages 122, 124, 161, 229 and 349, or Lentils and Rice (see page 254). Make a large bowl of yoghurt sauce with 300ml/½ pint plain yoghurt, some chopped mint, black onion seeds and 2 tablespoons of olive oil spooned over the top.

Three-minute Spelt Bread

Making spelt bread is completely different from making conventional wheat bread. The grain reacts aggressively to yeast, and does not have to be mixed, let alone kneaded, for more than a minute. There is also no need to let it rise.

This recipe is from Sybille Wilkinson, whose husband, Andrew, grows spelt in Northumberland. It really does take just 3 minutes to prepare.

500g/1lb 2oz spelt flour
10g/¼oz fast-action dried yeast
½ teaspoon sea salt
55g/2oz sunflower seeds
55g/2oz sesame seeds
55g/2oz linseeds
500ml/18fl oz warm water

Preheat the oven to 200°C/400°F/Gas Mark 6. Combine all the ingredients in a bowl, adding the water last. Mix well, then turn the dough into a greased 900g/2lb loaf tin. Put in the oven immediately and bake for 1 hour, until the loaf has risen, lifts out of the tin easily, and sounds hollow when tapped underneath. Take the loaf out of the tin, then put it back in the oven for 5–10 minutes to crisp up the sides and base. Remove from the oven and leave to cool on a wire rack.

'Saffron' Buns

A homage to the Cornish saffron bun but without the fruit. These light, soft rolls, hot from the oven, are exceptionally good with soups, dry-cured meats, or toasted with potted meat. I also love them buttered and stuffed with the freshest watercress, the vegetable that has historically been a substitute for meat in England.

The buns are saffron in colour only, since I'm more charmed by the tradition of using saffron in bread than I am by the flavour. Many bakers in Cornwall now use colouring in their buns instead. I've replaced the saffron with turmeric here. This spice is anyway very good for you, being rich in vitamin B6. Recent studies have found that it may help prevent the onset of arthritis.

Makes 24

250ml/9fl oz milk
1 teaspoon ground turmeric
1 tablespoon sugar
1 teaspoon fine sea salt
115g/4oz butter, softened

14g/½oz (2 sachets) fast-action dried yeast
175ml/6fl oz warm water
675g/1½lb strong white flour, plus extra for dusting
2 eggs – plus 1 egg beaten with 1 tablespoon water, to glaze

Heat the milk to boiling point in a small saucepan, then stir in the turmeric, sugar, salt and butter. Remove from the heat and allow to cool.

In a large mixing bowl, combine the yeast and water, then add the milk mixture. Add half the flour and mix well, then beat in the eggs. Add the remaining flour slowly, kneading to a soft, workable dough that pulls away from the sides of the bowl. You may not need to add all the flour. Turn the dough on to a lightly floured surface, cover and allow to rest for 10 minutes. Knead once again until smooth and elastic; this should take a further 5 minutes. Shape the dough into a ball, place in a clean bowl and cover loosely with cling film. Leave to rise in a warm, draught-free place for about an hour, until it has doubled in bulk.

Preheat the oven to 200°C/400°F/Gas Mark 6. Grease 2 baking sheets. Roll the dough into a square about 2.5cm/1 inch thick and cut it into 24 untidy squares. Arrange them on the greased baking sheets about 1cm/½ inch apart. Brush each bun with the egg glaze and then leave to prove (rise) for about 40 minutes. Bake in the oven for 12–15 minutes, until the buns are puffed and golden and the base sounds hollow when tapped with a finger. Eat hot.

Airy Buns

Made from choux pastry, these are light, hollow and good for stuffing with cream cheese and smoked fish.

Makes 12

150g/5½oz strong white flour
a pinch of fine sea salt
225ml/8fl oz cold water

115g/4oz unsalted butter, cut into dice
5 medium eggs, lightly beaten – plus
1 egg beaten with a little milk, to
glaze

Preheat the oven to 220°C/425°F/Gas Mark 7. Sift the flour and salt on to a sheet of greaseproof paper. Heat the water and butter in a saucepan until it boils; when it is boiling fast, tip in the flour and salt. Stir vigorously until the paste leaves the sides of the pan clean. Cook over a very low heat, stirring, until the mixture begins to stick to the bottom of the pan again. Remove from the heat. Add the eggs a little at a time, beating the mixture until it is smooth before adding more. After you have added about 4 eggs, the mixture should be sloppier and softer. Add the remaining beaten egg very gradually, and stop adding it as soon as the mixture is soft enough to drop slowly from the spoon.

Line a baking sheet with baking parchment. Spoon or pipe 12 pingpong-sized balls of the choux pastry on to the parchment, evenly spaced but not less than 4cm/1½ inches apart. Brush with a little of the egg and milk mixture, then place in the oven and bake for 15 minutes. Turn the oven down to 200°C/400°F/Gas Mark 6 and continue to bake until the buns are crisp and golden. Cool on a wire rack, then slit them open ready for filling.

Berkswell Cheese Scones

I like to make these small, to eat with smooth soups or serve hot with drinks. Make use of any cheese rind or drying bits – they will melt nicely into the dough.

Makes 20 small scones

450g/1lb plain flour, plus extra for
    dusting
1 teaspoon bicarbonate of soda
1 teaspoon cream of tartar
2 teaspoons fine sea salt
85g/3oz beef dripping or butter,
    or 6 tablespoons olive oil
225g/8oz Berkswell cheese, roughly
    grated
300ml/½ pint sheep's milk yoghurt

Preheat the oven to 200°C/400°F/Gas Mark 6. Sift all the dry ingredients into a bowl and rub in the fat, then stir in the cheese. Make a well in the centre and stir in the yoghurt to make a smooth dough. Turn out on to a floured board and roll out to a thickness of 1cm/½ inch. Cut into 5cm/2 inch squares and put on a baking sheet lined with baking parchment. Bake for about 10 minutes, until puffed and golden. Eat as soon as possible (they reheat well).

Farro with Potatoes and Basil Oil

An interesting naming debate arises with farro, an ancient wheat breed that is sold as a partly hulled whole grain to put in soups and braises. Pliny the Elder once noted that farro was called *adoreum*, or glory, which is appropriate for a grain that is so delicious to eat. There has been a revival of farro in Italy, but its real name is emmer and it is only being cultivated in small quantities organically in the mountainous Garfagnana region of Tuscany. You will, though, find packs from Italy labelled farro that contain another historic grain, spelt, which is being grown in lowland areas. For the real farro, look for mention of the co-operative body that certifies it, the Consorzio Produttori Farro della Garfagnana. If you get the spelt version, however, it is no real bad thing – both can be used in this recipe.

Serves 4

3 tablespoons unsalted butter
1 red onion, finely chopped or grated
200g/7oz farro (whole wheat grains, partly hulled)
1 wineglass of white wine
1 litre/1¾ pints vegetable stock (you may need more)

8 new potatoes, cooked and sliced
225g/8oz vegetable sprouts (see Kitchen Note below)
sea salt and freshly ground black pepper

For the basil oil:
a handful of basil leaves
4 tablespoons extra virgin olive oil

To make the basil oil, either liquidise the basil and oil together or pound them together in a mortar and pestle. Season to taste.

Melt 2 tablespoons of the butter in a large, shallow pan, add the onion and cook over a low heat for a few minutes until soft. Add the farro and wine, bring to the boil, then pour in enough stock to cover the grains by about 2cm/¾ inch. Simmer for 20–30 minutes, until the farro is soft to the bite. Next, beat in the remaining butter and stir in the potatoes. Taste and add salt and pepper if necessary, then stir in half the vegetable sprouts. Serve with the remaining sprouts and the basil oil spooned over the top.

 Kitchen note
Vegetable sprouts such as broccoli, fennel and leek are available from Goodness Direct: www.goodnessdirect.co.uk; tel: 0871 871 6611.

Spelt and Lentil Salad with Lots of Parsley

Try to find parsley with tender leaves, or this salad is unpleasant to eat.

Serves 4

100g/3½oz small brown Italian lentils
200g/7oz whole spelt
leaves from a large bunch of flat-leaf
    parsley, finely chopped
5 tablespoons extra virgin olive oil
sea salt and freshly ground black
    pepper

Put the lentils in a pan, cover them well with water and bring to the boil. Simmer for about 10 minutes, then add the spelt. Cook for another 15–20 minutes, until both are done. Do not overcook the lentils or they will turn to mush – so test regularly. Once cooked, drain immediately and tip into a bowl. Season, then add the parsley and olive oil. Eat with anything. You can even heat it up in a pan for a hot supper.

WILD SALMON

Poached Wild Salmon

Wild Salmon and Halibut Cured and Served in
   Soy, Lime and Garlic Broth

I miss wild salmon. My father liked fly-fishing and he was a man who ate his trophies. It was impossible not to notice, however, that the supply was running out. On my last holiday with him, we fished for a week (he had fished for another prior to that) on the Isle of Lewis in the Outer Hebrides and did not catch one. Not one, and this was on a river that, according to the book in the lodge he had rented, had once filled fishermen's bags full. By the time the week was up and we were about to pack our bags, the flies had been ditched and we were using diamante-studded spinners that we found by the river, dropped by poachers. Later I realised, having learned more about salmon, that the poachers were not the reason for the disappearing fish; the cages of farmed salmon in the sea lochs had more to answer for. Sea lice and escaped fish have been blamed for the demise of salmon stocks, but the netting boats outside the estuaries were culpable, too. Now netting is banned and the salmon farms have begun to clean up their act, wild salmon numbers are rising, but very slowly. I am still yet to buy a Scottish wild salmon. I buy sea trout instead, whose stocks are healthy.

Two summers ago I travelled to Southeast Alaska to see the Marine Stewardship Council-certified wild salmon fishermen. This is an area where netting and fish farming is banned. The wild life is extraordinary – there are so many whales that the fishermen complain about their breath as they breech. Five species of salmon were heading towards the rivers to spawn and every time the boats trolled their line of hooks, up came a number of fish, some enormous. Hook and line is low-impact fishing that allows large quantities of fish to escape into the rivers to breed. Numbers in the region are healthy, yet the catch is big enough to see this fish taken frozen to the UK, where it is sold with an MSC logo.

The salmon species in the Pacific Northwest are different. They include king salmon, coho, sock-eye, pink and chum. Perhaps it is hard to match the beauty of the troubled Atlantic salmon but king salmon is easy to love, and each of the others has characteristics that suit certain cooking methods.

The fish are cleaned immediately on landing and then blast frozen. They are not even in rigor, so after several months in a freezer they are still biologically a few hours out of the water. They are sea-freighted to the UK, so at least we have a supply that we can feel happy about eating, whereas farmed salmon can be questionable environmentally and the Atlantic salmon needs to be left, Garbo-esque, alone, reminding me that even with the glittering spinner, we never caught that Lewis fish.

Buying wild salmon

Marks & Spencer has committed itself to stocking wild Atlantic salmon, selling it fresh and smoked. Look for the MSC certification logo on Alaskan salmon in other shops. Do not buy unless it is present; other parts of Alaska are fished using nets.

Wild sea trout is available in season, from April to October – ask your fishmonger.

Poached Wild Salmon

1.5–2kg/3¼–4½lb whole wild salmon, scaled and gutted

For the stock:
1 litre/1¾ pints water
2 carrots, roughly chopped
1 celery stick, roughly chopped

1 onion, roughly chopped
1 bay leaf
4 cloves
6 peppercorns
1 wineglass of white wine vinegar, or white wine

Bring all the stock ingredients to the boil in a fish kettle and simmer for 30 minutes. Lower the fish into the simmering stock, cover the pan and turn off the heat. Even a 1kg/2¼lb fish will cook naturally in the cooling stock within about 20 minutes.

To serve, lift the fish from the kettle, let it drain a little and then transfer to a serving platter. Remove the skin just before serving. Eat warm or cold, with a butter sauce such as the one on page 372, or with Mayonnaise (see page 281).

Wild Salmon and Halibut Cured and Served in Soy, Lime and Garlic Broth

The freshest fish, cured, sliced and served with an aromatic Southeast Asian broth. All can be prepared in advance, the fish sliced and covered in cling film ready to serve.

Serves 8–10 as a starter

700g/1lb 9oz wild Alaskan salmon fillet, in 2 fillets cut from the same fish, skin on
700g/1lb 9oz halibut fillet, in 2 fillets cut from the same fish, skin on
40g/1½oz sea salt
30g/1oz caster sugar
12 black peppercorns, crushed
soft leaves from a fennel bulb, or 3 baby fennel bulbs with leaves attached (save some leaves for garnish)
chervil and/or fennel leaves, to garnish

For the sauce:
150ml/¼ pint naturally brewed Japanese soy sauce, such as Kikkoman
juice of 2 limes
1 garlic clove, very finely chopped

Put a fillet of each fish skin-side down in a shallow, oval ceramic dish. Mix together the salt, sugar, peppercorns and soft fennel leaves and scatter them over the fish. Cover each with its second fillet, skin-side up. Cover the whole dish with cling film, then put a wooden board that will fit inside the dish on top and a weight (such as 2 cans of tomatoes) on top of that to compress the fish. Leave in the fridge for at least 18 hours, turning once. Liquid will run out of the fish.

Remove the fish from the dish and slice each fillet across the grain, taking it off close to the skin. Lay the slices on a clean, non-metal plate, cover with cling film and put in the fridge.

Combine all the ingredients for the sauce, then refrigerate.

To serve, take 2 slices of each cured fish, wrap into a curl and put into a shallow dish for an individual serving. Pour over a little of the sauce, then scatter some chervil and/or fennel leaf on top.

WOODPIGEON

Pigeon Breasts with Buttered Shrimps
Potted Pigeon Salad with Celery and Mustard Dressing
Pigeon Rice with Figs and Whole Wheat

Here is a meat supply to tap into. Woodpigeons are plentiful, well-fed, loathed by farmers and therefore a target pursued with passion. Unlike other game birds, they are available all year round. My favourite time to eat them, however, is later in the summer, when the feathered gluttons have been at the loose corn left in fields after harvest. They couldn't get fatter at any other time of year, or better to eat. I eat the breasts roasted or fried, and when there is time, braise the small legs to make little pots of peppery meat with a mustard dressing.

In France, pigeon are farmed and usually sold as squab. These are easy to cook and have a milder flavour than the birds that scrabble for food all year round, jetting backwards and forwards between wood and field. Squab are penned, if not caged, so their meat is predictably easy to bite, but less interesting.

Last year I ate a dove that a member of a shoot had mistaken for a pigeon. It was paler, sweeter, and I was slightly sad to be doing it. Must be the association with peace, I thought – as I rubbed it with olive oil before putting it in the oven.

Buying woodpigeon

Ask your local butcher for woodpigeon and look for them in farmers' markets. Game birds including pigeon are available direct from game expert David Hammerson at the Everleigh Farm Shop (www.everleighfarmshop.co.uk; tel: 01264 850344), from Ben Weatherall at Yorkshire Game (www.yorkshiregame.co.uk; tel: 01748 810212) and also from The Thoroughly Wild Meat Company (www.thoroughlywildmeat.co.uk; tel: 01963 824788 or 07770 392041).

Pigeon Breasts with Buttered Shrimps

This was an accidental feast for two; a clean-out of the freezer section in the fridge that produced a remarkable dinner. You will need 4 pigeon breasts, some good brown or sourdough rye bread for toasting and 2 small pots of potted shrimps.

Season the pigeon breasts. Heat an oiled grill pan until it begins to smoke, then add the pigeon and cook for about 1½–2 minutes on each side, until pink droplets of juice seep through the skin. Remove from the heat, cover with foil and leave to rest in a warm place. Meanwhile, warm the pots of shrimps in a dish filled with hot water – the butter should go creamy and soft. Tip them on to a plate, slice the pigeon breasts thinly and put them beside the shrimps. Eat with mustard and cress or another leaf, and use the toast to scoop both up. Tabasco – as usual – is never far away when we eat this type of thing.

Potted Pigeon Salad with Celery and Mustard Dressing

Put 8 spare pigeon legs into a pan, cover with stock or water and bring to the boil. Turn down to a simmer and cook for about 45 minutes, until the meat is falling off the bone. Strain through a sieve, reserving the stock (it can be used in other dishes). Pick all the pigeon meat off the bone, throwing away any sinews. Put the meat into a bowl. Slice 2 celery sticks very thinly and add to the meat. Make a dressing with 1 heaped teaspoon of Dijon mustard, 1 teaspoon of sugar, ½ teaspoon of salt, 1 tablespoon of red wine vinegar and 4 tablespoons of olive oil. Mix with the pigeon meat and celery, then divide between small pots to eat with toast.

Pigeon Rice with Figs and Whole Wheat

An earthy rice and grain supper dish, eaten with pigeon breasts roasted on the bone. If you cannot buy whole pigeons but only the breast meat, fry the breasts for 1½–2 minutes on either side (see the recipe for Pigeon Breasts with Buttered Shrimps, above) and add them to the rice.

Serves 4

8 pigeons
2 tablespoons dripping
2 onions, finely chopped
2 garlic cloves, chopped
½ teaspoon ground allspice
150g/5½oz Arborio or Carnaroli rice

4 tablespoons whole wheat grains
1 litre/1¾ pints game or chicken stock
(see page 116)
4 green figs, quartered
2 teaspoons soft brown sugar
leaves from 4 sprigs of dill, chopped
sea salt and freshly ground black
pepper

Use a pair of kitchen scissors to snip the crown of bone that holds the breast away from the legs on each bird. Cut from the front of the cavity opening, above the legs and down under the wings. Sever the joint between the wing and carcass. Then repeat with the other side. You should be left with just the breasts, plus small wings attached to the breast bone – these are the pigeon 'crowns'. Keep the legs for another dish (see above).

Preheat the oven to 230°C/450°F/Gas Mark 8. Season the pigeon crowns, place them in a roasting tin and roast for 15 minutes. Remove from the oven, cover with foil and leave to rest for 15 minutes.

Meanwhile, heat the dripping in a pan and add the onions, garlic and allspice. Cook for about 2 minutes, then stir in the rice and wheat. Cook for another minute and cover with the stock. Cut a round of greaseproof paper and lay it on top. Bring to the boil, turn down to a simmer and cook for about 20 minutes, until all the liquid has been absorbed.

Put the quartered figs on a baking sheet lined with greaseproof paper and sprinkle the sugar on top. Place in the oven and roast for 10 minutes, until the figs are tinged with brown.

Stir the dill into the rice mixture. Fillet the meat off the crowns; you will find this very easy to do but it helps to use a sharp knife. Serve the roast pigeon on the rice, with the grilled figs thrown over the top.

Bibliography and Sources

Barham, Peter
The Science of Cooking (Springer-Verlag Berlin and Heidelberg, 2000)

Bell, David and Valentine, Gill
Consuming Geographies: We Are Where We Eat (Routledge, 1997)

Blythman, Joanna
Bad Food Britain: How A Nation Ruined its Appetite (Fourth Estate, 2006)

Boyd, Lizzie (ed.)
British Cookery, 2nd edition (Christopher Helm Publishers, 1988)

Clarke, Bernadette
Good Fish Guide (Marine Conservation Society, 2007)

Clifford, Sue and King, Angela, with Philippa Davenport
England In Particular: A Celebration of the Commonplace, the Local, the Vernacular and the Distinctive (Hodder & Stoughton, 2006)

Clifford, Sue and King, Angela
The Apple Source Book: Particular Uses for Diverse Apples (Hodder & Stoughton, 2007)

Cobbett, William
Cottage Economy, new edition (Verey & Von Kanitz Publishing, 2000)

Davidson, Alan
The Oxford Companion to Food (Oxford University Press, 1999)

Davidson, Alan
North Atlantic Seafood, new edition (Prospect Books, 2003)

Farmer, David
Oxford Dictionary of Saints, 5th edition (Oxford University Press, 2003)

Feltwell, Ray
Small-Scale Poultry Keeping: A Guide to Free-Range Poultry Production (Faber and Faber, 1980)

Grigson, Jane
Charcuterie and French Pork Cookery (Michael Joseph, 1967)

Grigson, Jane
English Food (Macmillan, 1974)

Harvey, Graham
We Want Real Food: Why Our Food is Deficient in Minerals and Nutrients – and What We Can Do About It (Constable, 2006)

Hix, Mark
British Regional Food (Quadrille Publishing, 2006)

Hodgson, Tony
Good Food Stories: Our Choices Make the World of Difference (Shepheard-Walwyn Publishers, 2006)

Kiple, Kenneth F. and Ornelas, Kriemhild Conee
The Cambridge World History of Food, Volumes I and II (Cambridge University Press, 2000)

Lang, Tim and Heasman, Michael
Food Wars: the Global Battle for Mouths, Minds and Markets (Earthscan Publications, 2004)

Lehmann, Gilly
The British Housewife: Cookery Books, Cooking and Society in Eighteenth-Century Britain (Prospect Books, 2003)

Levy Beranbaum, Rose
The Cake Bible (Macmillan, 1992)

Mabey, Richard
Food for Free, new edition (HarperCollins, 2001)

Masefield, G. B., Wallis, M., Harrison, S. G., Nicholson, B. E.
The Oxford Book of Food Plants (Oxford University Press, 1973)

Orwell, George
The Road to Wigan Pier (Victor Gollancz, 1937)

Orwell, George
'A Nice Cup Of Tea', taken from *Essays* (Everyman's Library Classics, 2002)

Papashvily, Helen and George, and the editors of Time-Life Books
Foods of the World: The Cooking of Russia (Time-Life Books, 1971)

Petrini, Carlo
Slow Food Nation: Why Our Food Should Be Good, Clean and Fair (Rizzoli International Publications, 2007)

Planck, Nina
Real Food: What To Eat and Why (Bloomsbury, 2006)

Pollan, Michael
The Omnivore's Dilemma: A Natural History of Four Meals (Penguin Press, 2006)

Prince, Rose
The New English Kitchen: Changing the Way You Shop, Cook and Eat (Fourth Estate, 2005)

Prince, Rose
The Savvy Shopper (Fourth Estate, 2006)

Pullar, Philippa
Consuming Passions: A History of English Food and Appetite, new edition (Penguin Books 2001)

Smith, Anthony
Life for Beginners: Balance and Moderation (Juniperland Publications, 2005)

Spencer, Colin
British Food: An Extraordinary Thousand Years of History (Grub Street, 2002)

Symons, Michael
A History Of Cooks and Cooking (Prospect Books, 2001)

Tannahill, Reay
Food in History, revised edition (Penguin Books, 1988)

Time-Life Books, the editors of
The Good Cook: Offal (Time-Life Books, 1981)

Trager, James
The Food Chronology (Henry Holt & Co, 1995)

Tudge, Colin
So Shall We Reap: What's Gone Wrong With The World's Food and How To Fix It, new edition (Penguin Books, 2004)

Visser, Margaret
The Rituals of Dinner: The Origins, Evolution, Eccentricities and Meaning of Table Manners (HarperCollins, 1991)

Whitley, Andrew
Bread Matters: the State of Modern Bread and a Definitive Guide to Baking Your Own (Fourth Estate, 2006)

Other Sources

Bioversity International
Via dei Tre Denari
472a 00057 Maccarese (Rome)
Italy
Tel: (39) 066118 1
www.bioversityinternational.org

Department for Environment, Food and Rural Affairs (DEFRA)
Nobel House
17 Smith Square
London SW1P 3JR
Tel: 020 7238 6000
www.defra.gov.uk

The Edible Schoolyard
Martin Luther King Jr Middle School
1781 Rose Street
Berkeley
California CA 94703
Tel: 00 1 510 558 1335
www.edibleschoolyard.org

The Food Commission
94 White Lion Street
London N1 9PF
Tel: 020 7837 2250
www.foodcomm.org.uk

Food Standards Agency
www.food.gov.uk

Marine Stewardship Council
3rd floor, Mountbarrow House
6–20 Elizabeth Street
London SW1W 9RB
Tel: 020 7811 3300
www.msc.org

New Economics Foundation
3 Jonathan Street
London SE11 5NH
Tel: 020 7820 6300
www.neweconomics.org

Soil Association
South Plaza
Marlborough Street
Bristol BS1 3NX
Tel: 0117 314 5000
www.soilassociation.org

Slow Food International
Piazza XX Settembre, 5
12042 BRA (Cuneo)
Italy
Tel: (39) 0172 419611
www.slowfood.com

Sustain
94 White Lion Street
London N1 9PF
Tel: 020 7837 1228
www.sustainweb.org

Watercress Alliance
www.watercress.co.uk

WRAP (Waste & Resources Action Programme)
The Old Academy
21 Horse Fair
Banbury
Oxon OX16 0AH
Tel: 01295 819900
www.wrap.org.uk

Index